PAUL TOURNIER

"A MAN SKILLED IN MEDICINE...
AND WISE TOWARDS GOD."
—*William Barclay*

A DOCTOR'S CASEBOOK
IN THE LIGHT OF
THE BIBLE

"A PHYSICIAN'S ATTEMPT to lay hold of biblical thought which will bear on the practice of medicine."—*Westminster Bookman*

"OF EXCEPTIONAL INTEREST to all who are concerned with the problems of healing."
—*Church Times*

"CONVINCINGLY DEMONSTRATES that the healing power of biblical faith directly fulfills man's emotional and physical needs today."
—*Christian Advocate*

"BIBLE STUDY IN PERSPECTIVE. Should be read by anyone who seeks to understand the meaning of illness."—*Eternity*

"SIMPLE, APPEALING, AND WARM."
—*Church Woman*

"AN EXCELLENT GIFT for a physician."

—*Presbyterian Action*

HARPER JUBILEE BOOKS

HJ 1   WILLIAM BARCLAY: The Life of Jesus for Everyman
HJ 2   ERNEST GORDON: Through the Valley of the Kwai
HJ 3   HELMUT THIELICKE: The Waiting Father
HJ 4   PAUL TOURNIER: The Person Reborn
HJ 5   A. W. TOZER: The Knowledge of the Holy
HJ 6   WALTER TROBISCH: I Loved a Girl
HJ 7   WALTER TROBISCH: I Married You
HJ 8   ELTON TRUEBLOOD: The Humor of Christ
HJ 9   ETHEL WATERS: To Me It's Wonderful
HJ 10   ELEANOR SEARLE WHITNEY: Invitation to Joy
HJ 11   SHERWOOD ELIOT WIRT: Not Me, God
HJ 12   JOHN R. BISAGNO: Love Is Something You Do
HJ 13   INGRID TROBISCH: The Joy of Being a Woman
HJ 14   RICHARD WURMBRAND: Victorious Faith
HJ 15   PAUL TOURNIER: A Doctor's Casebook in the Light of
            the Bible
HJ 16   ELTON TRUEBLOOD: Your Other Vocation
HJ 17   DIETRICH BONHOEFFER: Life Together
HJ 18   CLARENCE W. HALL: Adventurers for God
HJ 19   HERBERT LOCKYER: Everything Jesus Taught. Volume 1
HJ 20   HERBERT LOCKYER: Everything Jesus Taught. Volume 2
HJ 21   HERBERT LOCKYER: Everything Jesus Taught. Volume 3
HJ 22   HERBERT LOCKYER: Everything Jesus Taught. Volume 4
HJ 23   HERBERT LOCKYER: Everything Jesus Taught. Volume 5
HJ 24   ULRICH SCHAFFER: Love Reaches Out

A DOCTOR'S CASEBOOK

IN THE LIGHT OF THE BIBLE

PAUL TOURNIER

Translated by
EDWIN HUDSON

HARPER & ROW, PUBLISHERS

New York, Hagerstown, San Francisco, London

A DOCTOR'S CASEBOOK IN THE LIGHT OF THE BIBLE

Printed in the United States of America

The original edition of this book
was published under the title
Bible et Médecine
by Delachaux & Niestlé,
Neuchâtel and Paris

First published in English 1954
First American edition 1960

First Harper & Row Jubilee edition published in 1976.

Library of Congress catalog card number: 60–8140

ISBN: 0-06-068389-9

75 76 77 78 79 10 9 8 7 6 5 4 3 2 1

TO MY WIFE,
WHO FOR MANY YEARS HAS
BEEN MY COMPANION IN
BIBLE-READING AND MEDITATION,
I DEDICATE THIS BOOK

TRANSLATOR'S NOTE

In dealing with the Biblical quotations it was found that the English Revised Version text agreed in nearly every case more closely than other versions with Dr. Tournier's French quotations.

E. H.

CONTENTS

Part One

THE BIBLICAL PERSPECTIVE

1. THE TWO DIAGNOSES 11
2. STUDYING THE BIBLE AS LAYMEN 17
3. THE BIBLE AND SCIENCE 25
4. THE MEANING OF THINGS 33
5. THE MEANING OF NATURE 42
6. MEDICINE AND NATURE 47
7. THE BIBLICAL ATTITUDE 54
8. THE MEANING OF THE INSTINCT OF SEX ... 62
9. THE MEANING OF DREAMS 70
10. THE MEANING OF EVENTS 76

Part Two

THE PROBLEM OF MAGIC

11. BELIEF IN MAGIC 87
12. SCIENCE AND MAGIC 96
13. THE BIBLE AND MAGIC 104
14. THE TEMPTATION OF MAGIC 111
15. THE PERSONALISM OF THE BIBLE 121
16. THE INTEGRATION OF THE PERSON 128

Contents

Part Three

LIFE, DEATH, DISEASE AND HEALING

17.	THE MEANING OF LIFE	139
18.	VITALITY	146
19.	DIVINE BLESSING	154
20.	THE MEANING OF DEATH	162
21.	THE MEANING OF DISEASE	169
22.	THE MISSION OF THE DOCTOR	178
23.	SIN AND DISEASE	188
24.	THE MEANING OF AFFLICTION	197
25.	THE MEANING OF HEALING	205
26.	THE MEANING OF MEDICINE	215

Part Four

THE CHOICE

27.	LIFE OR DEATH	227
28.	THE HIGHEST GOOD	236
	Indexes	247

PART ONE

THE BIBLICAL
PERSPECTIVE

1

THE TWO DIAGNOSES

ONE DAY the wife of one of my colleagues came to see me in Geneva. 'Please,' she said, 'can you do something to help my husband? I don't know what is on his mind, for he seldom talks about himself, but I have the impression that he is heading for some disaster. He is over-tired, and his nerves are on edge. For several years now he hasn't taken a holiday, and says that it is because he cannot afford it. Nevertheless he works feverishly from early morning until late in the evening. In spite of taking several sleeping tablets every night, he sleeps badly. He has deserted his friends, and has scarcely any time either for them or for me and the children, or for any interesting activity outside his work. His life is just a maelstrom, and looking at his contorted face I can tell that he is suffering some terrible and mysterious agony of mind.'

'Last year,' she added, 'he had a serious illness; he spent several months in hospital. His doctors were surprised that he responded so badly to treatment. But you can imagine that with so much over-work his strength was exhausted. The least I hoped was that this long illness would bring about a change in his life. On the contrary, he would not even go away to convalesce, as I begged him to. No sooner had he recovered than he threw himself into his work more strenuously than ever. If he goes on like this, he will make himself ill again.'

I decided to write to my colleague. Would he take it badly? Would he reproach his wife for having appealed to me? I wondered.

On the contrary, however, it was in the most friendly frame of mind that he came to see me.

'For several years I have been promising myself to come here,' he said as he entered my study, 'but I haven't had the courage. Today, I am determined to tell you everything.'

Then he related the drama of his life. A first lapse, when he was a student, had brought others in its train. This world is like that: one evil brings on another in a terrible chain. These errors had made him a lonely man, for he had dared to unburden himself neither to a priest nor to his wife. This further aggravated his bad conscience and his distress. From then on his mastery of himself had weakened more and more; he had let himself become further involved, and had no longer the strength to put things right.

'All day long,' he said, 'I give advice to my patients, for I believe that the practice of medicine means straightening warped lives as well as prescribing medicines; but though I know what I myself ought to do to regain peace of mind and health of body, I am incapable of doing it.'

His faults had also brought him financial difficulties which he had wanted to hide from his wife, because it was on his conscience that he had used her money. He was always hoping to extricate himself by incessant work, but still his debts mounted. For he did not dare to charge fees in proportion to the time he gave to his patients. One knows those generous people who insist on under-rating themselves. This over-work was to some extent a false self-immolation, an expiation and also a flight from himself.

Then he spoke to me of his time in hospital. An unimportant local infection had rapidly developed into serious septicaemia. It had not surprised him: for several years he had been expecting disaster. This illness had a meaning for him. It was like a due that must be paid. It could also, he thought, become a providential opportunity of recovery, for it had for a moment cut through the infernal toils in which he had allowed himself to be caught. But would he manage to seize the opportunity?

This deep significance of his illness, this remorse from which he could not free himself, those resolutions which he had so often made already and which he doubted his ability to keep any better in the future, haunted him during the long hours of fever. He would have liked to unburden himself to his doctors. They were his friends, full of affectionate attention towards him. The senior doctor, a distinguished clinician, had his full trust and looked after him most conscientiously, never failing to offer him some word of encouragement to keep up his morale.

The Two Diagnoses

The reader will understand that something different was needed: the patient had his secrets, and so personal and poignant were they that every day the professor, surrounded by his staff, went away from the sick-bed without his having been able to confide them. Each time, there was talk of blood-cultures that remained obstinately sterile. This, and the resistance of the infection to anti-biotics, was a puzzling problem for the scientist. How could one turn abruptly from these subjects to those other quite different problems which were gnawing at the heart of the invalid?

Clearly, any kind of illness raises questions of two quite distinct orders: firstly, scientific—questions concerning the nature of the malady and its mechanism: diagnosis, aetiology, pathogenesis; secondly, spiritual—questions concerning the deep meaning of the illness, its purpose. We may say, then, that every illness calls for two diagnoses: one scientific, nosological and causal, and the other spiritual, a diagnosis of its meaning and purpose.

The first diagnosis is objective. It is we doctors who make it on our patient. Of course we need his collaboration, but it might be termed a passive collaboration. It is much more difficult to tend a brother doctor than any other patient, precisely because the former seeks to take part in the working-out of the diagnosis. All we require of our patient is that he furnish us with the data on which to base our judgement, to tell us what he feels and the diseases he or his forebears have had previously. But apart from this our task does not differ from that of the veterinary surgeon who receives this information from the owner of the animal.

The second diagnosis, on the other hand, is subjective. It is the patient himself, and never the doctor, who can make it through the impulse of his inmost conscience. We in our turn can help him to establish this diagnosis, but here again passively; that is to say, not by suggesting a diagnosis to him, but through the climate of spiritual fellowship that we offer him.

From the point of view of the patient's eternal destiny, the second diagnosis is much more important than the first. But from the strictly medical point of view they are of equal importance. This was clear in the case of my colleague who knew well that the solution of his personal problems could hasten his cure and safeguard his future health.

That sickness has a 'meaning', that it tends towards an often salutary end, that it plays a definite role in the destiny of the patient, I think all doctors who stop to reflect will agree. They will more readily admit it in the case of neuroses, for psycho-analysis has plainly shown it to be true. The school of Jung has adopted a definitely purposive interpretation of neurosis. That of Freud claims to remain exclusively in the field of causal determinism. Nevertheless it was the latter which first spoke of the 'language of the organs' and of the symbolic meaning of illness. But I have here intentionally chosen a case of septicaemia in order to show clearly that an organic, physical disease has a 'meaning' quite as much as one that is nervous and functional.

Now, though science helps us to make the first diagnosis, it is of no use to us for the second. A doctor whose only preparation for his career is his scientific training will remain blind to the part played by spiritual problems in sickness, and powerless to sustain his patient in his efforts to resolve them.

Of the 'meaning' of disease, science has nothing to say: from the standpoint of science, nothing has meaning—neither the universe, man, life, death, illness, nor cure. The scientific view of the world is a stupid one. We see this clearly in the anguish that can take possession of a man when suddenly he realizes that nothing has meaning for him, neither his existence, his actions, nor his destiny. Science shows us only phenomena, a universal and impassible chain of phenomena, without beginning or end, without origin or goal. Whether it rains or the sun shines, whether we are miserable or happy, sick or well, is but a matter of physical, chemical, or psychological reactions, which unfold imperturbably and entirely without significance. As Lecomte du Nouy[1] has shown, the scientific explanation of the world is never, in the last analysis, more than chance. It is by chance that what is exists, that there were produced those circumstances that were favourable to life, and caused its beginning, or that a being, man, happened to come to such a state of differentiation that self-consciousness arose in him. Lastly, when science today seeks to impose upon us the notion of an 'anti-chance', and at the same

[1] Lecomte du Nouy, *Biological Time*, Methuen & Co., London, 1936

time that of a 'principle of indeterminism', the absurdity of a purely scientific explanation of the world is obvious.

I knew my colleague to be a believer. I asked him therefore if his faith and his Church had not been able to help him.

'That's the most tragic thing about it,' he said. 'I pass for a militant Catholic, and yet it is years since I went to confession or Communion. I was once bound by a close tie of friendship with my confessor, whom I trusted completely. But he has moved to another town, and I haven't been able to summon the courage to choose another. This contrast between my reputation and my real life hurts me terribly; and that too has sapped my moral strength. I was thought by all to be a good Catholic, and yet as the years passed it became increasingly difficult for me to return to my religious duties. I thought about it all the time I was in hospital, and I promised myself that I would really take the decisive step. But I have not been able to do it.'

I have often thought about my colleague's sojourn in hospital, about the tragedy of those daily visits of the specialist, the moral loneliness in which his patient remained locked in spite of all the kindness he showed him, and the impossibility of communion between those two minds that moved on two planes utterly unrelated the one with the other. If the mind of the doctor is filled exclusively with scientific preoccupations, if he thinks of nothing but microbes, chemical doses, or psychic complexes, the patient will never speak to him of the questions which torment him and which concern the meaning of his illness, rather than its mechanism.

Some day this doctor, as a result of some personal experience, will widen his horizon. Without neglecting the scientific study of phenomena, he will open his eyes also to their 'meaning'. With astonishment, without his having said anything about this new development in himself, he will see his patient open his heart to him on this other no less important aspect of his illness, that of its inner meaning. He will feel he is making a wonderful discovery: everything will take on a meaning, each success, each setback, each utterance, each silence, every improvement and every relapse. The world too, and each incident in his own life, will be seen in a strange new light: for him, there will be no more chance; everything will speak to his heart and open his mind to new questions: 'What is the meaning of this event? What does God wish to tell me through it?'

Of the meaning of things, the meaning of sickness and cure, of life and death, of the world, man, and history, science tells us nothing; here it is the Bible that speaks to us. For this reason the study of the Bible is as valuable to the doctor as the study of science. This is what I hope to show in this book.

But first I must finish the story of my colleague and of his visit to me. He had come to the end of his account. I made no reply; I had none to make. In a matter of science, we must teach, advise, instruct. In a matter of the spiritual life, we must only listen, understand, love, and pray. It is God who replies. Thus, after a long silence, my friend began to say aloud what it was that God was requiring of him. Very simply and clearly he enumerated the amendments necessary if order and obedience were to be put back into his life. I confined myself to asking him to make certain points more explicit, knowing how such questions can help: 'That letter you want to write, when do you reckon to write it?' 'As soon as I get back home.'

A few weeks later he was writing another letter, which I received with deep emotion: a song of thanksgiving to God for blessings received. My friend had carried out the decisions made in my study; he had returned to the Confessional and to Communion. He had told his wife everything, and had fixed with her the date of the holiday they were going to take together, and which was to be like a second honeymoon.

2

STUDYING THE BIBLE
AS LAYMEN

M Y FRIEND Dr. Armand Vincent, of Paris, was asked recently to address a congress of doctors on the subject: 'Towards a humane medicine.'[1] He began by quoting a remark made by one of his patients:

'We are prevented from dying,' she had said; 'we are not helped to live.'

If we wish to practise a humane medicine we must answer that appeal. Then inevitably we are confronted by those questions which medical practice raises and to which science has no answer: what are life, death, man, sickness and health?

On this subject medicine as taught in our faculties and text-books remains silent. Behind its silence there lies, albeit unexpressed, the perplexity it experiences as it attempts with its purely scientific methods to grapple with the fundamental problems of which we as doctors are aware, such as that of the nature of sickness. As Dr. Leriche, a professor at the Collège de France, has ventured to write: 'If we begin to ask why things are as they are, or seek to understand the secret springs of disease, the text-books give us scarcely any but superficial, even childish, explanations, with little or nothing behind them.'[2]

Science, then, analyses phenomena, but provides us with no clear, sure and general notion concerning man, life, sickness, or death. We turn, therefore, towards the Bible, as Pascal invites us: 'We know life and death only through Jesus Christ. Apart from Jesus Christ we know not what our life is, nor our death, nor God, nor ourselves. Thus, without the Scriptures, whose only object is Jesus Christ, we know nothing, and can see but obscurity

[1] 'Pour une médecine humaine', in Le médecin français, special number: Journées d'étude, Paris, 23 April, 1950, X[th] Year, No. 13, 10 July, 1950

[2] R. Leriche, Thromboses artérielles, Paris, Masson, 1944

and confusion in the nature of God, and in our own nature.'

But how are we going to study the Bible?

Being doctors we are called to study it as doctors, not as theologians. The theologian starts from the Bible and moves towards men. He studies the Bible in terms of exegesis and historical criticism; he meditates upon it and recognizes in it the Word of God. He derives from it dogmas and doctrines which he presents for our religious instruction and our edification. That is his vocation: it is not ours.

I suggest for doctors the reverse process: starting from our practical concerns, from the questions raised daily by our work, and going to the Bible to seek an answer. 'Let us read the Bible,' said Professor Emil Brunner to me once, 'thinking constantly of our daily lives, and let us live our lives thinking constantly of the Bible.'

The doctor is a practitioner. If we invite him to study the Bible, he will ask if it will help him to tend his patients better. I write this as a man committed, terribly committed: I am grappling daily with actual cases. Faced with their difficulty, I am intensely conscious of the insufficiency of our methods. In working out this book I have been guided by those urgent practical needs.

More than ten years ago I published *Médecine de la personne*. In a chapter on the Holy Scriptures I suggested that doctors should seek there the laws of life and health. I added that I intended one day to write another book on the subject. Since then I have frequently been asked how the work was progressing. I did in fact throw myself zealously into the task. But I came to an impasse. I set to work to read the whole of the Bible, noting down all the passages that had any bearing on medicine, psychology, disease, and the conduct of life.

The first discovery I made was of the incomparable richness of the Bible. The Bible is the book of the drama of human life, and for us doctors, acting as we are all day long in that drama, it is of absorbing interest. And then the Bible is infinitely human. Think, for example, of the matchless tenderness shown by Jesus, even on the Cross, towards His mother and the Apostle John, 'the beloved disciple', as they are about to lose Him. 'He saith unto his mother, Woman, behold thy son! Then saith he to the disciple, Behold thy mother!' (John 19.26-7).

Another striking feature of the Bible is its realism. It shows us man as he is, and as we know him, with all his afflictions and all his greatness, all his certainties and all his doubts, all his aspirations and all his vileness. Doctors will be interested to find that even feigned illness is described in the Bible (II Sam. 13.1-22). It is the story of Amnon, one of the sons of King David, who was infatuated with his sister Tamar. On the advice of his cunning friend Jonadab, Amnon went to bed and pretended to be sick so that his sister might come alone into his chamber to tend him, for he wished to violate her. They will be interested too in the affectionate words of Absalom, another of Tamar's brothers. Seeing his sister greatly distraught, tearing her garments and crying aloud, he takes her under his protection and says to her: 'hold thy peace, my sister: he is thy brother; take not this thing to heart.'

But in recalling here the extreme realism of the Bible, I should like particularly to show the reader that it is this that explains the contradictions which we find in it, and which are often very perplexing for us. The Bible is, in fact, a mirror of the human heart, and the human heart is full of contradictions; it never grasps more than a part of the truth, and that part it then generalizes as if it were absolute.

Thus, St. James tells us that temptation does not come from God (Jas. 1.13), and yet in the Lord's Prayer Jesus teaches us to ask God not to lead us into it (Matt. 6.13). Similarly, numerous passages affirm that disease and death do not come from God, but from His enemy, from Satan, from the Devil (I Cor. 15.26; Luke 13.16); and elsewhere it is written: 'If thou wilt not hearken unto the voice of the Lord thy God . . . the Lord shall smite thee with the boil of Egypt, and with the emerods and with the scurvy, and with the itch, whereof thou canst not be healed. The Lord shall smite thee with madness, and with blindness, and with astonishment of heart' (Deut. 28.15, 27-8); and again: 'See now that I, even I, am he . . . I kill, and I make alive, I have wounded, and I heal' (Deut. 32.39).

Let us not look in the Bible for logic, but for life; for logic is powerless to grasp and to express life. As doctors we are well aware of that.

It is in fact life that we find in the Bible, and not a system of thought. We know that there is something true and vital in each of those apparently contradictory affirmations, whereas no logical system would be true. A philosophical system necessarily juggles with the truth. We are nearly always longing for an easy religion, easy to understand and easy to follow; a religion with no mystery, no insoluble problems, no snags; a religion that would allow us to escape from our miserable human condition; a religion in which contact with God spares us all strife, all uncertainty, all suffering and all doubt, in short, a religion without the Cross. In the Bible, God does not take man out of his drama; but He lives it with him and for him. The Bible avoids nothing. It enters realistically into our life as it is. It expresses all our feelings, all our aspirations, all our fears and all our contradictory intuitions. On every page it utters the cries of human suffering, from the anguish expressed so poignantly by Job:

> *Why died I not from the womb?*
> *Why did I not give up the ghost when I came out of the belly?*
> *Why did the knees receive me?*
> *Or why the breasts, that I should suck?*
> *For now should I have lain down and been quiet;*
> *I should have slept; then had I been at rest* (Job 3.11-13).

to the agony of Christ on the Cross: 'My God, my God, why hast thou forsaken me?' (Matt. 27.46). On every page, too, it proclaims the certainties of faith: 'Fear thou not, for I am with thee' (Isa. 41.10).

The amazing wealth of the Bible is precisely what makes it a difficult book to study. As I read, my notes accumulated; and the further I progressed the more gigantic and overwhelming did the task appear. I felt that it was really a theologian's work; that it required dogmatic and exegetical knowledge that I lacked.

Fortunately I was led along another road. In 1947, at the request of a number of our colleagues, an international conference of doctors was organized at the Ecumenical Institute of Bossey by Dr. A. Maeder of Zurich, Dr. J. de Rougemont of Lyons, and myself. There we were, drawn from the most varied backgrounds: university professors and general practitioners; housemen, surgeons, psychiatrists, and other specialists; Calvinists,

Roman Catholics, Lutherans, Orthodox, and even a Jew. The bond between us was our common concern over the insufficiency of modern medical practice, its excessive specialization, the premium placed on technique which makes it less humane, and our common desire for a more complete committal of ourselves, as well in our relations with our patients as in this friendly community which we wished to set up.

I realized that Bible-study, as practised in different denominations, was likely to divide rather than unite us; to divide Christians of various confessions among themselves, as well as Christian doctors from their colleagues outside the Church. I had seen it happen in Germany at a joint conference of doctors and theologians, even though they all belonged to the same confession. The advanced specialists went for a walk in the park while the rest listened to a pastor lecturing on the Bible.

We began therefore by discussing medicine and personal experience, not the Bible and theology. But of course in discussing medicine along the lines we had chosen we found that we had first of all to debate our conception of the nature of man. In avoiding shipwreck on the rocks of dogmatic controversy, however, we were running into another danger: that of being without any stronger guiding principle than a vague idealism of no practical value.

So, after three days of most interesting discussion on 'Body, mind, and spirit,' we approached one of the teachers at the Ecumenical Institute, Suzanne de Dietrich. We told her that we wanted to know what the Bible had to say on the subject. I hope that Mlle. de Dietrich will one day publish the remarkable paper she read to us. However we might differ in spiritual outlook, we all listened to her with interest, for this was no Sunday-school lesson, but the flooding of new light on the problem set for us by our daily lives as doctors.

I especially remember her saying that the thought of the Bible is far removed from that of today, so that in undertaking Bible-study we have to make an effort to put ourselves into its perspective, which is less intellectual than ours. The Bible is not concerned to give precise definitions of such ideas as the spirit or the soul, or to set forth a systematic philosophy of the nature of man. It uses several different words in turn for one and the same reality such as the soul, and one and the same word may be used to mean successively things which we distinguish: the mind and the heart. It is more poetic, more intuitive, and above all more dynamic, than we are. It gives a picture of man living, moving, perpetually becoming, rather than a static image dissected into its component parts. Thus, that which man has received from God, that which makes him different from the animals, his spirituality, his mind, his soul, whatever name we give it, is not described in the Bible as a thing, a part of man, a substance, but as a breath, a movement, an impulse, an echo of God's voice.[1] I am reminded here of a penetrating remark made by Professor Siebeck at one of our Bossey meetings: 'It is in his vocation, that is to say because God calls him, that man becomes a person.'

Now we had found a method of studying the Bible that was particularly suitable for doctors. Day after day, in the weeks that we have spent at Bossey each year since then, we have together pursued this inquiry: what does the Bible teach us concerning those matters which are the subject of our work and of our discussions? This book, written at the request of my colleagues, is the reflection, necessarily incomplete, of those conferences in which we examined in the light of the Bible each of the problems that we as doctors have to face: the person, life and death, disease and sin, the meaning and aim of medicine, the gift of healing, relations with the patient, the team spirit, social medicine, sex, love, marriage and celibacy, the laws of health, and so on.

I believe that we have here a most rewarding field of study for laymen. I was asked recently by a group of German architects to give a paper on the Bible and architecture. I found the work intensely interesting. I had to delve into the account in the Book of the Revelation of the heavenly Jerusalem, a passage which I had until then rather neglected, but whose riches I now discovered. It was one of the sessions of the Evangelical Academy of Bad Boll, which, under the energetic direction of its founder, Dr. Eberhard Müller, has made its influence widely felt. To it come in turn members of various professions—lawyers, teachers, peasants, factory workers, railwaymen, students, local government officials, and others—to spend a week or so examining their professional problems in the light of the Bible. I have of course

[1] Gen. 2.7; Acts 17.28; Ex. 3.4; Isa. 49.1

been there several times at conferences of doctors, and on one occasion for a conference of artists, which included poets, painters, scenario-writers, sculptors, and radio artists. A large number of books has been produced as a result of all this effort. One in particular may be mentioned: Professor Otto Michel's book[1] on the work of one of the medical conferences.

In Switzerland a similar experiment has been made over the last few years, on the initiative of the Church of Zurich, at Boldern-Männedorf, under the direction of Dr. Rinderknecht. In Greece a professor of law, Dr. Tsirintanis, a true apostle of the intellectuals, has founded the Christian Union of Greek Intellectuals, which includes many members of all faculties at the universities, and publishes a remarkable review, 'AKTINE'. As a result of the work of this Union there has been published an extensive study[2] of the fundamental principles which must guide a truly Christian civilization, dealing in turn with each field—law, economy, science, art, and so on. The medical section, directed by Dr. Aspiotis, has recently published, under the title *Sickness and the Soul*,[3] a first and most important work on the questions we are here examining. Finally I shall mention the Protestant Study Centre, founded in Geneva by Pastor J. de Senarclens, which also has several sections, and to which we are indebted for some important publications; the Protestant professional associations in France, and the 'Church and World' organization in Holland.

Perhaps, on reading this, some lawyer, musician, sociologist, business-man, farmer, teacher or housewife will in his or her turn be encouraged to seek, each in his own domain, the answers made by the Bible to his professional problems. The housewife should not fail to note the passage in St. John's Gospel (John 21.9) which shows us Jesus, shortly after His Resurrection, roasting fish for His disciples over a coal-fire. We tend always to oppose the spiritual to the material; it is not thus that we should expect to see Christ, after His Resurrection, and on the eve of His Ascension, preparing for one of His last interviews with His disciples. Nevertheless, He chooses to show His love for them by

[1] *Medizin und Theologie im Gespräch*, Tübingen, Furche-Verlag, 1948
[2] *Towards a Christian Civilization*, Damaskos Publications, Athens, 1950
[3] A. Aspiotis, Ἡ ἀρρώστεια καὶ ἡ Ψυχη, Damaskos Publications, Athens, 1951

23

this simple every-day act, like any mother preparing a meal for her husband and children.

I am reminded of an amusing remark made once in Lausanne at a meeting of theologians, lawyers, and doctors to discuss marriage problems. We were straying rather too far into learned dialectics when the wise, quiet voice of Dr. Lucien Bovet interrupted us: 'It isn't as complicated as you think,' he said. 'When I ask one of my patients if he is happy in his marriage, as often as not he will reply: "Oh! yes—she's a good cook."'

When, a few months ago, I wrote these lines, and recalled the well-loved figure of Dr. Bovet, I did not think that before they appeared in print he would be so tragically and prematurely taken from us. He had the sense of incarnation which permeates the whole Bible, and which the kind of professional study I have indicated can recover for us. Such study will help to enrich our knowledge of the Scriptures, give us a better appreciation of their value for our daily life, and a new vision of our professional vocation. It will help also to cure our modern world of the exaggerated intellectualism to which it is prone.

3

THE BIBLE AND SCIENCE

WE RETURN now to medicine. One of the first questions that strikes us when we open our Bible is that of the relationship between science and faith. In connection with the two diagnoses I spoke of the two kinds of problem—the scientific and the spiritual. I said that they were absolutely distinct. By this I mean that they neither conflict nor are confounded the one with the other.

Many people think that the Bible and science are fundamentally opposed. When we speak of taking account, in our work, of our religious beliefs, many doctors think that we are rejecting science. Many believers, for their part, think that to have recourse to science in treating illness is to reject faith. The other day I was examining a hernia patient. I advised her to consult a surgeon. But she refused, with the remark: 'I don't want to depend on anyone but Jesus Christ.' Today I have seen a friend whom I have been tending for many years, in collaboration with a psychiatrist who has treated him during the more acute periods of his illness. He tells me that he went to see the psychiatrist again recently, and that my colleague prescribed him a sleeping-draught to be taken regularly every night.

'I take it,' he told me, 'and it does me good. I am more relaxed, and less nervous, and I work better; and yet I must confess that I never take it without a twinge of conscience. It is as if to use an artificial method were a sign of lack of faith in God.'

'But,' I said, 'that medicine is also a blessing from God, just like the bread He gives us every day!'

I do not deny that, under God's especial command, a man may refuse medical aid. Similarly, hermits, or Eastern sages, have sometimes felt themselves called to abstain from food for long periods. But it is not a sign of lack of faith to eat the daily bread for which we ask God, provided we give thanks to Him for it.

The Biblical Perspective

To have recourse to the doctor's skill, or to eat the baker's bread, these are one and the same thing. It is the same as wearing the tailor's clothes, living under the carpenter's roof, or going aboard the fisherman's boat. Here already is the life of Jesus Christ in all its humanity; Jesus Christ the carpenter—the technician therefore, the builder (Matt. 13.55), all His arguments with the Pharisees about food (Matt. 11.19), His miracle at the marriage in Cana (John 2.1-11), His many journeys by boat (Matt. 8.23), although He could also walk on the water (John 6.19).

Let us beware, then, of generalizations. A systematic refusal to accept the benefits of the technique and progress of science may be due to this idea of a conflict between the spiritual and the material, which I mentioned just now.

The notion that science and faith conflict does not seem to me to be Biblical. The Bible tells us of the institution of science as a gift from God. When God created man He commanded him to give names to 'every beast of the field, and every fowl of the air' (Gen. 2.19). The giving of names is the basic principle of science. It is the function of natural science to give a clearly-defined name to each living species, as also to each chemical element and each physical force. And as for mathematics, it was Poincaré who said[1] that they are only a conventional language.

The foundation of science may also be seen in the unique power given by God to man and woman when He said to them: 'Replenish the earth, and subdue it; and have dominion over the fish of the sea, and over the fowl of the air, and over every living thing that moveth upon the earth' (Gen. 1.28). There is a passage in the Epistle of St. James that should be compared with this text (Jas. 3.7-8). He speaks of the tongue, of its misdeeds, and of man's inability to tame his own tongue, although he has tamed every kind of animal. The whole drama of science is present in this paradox: man controls Nature, but does not control himself. The Bible condemns neither science nor man's power: it presents them as gifts of God which man must manage in submission to his Creator. The catastrophes brought about by science are not, in fact, the work of science, but that of the

[1] H. Poincaré, *Science and Hypothesis*, Walter Scott Pub. Co., 1905

26

untamed heart of man using his power against God. 'The atom bomb is not in the least dangerous,' writes Denis de Rougemont.[1] 'It is a thing. What is fearfully dangerous is man. . . . Clearly, if the bomb is left alone, it will do nothing. Let us have no more nonsense, then. What we need is control of man.' The Bible condemns science when, being the gift of God, it tries to set itself up as a god; when it is proud, when it claims to set man free from God. 'Cursed is the man that trusteth in man' (Jer. 17.5).

This brings us to the well-known story of the Fall, and the temptation by the serpent: 'Ye shall be as gods' (Gen. 3.1-19). But notice in this connection that the tree of the forbidden fruit was 'the tree of the knowledge of good and evil' (Gen. 2.9), and not, as is often said, 'the tree of knowledge'. What God forbade was not the knowledge which man might acquire through the intellect with which He had endowed him, but the claim to judge good and evil for himself, to judge, that is, the use to which he might put this knowledge.

Without going further into this more general discussion, I should like to return now to our daily medical practice. Dr. Vincent, whom I have already quoted, speaks in his book, *Le jardinier des hommes*,[2] of the formidable and invisible barrier set up by the medical knowledge of the doctor, a barrier which may make contact with his patient difficult. Human contact is possible only in so far as we feel our deep equality as men. The patient often feels himself inferior to the doctor, and the doctor quite as frequently has a false feeling of superiority. Dr. Jean de Rougemont has described this in his *Culture et misère humaine*.[3] It is never as a scientist that the doctor establishes real contact with his patient, but only as a man who feels himself, in spite of his science, as wretched a creature as his patient, sympathizing with him in the true sense of the word: suffering with him. 'Knowledge puffeth up, but charity edifieth,' writes St. Paul (I Cor. 8.1).

There is a grave danger here for us doctors. If we pin our faith

[1] Denis de Rougemont, *Lettres sur la bombe atomique*, N. R. F., Gallimard, Paris, 1946

[2] Armand Vincent, *Le jardinier des hommes*, Collection Esprit, Editions du Seuil, Paris, 1945

[3] Jean de Rougemont, *Culture et misère humaine*, Imprimerie Nouvelle Lyonnaise, Lyons

to our science, we pay but little attention to our patient's often naïve explanations of his troubles. He senses that we are not taking him seriously. He feels in us that self-sufficiency, that cocksureness, which thinks it has nothing more to learn. Contact between him and us is broken; and, moreover, we cut ourselves off from that true science, which is to be learned from our patients rather than our books.

There are two sorts of minds. The first is the superficial mind. For these people there is no mystery. They always know what to do. They are more ready to give advice than to listen to it, to understand, or to change their opinions. On the other hand there are those who possess the sense of mystery, who are conscious of the gaps in their knowledge and of its limits, for whom every sick person is an enigma that will never be completely explained. It is not the first who are the more scientific of the two.

But we all have in us these two tendencies. None of us can flatter himself that he has escaped the danger of the 'knowledge which puffeth up'. But we are protected from it by reading the Bible. However powerful and learned he may be, the Bible always sets man face to face with God, reminding him thus of his frailty and his weakness: 'Put no more trust in man, with his mere breath of life: of what account is he?' (Isa. 2.22, Moffatt's translation).

Science, then, in the Biblical view, is a precious gift from God, entrusted to us so that we may care better for our patients. But with it goes the risk of losing that humility without which there can be no true science and no true medicine. This humility can be recovered only through that reflection on our own conduct, the repentance spoken of throughout the Bible.

Nor does the Bible condemn medicine. I shall return later to this subject: but meanwhile let me quote, in this connection, a beautiful passage from Ecclesiasticus: 'Honour a physician with the honour due unto him . . . for the Lord hath created him. For of the Most High cometh healing. . . . My son, in thy sickness be not negligent: but pray to the Lord. . . . Then give place to the physician, for the Lord hath created him: let him not go from thee, for thou hast need of him. There is a time when in their hands is good success. For they shall also pray unto the Lord,

that he would prosper that, which they give for ease and remedy'
(Eccles. 38.1-2, 9, 12-14).

Secondly, if science and the Bible are not in conflict, nor
are they confounded the one with the other. Here I must make
an important observation on the spirit in which we doctors are
to study the Bible. It was suggested to me by a talk given by
Professor Eichrodt, of Bâle. He was dealing with law, economics,
politics and sociology, and discussing to what extent the Christian
might draw his inspiration from the Bible for the organization of
society in these spheres.

He mentioned three possible attitudes: the literalist attitude,
seeking to impose on our modern society all the precepts of the
Mosaic law, on the grounds that it is the only legislation inspired
by God. Then there is the sceptical attitude, which holds that all
the many Mosaic precepts belong to a long-dead past, that we
can retain only the strictly religious message of the Bible, and
that as regards social organization, we have no other help but
that of science. The third attitude, which was the one advocated
by the speaker, lies between the first two. The Biblical vision is
never that of a religion cut off from the world of events, but
rather an incarnate religion, moulding the life of man and of
society. Here then, he said, was the course to follow: take the
Mosaic law, not in this detail or that, but as a whole; understand
its underlying principles, as for example that of the protection
of the weak which is one of its chief characteristics, and seek to
apply it to present-day conditions.

Listening to that talk, I thought of medicine. The literalist
attitude would, in prescribing diets for the sick, forbid pork and
the meat of all the animals enumerated in Chapter 11 of Leviticus;
it would adopt the differential diagnosis of leprosy given in
Chapter 13, or all the rules of sexual hygiene in Chapter 15;
the sick would be treated as they were in the days of David or of
Jesus Christ, applying Isaiah's plaster of figs for boils (II Kings
20.7), or mud for blindness (John 9.6), or prescribing wine for
dyspepsia, as Paul recommended to Timothy (I Tim. 5.23).
In short, one would be falling into a confusion between science
and the Bible, seeking in the latter scientific teaching which it
does not give.

The opposite attitude, sincerely adopted by many doctors, is to think that only science can guide us moderns in our professional work; that we may seek in the Bible precepts for our moral or religious life, but that it has nothing to teach us about medicine. 'Medicine,' the great German specialist Naunyn used to say, 'will be scientific, or will not be at all.'

With Professor Eichrodt, I adopt the third attitude. It will lead us to seek in the Bible not, of course, scientific teaching properly so-called, but truths, nevertheless, of real practical importance in the exercise of our vocation. Without adhering narrowly to each detail of the Mosaic law, we shall see in its general inspiration the laws of healthy living. As regards marriage, sex and psychology in general, we shall find much valuable teaching that agrees singularly well (as Dr. Georges Liengme has remarked[1]) with the most recent advances in psychological study. Thus Dr. Mentha[2] calls Psalm 32 the Psalm of psychoanalysis. 'While I held my tongue, my bones consumed away' (Prayer Book version). Elsewhere he has pointed out the importance, medically speaking, of Christ's exhortation: 'Seek ye first his kingdom and his righteousness; and all these things' (the things that are necessary to our life) 'shall be added unto you' (Matt. 6.33). This word righteousness means in the Bible a right relation with God, with man, and with nature, a relation in conformity with God's purpose. Dr. Mentha sees in this text the statement of a law of happiness whose validity we may constantly verify in our consulting-rooms. How often people come to us to tell us of their despair: by seeking first their own happiness all they have done is to destroy it. By trying to satisfy all their gluttonous appetites —of the intellect, the stomach, the emotions, or of sex—they have brought themselves to misery, sickness, loneliness, or to sexual frustration.

Here is another example of the sound psychology of the Bible. To the account of the institution of marriage there is added this sentence: 'Therefore shall a man leave his father and mother, and shall cleave unto his wife' (Gen. 2.24). According to God's plan, in order to marry one must first detach oneself from one's

[1] Georges Liengme, *Pour apprendre à mieux vivre*, Victor Attinger, Neuchâtel, 1936

[2] Henri Mentha, 'A propos de médecine psychosomatique', in the *Revue médicale de la Suisse romande*, 27 June, 1947

parents. There come to consult us many couples whose marital conflicts are at bottom due to failure to recognize this divine law. A careful examination of their case reveals that one or the other, or sometimes both, have remained in a childish psychological dependence on their parents, even sometimes after their death. Usually with the husband it is his mother, and with the wife her father, who after marriage remains for them the person with whom they have the closest tie.

Of course, they are not usually aware of the fact. They are the victims of what the psychologists call an unconscious father or mother fixation. The parent is still the centre of their life, their chief support and inspiration, retaining the place that should have been taken by the marriage partner. There are even cases where a man has never outgrown his adolescent revolt against his father. He criticizes him continually, contradicts him by every attitude in life that he adopts, but by this very fact he remains, in spite of his hostility, dependent on him, since it is this opposition that determines everything he does. He has married without being free, without being free to give himself unreservedly to his wife. There is a lovely story in the Bible that illustrates the command in Genesis to which I have just referred. Owing to a famine, an Israelite named Elimelech, and his wife Naomi, took refuge in the land of Moab. Their two sons there married Moabite women. Then Elimelech and his two sons died, and Naomi wished to return to her own country, where the famine had ceased. But she was unwilling to take her two daughters-in-law away with her into a strange land where they would doubtless be unable to marry again. She said to them: 'Go, return each of you to her mother's house' (Ruth 1.8). One of them did so, but the other, Ruth, had really understood the nature of marriage; she had committed herself and her whole life to it, and she replied to her mother-in-law: 'Intreat me not to leave thee, and to return from following after thee: for whither thou goest, I will go; and where thou lodgest, I will lodge; thy people shall be my people, and thy God my God: where thou diest, will I die, and there will I be buried' (Ruth 1.16).

Often we find cases of parents who will not loose their hold on their grown-up married child. Usually these are well-educated people, of excellent intentions, enlightened, and even devoutly religious. They think they are doing right in continuing to surround their married daughter or son with their care and protection, and in giving them the benefit of their advice in everything. But they are keeping them in a state of dependence which is contrary to what the Bible teaches. And this protective instinct, that of the hen which keeps her chicks under her wings, can be extraordinarily strong. Recently I interviewed a woman whose mother-in-law had installed herself in the young couple's bedroom on their return from their honeymoon.

It is not, of course, only on their children's marriage that parents must abdicate their position. It must be happening throughout their children's childhood and adolescence, so that they may be allowed to become themselves, to become real persons. There is a telling instance of this recounted in the Bible. It is actually a doctor, St. Luke, who reports it (Luke 2.41-51). Jesus was twelve years old; He had accompanied His parents to Jerusalem; but instead of leaving Jerusalem with them, He had stayed behind in the Temple, talking with the theologians. Naturally, His mother, not realizing that He could have any other duty apart from that of pleasing her and avoiding trouble to her, reprimanded Him sharply when she found Him again. But Jesus replied firmly: 'Wist ye not that I must be about my Father's business?' At twelve years of age He is in the process of detaching Himself from His mother, of becoming Himself, discovering His own vocation; He is not destined to be what His mother imagines, but what God is calling Him to be.

There are in the Bible other examples of maternal domination, of the 'mother complex', as the psychologists call it. We shall see later the case of Rachel and Joseph. And there is the passage in the Gospel where we see the mother of the two disciples James and John coming to Jesus and asking Him: 'Command that these my two sons may sit, one on thy right hand and one on thy left hand, in thy kingdom' (Matt. 20.20-1). Here we have that naïve projection of a mother's ambitions on to her sons, which we so often meet.

We shall have occasion to note many other characteristic examples of the psychological wisdom of the Bible; but first I should like to return to Professor Eichrodt's method, to the search for what may be called the Biblical perspective.

4

THE MEANING OF THINGS

IT IS POSSIBLE, then, as I have just shown, to study a
particular Bible passage and discover its message, its inner
meaning and its practical application. But the Bible can also be
considered as a whole. I cannot too strongly urge this upon
scientists, haunted as they are by the enigma of the world and of
man. The Bible seems diverse and uneven in its various parts.
But these parts have not been brought together by chance. The
more one studies it, the more one becomes aware of an underlying unity beneath this apparent incongruity. All the men of the
Bible share a common outlook, the same way of thinking. There is a
perspective, an over-all plan, that is co-ordinated and harmonious.
On this point I found a book by Suzanne de Dietrich, *Le dessein
de Dieu*,[1] most enlightening. She takes us away from details to
a view of the whole Bible, and of its way of looking at the world
and at history, which differs radically from that suggested by
our modern culture.

Here I pick up again the thread of our reflections concerning
my colleague and the two diagnoses. We were saying that from
the standpoint of science there is only a blind concatenation of
events; nothing has meaning. In the Biblical view, however,
everything has meaning. The certainty of this permeates the
Bible from cover to cover. Nothing that happens is without
meaning—neither the creation of the world nor its end, nor the
smallest event in history, nor anything that happens to a man in
the course of his life. There is no such thing as chance. There is a
divine plan. Through every circumstance in which we find
ourselves the divine combat is waged, as God puts to us His
question that must be answered one way or the other: yes or no
(I Kings 18.21). For it is in terms of God that all things take on
meaning.

[1] Delachaux et Niestlé, Neuchâtel and Paris, 1945

The sphere of science is that of quantities. Meaning pertains to the realm of quality, the realm of values. It is like a mathematical + or — put before a quantity. And what is it that gives meaning to things? It is the positive or negative relation with God. Apart from God, everything is neutral, as Sartre has said; there are no values. With God, everything takes on meaning, everything has value, either positive or negative.

I am colour-blind. In Lausanne one day my friend the late Professor Carrard put me for fun through the tests used by psychologists to discover colour-blindness. The subject is shown a number of cards dotted all over with little circles of different colours. On one of these cards all the little green circles, whether light or dark, traced out the letters of a word. To Dr. Carrard's eyes this word leaped out, since, being well able to distinguish this colour, he automatically isolated the circles outlining the word from all the circles of other colours. I, on the other hand, not being able to distinguish green, could not read the word. There was also a control-test: one of the cards contained a word outlined by the green, grey and brown circles, all of them colours which I confuse together. This word I was at once able to read, while Dr. Carrard was not able to see it.

I am reminded of that experiment by the two views I am speaking of here—the scientific and the Biblical. We all look at the same object, the world, or man. According to our personal dispositions we read there a physico-chemical story or a spiritual one. If we lack a certain inward disposition we will no more be able to perceive the spiritual meaning of things than I was able to read Dr. Carrard's word, or he mine. So there is no discussion possible between those who see in man or in nature merely a vast physico-chemical or psychological mechanism, and those who discern in them a meaning, just as there could have been no discussion between Dr. Carrard and me on the basis of the cards we were looking at together. If one is colour-blind, or wants to be so, one will remain unable to see the spiritual aspect, the meaning, of things.

Today most doctors are colour-blind on principle. One must bear in mind that science had to struggle for hundreds of years to free itself from the fetters of philosophy and the Church. Doctrines concerning the meaning of things, that is to say

34

concerning 'first causes', were invoked to prevent the study of the mechanism of things, that is to say, of 'secondary causes'. To succeed in this study, and to construct the solid and gigantic edifice of modern science, scientists had to exclude from their purview all notions that were not 'positive'. This was legitimate; and it has borne much fruit; it must remain the condition of all purely scientific research; but it is a method which explores only one aspect of reality; it gives us only a mechanicalist, causal view of man and of the world; it excludes entirely any spiritual and purposive view. Medicine, to be complete, must include both.

I do not deny that there are on the one hand physical phenomena, such as disease, which pertain to the realm of science, and on the other, spiritual phenomena, such as sin, which pertain to the realm of theology. I assert that every phenomenon, however material or however spiritual, may be looked at from the scientific point of view, as to its causal mechanism, or from the spiritual point of view, as to its inner significance. For this reason we may not say that scientific treatment is the doctor's province, and the cure of the soul the theologian's. To say this would be to condemn both doctors and theologians to see, each of them, but one half of reality, just as Dr. Carrar . and I each read our own word.

From science, then, the doctor learns the mechanism of things, and from the Bible their meaning. We sometimes hear talk of a 'Christian medicine'. For my part I do not believe there is a Christian medicine distinct from ordinary medicine. What the Bible teaches us about nature and about man is true for the whole of medicine. Every sick person is faced with the problem of the meaning of things. Doctors, whether or not they are believers, can find real enlightenment on this subject only in the Bible. They will discover that all the men of whom the Bible speaks are, as it were, listening-in to God; that it is in that perspective that they view everything that happens to them. 'What is God saying to me through this?' is their constant question. That is the meaning of things. It is to ask myself what God is saying through that star that I am looking at, through this friend who is speaking to me, through this difficulty which is holding me up or through this trouble which befalls me. Once awake to this way of thinking, one discovers the true savour of life. Everything becomes throbbing with interest. There is no more chance. A patient tells me of one of Mauriac's books[1] about Jesus Christ which has come into her hands, and made a great impression on her. 'I don't think it is just chance,' she says; 'as long as my parents were alive, I felt secure; but now that they are dead I am faced with many questions; and I think that it is to find an answer to them that I have been led to read this book.' Thus, everything becomes an opportunity of seeking God, His will, and His call. He is no longer only the distant inaccessible master of the universe; He becomes the personal God, who speaks to us personally, or whom at least we seek personally to hear.

For of course I do not pretend that in this search for the true meaning of things we never make a mistake. So limited is our mind, so dull our intellect, so dim our eyes, and so deaf our ears, that God must often compel us to understand by means of many converging signs. And even then we are not certain to have understood. The search for the meaning of things demands unyielding self-criticism. But science demands a similar critical vigilance, and it too is constantly seeing thrown into the melting-pot the things it believed to be firmly established.

But perhaps the word 'criticism' is not the right one to use. It is too intellectual. God is understood in the heart. Rather let us say that this search demands humility. It is just when we are most sure of having properly understood God that we run the risk of being most mistaken.

It is less a matter of finding than of seeking, or, one might say, of finding that attitude which consists in seeking. This is no paradox. Like many of my readers, no doubt, I am perplexed by certain pages of the Bible. Those, for example, where the Israelites believe themselves to be obeying God when they deceive or massacre their enemies. Perhaps objectively they were mistaken. But by their faith they enter that great company of men who accept the risk of making mistakes rather than remaining prudently in disillusioned and sterile scepticism. There they have a message for me. They speak to me in God's name, in spite of the fact that they may have been mistaken. I say 'may have been,' for who am I to set myself up as a better judge than they? They tell me that we always come closer to God when we try to obey

[1] F. Mauriac, *Life of Jesus*, David McKay, New York, 1951

Him, even if we are making mistakes. There is a striking Biblical illustration of this in the sacrifice of Isaac (Gen. 22.1-18). God Himself, through an angel, stops Abraham at the last moment, when his hand is raised, and tells him he was mistaken when he thought he was being commanded to butcher his only son. But the angel adds: 'Because thou hast done this thing, and hast not withheld thy son, thine only son. . . . I will bless thee' (Gen. 22.16-17).

Thus, even by his error, Abraham was led to a greater experience of God, an experience quite new in his day, when human sacrifices to the divinity were still common. And Abraham thus became the first of all the long line of believers, of those who in every circumstance of life seek to know what message from God that circumstance brings them. They are not for that spared error and hesitation. Look, for example, at Gideon (Judg. 6.11-40): he is the lowliest member of the lowliest family in Israel; and suddenly a man comes to him telling him that God has chosen him to lead His people to victory over their powerful oppressors. The thing seems so unlikely that Gideon asks for proof. 'And Gideon said unto God, If thou wilt save Israel by mine hand, as thou hast spoken, behold, I will put a fleece of wool on the threshing-floor; if there be dew on the fleece only, and it be dry upon all the ground, then shall I know that thou wilt save Israel by mine hand, as thou hast spoken. And it was so.' But that is not enough for Gideon, who demands a second proof from God: this time he asks Him to 'let it be dry only upon the fleece, and upon all the ground let there be dew'. And God does not resent Gideon's prudent insistence: He grants him his second proof.

Thus, to seek the meaning of things and God's will does not spare us either from error or from doubt; nor does it resolve all the mysteries of our destiny, all the insoluble problems which are set us by any event in Nature or in our lives; nevertheless, it does give a new meaning to our lives.

We see this clearly in our patients. Patients who are sceptics endure a threefold suffering: they suffer from their disease, and they suffer on account of its meaninglessness for them. It is in their eyes nothing but a more or less serious vexation, the result of blind chance; they suffer again because it suspends their life:

they wait passively, as it were, for their cure, in order to begin living again.

The real believer, on the contrary, even though his faith may not deliver him from his disease or diminish the suffering it causes him, continues to live as intensely as before, and even more so. For to him life consists in seeking and listening to God. He can seek God in the silence of sickness as well as in the fire of action. His ears are open to what God says to him through his sickness, and that may sometimes be for him such a fruitful experience that he will bless his sickness.

The sceptic will be asking: 'Do you claim that disease is sent by God? And if it does not come from God, why do you want me to seek God's will in it?' His logic is impeccable, but his triumph is sterile; and the bitterness in his heart will compromise his recovery.

The believer, on the other hand, is so absorbed in seeking what God means to say to him that he does not trouble to ask unanswerable questions.

Thus throughout the Bible we meet men as human as we are, who may make mistakes, who like us are feeling their way in this discovery of God, but who have this in common, that they believe that everything has meaning, that everything can help us to get to know God better. To understand them we must put ourselves in the same perspective as they.

In that perspective, Nature has a meaning:

> *The heavens declare the glory of God;*
> *And the firmament sheweth his handiwork.*
> *Day unto day uttereth speech,*
> *And night unto night sheweth knowledge.*
> *There is no speech nor language;*
> *Their voice cannot be heard* (Ps. 19.1-4).

I ought here to be evoking all the poetry of the Bible. The word is not accidental, for is not poetry precisely the expression of the meaning of things? Professor Marcel Raymond admirably demonstrated this in a lecture to the students of Geneva on the function of literature in the search for truth.[1] He shows us a

[1] Marcel Raymond, *Le sens de la qualité*, La Baconnière, Boudry, 1948

poet and a scientist before a sunset on the sea. For the scientist the whole thing is a matter of physical and chemical phenomena which he may study, an affair of radiations and of molecules; they may be studied equally well in a piece of wood. That, though true, is not the whole truth. The spectacle touches the soul of the poet and speaks to him; that also is true. Are we not back again at the two diagnoses, both of them true, yet neither confounded with each other nor opposing each other? The poet feels and admires. To feel is to recognize a meaning in things; to admire is to recognize something greater than ourselves, something which comes from God.

Dr. A. Tzanck, in *La conscience créatrice*,[1] speaks also of admiration, that beneficent and stimulating virtue of which a purely scientific view of the world tends to rob us. He tells of an early experience in the dissecting-room. Full of confidence in his scientific studies, he expected to find in the body what his text-book said was there. And then he suddenly saw that in the part he was dissecting there were two arteries instead of one. Full of wonder, the future professor dashed off to find the laboratory chief to show him his find. The latter merely said: 'It is an anomaly.' Yes, it is an anomaly. With this word the scientist has said everything. A genius, a saint, a miracle, are doubtless also anomalies.

I do not know what has become of the laboratory chief, but I doubt whether he has kept the astonishing youth of mind of Dr. Tzanck. I believe I may say that God had spoken to the future Dr. Tzanck through that corpse that he was dissecting. In the emotion he felt, a new realization was dawning upon him: the realization that science is not the only road to truth. Throughout a long career as a scientist, brought up as he was outside the influence of any religion, this intuition has never stopped growing and setting before him its disturbing question mark. It eventually led him to write *La conscience créatrice*, a most unexpected book, in which the laboratory worker, the biologist that he has now become, sets out the conclusions of his thoughts about life: that even the smallest manifestation cannot be understood without admitting the existence of a spiritual reality.

A good friend has taken me to task over what he calls my naïve admiration in quoting enthusiastically books which he regards

[1] Charlot Publications, Algiers, 1943

with the utmost reserve. Together we have discussed the subject at length, and I have realized that there is between us a difference of attitude similar to that that I have just mentioned in regard to Dr. Tzanck. I read little, but always passionately. I am seldom disappointed in a book. On the contrary, it arouses my interest, while my friend nearly always arrives at the last page with an air of disillusion, repeating the celebrated formula: what is new in it is not true, and what is true in it is not new!

Since my friend and I are both psychologists, we have tried to find the underlying cause of this difference of attitude. I have noticed that in reading a book I do not only read what the author writes; I read as well every train of thought which his writings start in my mind, all the many associations of ideas. He speaks of law: I think what that means for medicine. Even—perhaps most of all—parts of the book with which I am in no sort of agreement, awake in me so many exciting ideas that my pleasure exceeds my dissatisfaction. I have always liked people who are ready to argue.

Perhaps I should be doing violence to the truth if I said that God speaks to me through every book I read. Nevertheless there is something here of that attitude of which I was speaking just now when I said that the believer is always 'listening-in' to God. Similarly, my patients very often say to me: 'I admire the patience with which you listen to everything I tell you.' It is not patience at all, but interest. Everything is of absorbing interest to the person who is always looking for the meaning of things. There is so much to learn from the least important case if one is animated by this spirit of curiosity. There are no ordinary cases. All the greatest problems of human destiny are fundamentally present in the life of every person and in every situation we meet.

I am always surprised to find people so uninterested in understanding others. They would rather read their own party newspaper than that of the opposing party; or if they do read it, it always rouses their anger. A husband speaks to me about his wife; every sentence begins with: 'I don't know how she can say this or do that . . .', which means: I do not admit that anyone should think or act differently from me, and I don't in the least want to understand why.

After all, if woman were exactly like man, would marriage be marriage? Would it bring the stupendous enrichment that we find in it? Following in the steps of his master, C. G. Jung, Dr. Aloys von Orelli has described[1] this function of marriage, which, through the encounter with the opposite sex, assures the evolution and the development of the person. As a Christian, he sees in it the divine 'meaning' of marriage, the purpose of God in marriage. 'God created man . . . male and female' (Gen. 1.27), the Bible says, literally. That is to say that what He created was not an individual, but a community, the couple. He did not create two complete and independent beings who would then associate together as a matter of convenience. The complete being is the couple. The encounter with the opposite sex, with all its difficulties of mutual adaptation and comprehension, is one of the factors in the integration of the person. Dr. Paul Plattner, in his book[2] on marriage problems, has also shown quite practically the role that these problems can play in the personal development of both husband and wife.

We always find it more acceptable to have God speaking to us directly rather than through our wives! But we may learn a great deal by listening to what He says to us through them.

[1] A. von Orelli, 'Schatten, animus und anima', in *Die neue Sendung des Arztes*, Tyrolia-Verlag, Innsbruck-Vienna, 1947

[2] Paul Plattner, *Glücklichere Ehen*, Verl. Hans Huber, Berne, 1950

5

THE MEANING OF NATURE

IN THE BIBLICAL perspective, Nature has a meaning. It speaks to us of God; not only of His greatness or His wisdom, but also of His love. The creation, according to the Bible, is a manifestation of the love of God. God created the world for love. Love, and love alone, is the reason for the world's existence. The world is a part of God's plan, of His design of love. The Bible, throughout its revelation, including what it tells us of God's plan of Redemption, remains in a perspective of incarnation: the love of God, according to the Bible, is not active only on the level of pure spirit; it manifests itself also on the material level. 'In the beginning,' run the first words of the Bible, 'God created the heaven *and* the earth' (Gen. 1.1); that is, He manifested His love not only in the spiritual order but also in the temporal. Nature participates in the Fall and in the Redemption: 'The whole creation,' writes St. Paul, 'groaneth and travaileth in pain' (Rom. 8.22); and in his vision of the end of the world St. John sees not only a new heaven appearing, but also a new earth (Rev. 21.1).

Perhaps the reader is thinking that I am wandering off into theological considerations that have no bearing on medicine. But surely it is very important to us doctors, concerned as we are with the body and with matter, to know that God cares about them as much as about the soul.

When we recover this awareness of the meaning of things, our attitude towards Nature undergoes a marked change. We have said that looked at from a purely scientific point of view the world appears irrational.

An irrational world is a hostile one. A little thought will show the far-reaching implications of this truth. Think how many people live today as if hounded by a host of enemies: cold, heat, wind, rain, sun, microbes, poisons, men, society, psychological complexes. They spend their time in being irritated, in complaining, in protecting themselves, and in being afraid.

As I write these lines I remember that I dislike working in the open air, because when I am working I spread about me a large number of little sheets of paper. There is a sudden puff of wind. Seeing my irritation my wife calls out: 'There goes your enemy the wind again!' Is it really my enemy? Has it no message from God for me? Is it not here to remind me that I am taking myself and my little bits of paper too seriously? That these pieces of paper are, for Nature, no heavier than all those in which the modern State is submerging us? That what matters is what is in my heart!

To be surrounded by enemies is to live in a state of constant annoyance and under a constant threat; it is to be also more vulnerable to all those threats. Consider the old gentleman who refuses to accept the modern age, and is always singing the praises of the good old days when there were no cars in the streets. All this dense traffic seems to be aimed at him. A swarm of cars pursues him, its number seeming to increase with his panic. He advances, steps back, throws himself to this side and that, and finishes up under the wheels of a lorry.

Perhaps you think I am broadening the discussion too much; that I am no longer talking about Nature. But we have here that negative attitude towards the external world which has largely been suggested to us by modern science, medicine and psychology, and which invades the whole being; and we see the disastrous consequences which follow from that attitude as well for our physical as our mental health. You know those people who are obsessed and made bitter by this hostile irrational world: they hate the cold because it freezes them, heat because it stifles them; they hate men because they are egotists and women because they are jealous; they hate old people because they are cautious and young people because they are forward; they hate talkative people because they are bored by them, and taciturn people because they are paralysed by them; they hate tradition because it is dull and revolution because it is uncomfortable; they hate the government because it restricts them and the anarchist because he threatens them.

I could easily prolong the list, but I do not want the reader to misunderstand me: for the man who has learnt to seek the meaning of things, there are, behind the negative appearance of these torrents of complaints, great positive aspirations; aspirations towards justice, love, understanding, and true living.

But that is precisely the point: modern man has largely lost the sense of his own responsibility for his destiny. He feels himself hunted, as it were, by external enemies, before whom he is reduced to running away or to waiting passively for help, this also from outside. And this false attitude he owes chiefly to the conception of the world that he has gained from science. The fact is that science shows him only the mechanism of things and not their inner significance. It has peopled his universe with blind, inexorable, automatic forces which prowl ceaselessly around him and in him: gravitation, chemical affinities, bacteria, heredity, and psychological complexes.

Now this generalized determinism, even when it is at work within his own body, seems to him to be impersonal, external to himself, foreign to him: it is an endless chain of cause and effect, for which he himself feels no responsibility whatever.

If he falls ill, it is because of his liver, or his blood-pressure, the chromosomes of his parents, or the emotional shocks that he has suffered, the draught or the bacilli which he happened to encounter. Against those misfortunes which befall him he waits for help that is itself external, foreign to him. He waits passively for technical medicine to attack them in its turn with irradiations, disinfectants, intravenous injections, or psycho-therapy.

Thus the patient tends to become a battlefield on which formidable armies confront each other. A sort of armaments race takes place, and health seems to depend no longer on anything but the discovery of a bomb more powerful than the ones before it. The analogy goes deeper than at first appears. Just as a new weapon of war is soon matched by new defensive methods, so, it seems, do the microbes adapt themselves and train themselves gradually to resist new techniques which at first seemed devastatingly successful against them. Cases of 'penicillin resistance' seem to be becoming more common.

I was staying in Florence recently with a doctor friend. He called me to the bedside of an apparently moribund old woman. She lay there, her eyes vacant, making no more resistance to what was happening to her than would an inanimate object. She had passed through the hands of many doctors who had treated her heart with the powerful weapons of our various modern cardiac stimulants. My colleague leant over her and said gently: 'My dear, you must not rely only on medicine: there is yourself first, and God, and only after that the doctors.' I saw in him the man of the people that he is, who knew how to talk to this woman of the people, recalling her to those basic truths whose importance is as great as ever in medicine, in spite of all our technical progress.

The patient looked in astonishment at this doctor, the first one to treat her as a person and not only as a case of heart-trouble. She began to wake out of her passivity, to become once more aware of the part that she also had to play in the struggle; she was becoming a person again. 'Science,' writes Dr. Carrel,[1] 'has miraculously taken the edge off the bitter struggle for every-day life. We are fed, clothed, sheltered, transported and even educated by the work of machines. Thanks to the progress of technology, the greater part of the restraints imposed on us by the cosmos have disappeared and, along with them, the creative personal effort which those restraints demanded.'

I do not wish to belittle the powerful weapons placed in our hands by medical progress and by the wonderful work done in the laboratories of our chemical factories. In this respect my generation has seen more changes than have taken place over several centuries. As a young doctor, I was assistant to Dr. Wiki, a professor of therapeutics, who was fond of saying: 'If you are told that a medicine is harmless, you may take it that it also lacks any healing properties.' That was about the time when Charles Fiessinger published his *La thérapeutique en vingt médicaments* ('Therapeutics in Twenty Remedies'). It did not take long, then, to reckon up the total of tried remedies and effective techniques. Today we should have to put it at a good forty, since the introduction of the sulphonamide drugs, vitamins, synthetic hormones, penicillin, streptomycin, narco-analysis, electro-convulsive therapy, lobotomy, and so on.

But everyone knows that it is dangerous suddenly to become

[1] Alexis Carrel, *Reflections on life*, translated by Antonia White, Hawthorn Books, New York, 1953, p. 21

very powerful. Dr. Kressmann has rightly examined this question in his *Misère et grandeur de la médecine*.[1] He writes: 'I was seeing yesterday a doctor who described to me the tragic end of one of his patients who suffered from secondary carcinoma in the bone. Explaining to me that this youth of eighteen had received, since the age of nine, two injections a week of synthetic male hormone to promote growth, the practitioner concluded: "It is difficult to know whether this intensive therapy contributed to the formation of the tumour, but I should not care to have prescribed it." '

Dr. Kressmann continues: 'Faced with the great mass of unknown quantities which we handle every day, I confess that I tremble at the carefree way in which our researchers nowadays advocate new methods, without giving a thought to their attendant risks.'

[1] Delachaux et Niestlé, Neuchâtel, 1950

6

MEDICINE AND NATURE

A PATIENT of mine who had just returned from Paris described to me one day the confinement of a young relation of hers. The present fashion is to bring on the confinement at eight and a half months instead of respecting the period ordained by God. The year before, a good dose of quinine had sufficed. But this year, since quinine had no effect, the expectant mother was taken to the nursing-home. There followed an injection of posterior pituitary extract, and labour began. But it soon ceased. A second injection of extract was given, several more interventions including narcosis were tried, with the result that at two o'clock in the afternoon the patient came round to find herself the happy mother of a fine baby. The next morning, the young mother was already back home, armed no doubt with injunctions from her doctor to be careful. But such is the progress of science that these warnings are seldom heeded. The young mother got up to be weighed, received visitors, and did not give herself a moment's rest until suddenly, at midnight, she had a violent fit of shivering and frightful pains. The doctor was telephoned for. When after some delay he arrived, he administered strong doses of penicillin. Examination was impossible; further narcosis and an operation was decided upon. Meanwhile, fortunately, a large clot was expelled. Thanks to the penicillin, the fever was reduced. Wonderful! So wonderful that a day or two later when her husband was getting ready to go to a big society reception, his wife suddenly said to him: 'Wait for me! I'm coming with you.' In the middle of the festivities she had a fearful haemorrhage, was rushed to the nursing-home where she had an emergency operation, and blood transfusions. Victory! Then phlebitis threatened—more penicillin treatment, and all was well.

I tell this story in no spirit of ill-will—even with admiration for the fine courage and devoted zeal with which my brother doctors carry on daily these heroic struggles against death. With reserve, too, for patients cannot always understand why the doctor acts as he does. In any case that young mother has nothing but admiration and gratitude for the doctor who delivered her, and rightly so. But that story is symptomatic of a state of mind which is gaining ground both in the medical profession and among the public. It is a state of mind to which we must now give some thought. The more powerful medicine becomes, the more it becomes interventionist, and the more do patients impel it to become so, thinking thus that they can flout the demands of nature.

It is quite true that the penicillin, the blood-transfusions, and the operations saved that young woman's life several times over. But the modern mentality also contributed to her exposure to death. Though death was warded off in this case, it is not always so. And in the future, will not this exciting adventure-film leave that woman less resistant than would have been the case with a good old-fashioned confinement, with its wise, lengthy after-care in the nursing-home, teaching the mother right from the start that she must make sacrifices for the sake of her child? 'He who tries imperiously by force to shorten his ills,' wrote Montaigne, 'does but lengthen and increase the sum of them.'

The same tendency is evident in psychiatry, which has been endowed with new, efficient and quick acting weapons in rapid succession: malarial therapy, insulin treatment, E.C.T., narco-analysis, and now brain surgery.

These methods are of value. They have restored to health or at least afforded relief to very many sick people for whom twenty years ago we felt we could do nothing. But there is a temptation to put them into general use without due caution. The temptation is so great that many clear-sighted people, both within and without the medical profession, have in recent years become nervous of it. There have been some much-publicized court cases as a result of the use of narcotics in interrogation by the police. I took part in a wireless interview on this subject, along with several lawyers. The 'debate' which we were supposed to conduct before the microphone was not one at all, for we were all agreed that the practice ought to be condemned on the grounds that it violated that respect which is the inalienable right of the human person.

That is indeed the heart of the matter, as the late Emmanuel Mounier clearly showed in the great investigation he made into 'medicine, the fourth estate,' the results of which he published just before his death in his review, *Esprit*. I invite the reader to consult it for himself—I could not in a few lines do justice to such a valuable work.[1]

To what extent, Mounier asked, has the doctor the right to use methods which bring about serious changes in the personality? This is the case, especially, in leucotomy, the severing of the nerve fibres connecting the frontal lobe with the rest of the brain. Some doctors reply with a categorical negative: such intervention, permanently modifying as it does the character, behaviour and emotional make-up of the patient, seems to them inadmissible. A similar concern for the respect due to the human person leads also to condemnation of the use of shock treatment in psychiatry. Other doctors, however, are enthusiastic about the immense new possibilities opened up by these methods, and see in the opposition to them only the vestiges of old-fashioned prejudice; throughout its history science has had to overcome similar prejudice in order to bring to men its incomparable benefits.

For my part, I cannot take up either of these extreme positions. A little thought will show that all medical action, and even all action in education, constitutes an intervention implicitly aimed at modifying the personality. Whether I make an injection of thyroid extract, or practise psychotherapy by means of a fireside chat, or give a lesson on natural history or geological periods, I am bringing my patient or my pupil into contact with new elements which will change his ideas, his character, his social behaviour and his emotional outlook. To condemn every interference with the personality would be to condemn the whole of medicine and education. The scale runs in insensibly progressive stages from the most ordinary conversation right up to leucotomy. To draw a hard-and-fast line anywhere between them is to engage in arbitrary casuistry.

The discussion requires us to have a clear idea of the distinction between the person and the personality. Our personality is not

[1] 'Médecine, quatrième pouvoir?' in *Esprit*, special issue, March, 1950

static; it is the result of innate tendencies and of physical factors which we owe to our heredity. But it is also the result of the whole of our experience, of the teaching we have received, of the influences under which we have come, of the people we have met, of the books we have read and the films we have seen. And with each new day, even on a desert island, our personality will go on changing.

The intangible thing, it seems to me, is not the personality but the person; that which is immutable in us; that which is or is not; that which is specifically human, distinguishing the man from the animal. We are no more than animals if our freedom of choice and our sense of responsibility are taken from us; if we are deprived of our right to choose the influences which will modify our personality, and, in the last analysis, our right freely to obey or disobey God. We are persons when these possibilities and this right are safeguarded. For this reason, to speak of the person and of respect for the person, is to speak, not of that in man which is physical, psychological or intellectual, but of what is spiritual in him, his moral conscience, his sense of responsibility, his freedom of choice.

The doctor who administers an intravenous injection, however harmless and discreet, without giving any reason to the patient for it, or indicating the results anticipated, or the risks run, is treating him as an animal, as a thing, simply as a passive battle-field, as we said just now. To employ narco-analysis, as I have had occasion to do, with the full understanding and consent of the patient, after having thoroughly explained to him that in the state of half-sleep he may well reveal secrets which he would rather have kept to himself, seems to me to be respecting the patient's person. It leaves him, in fact, free to judge for himself according to his own conscience whether he will accept the intervention as a gift from God or refuse it as a violation of his essential self.

Recently I took part in a medical conference at Annecy, convened by Professor Delore of Lyons, and devoted to the problems of doctor-patient relationships. As Dr. Delore pointed out in his concluding speech, the thing that stood out most in numerous reports and in our discussions, was the importance of giving the patient as much information as possible about his disease and the treatments being used on him. What makes the patient feel that he counts as a person is the doctor's appeal to his judgement and personal co-operation.

In an article on 'Neuro-surgery and the Human Person,'[1] Dr. Trotot, of Paris, maintains that respect for the person implies essentially the 'express consent of the subject' to every intervention, provided, of course, that he is in full possession of his faculties. He quotes, further, a wise suggestion by Cushing: 'The day before the operation, the neuro-surgeon must have a personal talk with his patient, in order to prepare him morally, to give him confidence, and to enlist him as a team-mate in the difficult enterprise to be undertaken on the morrow.'

It seems to me, then, that respect for the person depends not so much on the nature of the medical intervention as on the spirit in which it is carried out. Now, whatever technique we are using, it is not within the province of science to furnish us with this spirit, this idea of the person and the respect due to it. As we have seen, man is to science but a collection of atoms, cells and organs, an interplay of physical, chemical and psychological phenomena. Why should we respect that more than a stone or a dog? Be it noted that there is no objection, scientifically speaking, to such experiments on living human beings as were practised in the Nazi concentration-camps. Doctors, in Germany as well as elsewhere, who protested vigorously, confessed in so doing that man is a spiritual being and not a mere machine, and that the doctor cannot be guided by science alone in his professional activity.

By whom then is he to be guided if not by God? Some will reply: by his human ideal. I have no objection; but it must be admitted that this human ideal is convincing, when confronted by a purely scientific conception, only to the extent to which it tallies with the conception of man and of Nature provided by Revelation. We are brought back to the Bible, the object of our study.

Over against technical medicine, which multiplies its doses, injections, interventions of all kinds, stand the naturist, homoeopathic, and neo-Hippocratic schools of thought. Technical medicine, as we have seen, tends to make us regard Nature as a

[1] As yet unpublished

world of enemies that must be attacked, coerced, and outwitted by every means at our disposal. The adherents of the second group, on the contrary, retain a sense of the organic links binding man to Nature. They emphasize the wisdom of submission to the laws of Nature, and the priority of hygiene and right living over aggressive therapeutics. In many respects their views are similar to those of the Bible which I am here discussing.

But in the absence of a firm Biblical foundation, there appears another danger, that of making Nature herself a god, so that naturism becomes a religion, and an exceedingly fanatical one. Every doctor must, like me, have seen large numbers of its adepts who have become real slaves of their dogma. To this state of affairs is due the note of violent and implacable polemic against orthodox medicine which detracts from the otherwise useful work of, for example, Carton. Maxence van der Meersch's fine book, *Bodies and Souls*[1] is similarly marred, and we find it again in Hahnemann.[2]

Through the reading of such books patients can become thoroughly obsessed. A new world of enemies has arisen: a grain of refined sugar, a tomato, a medical injection, a surgical operation, a pneumothorax, are feared as if they were serious crimes. While scientific medicine tended to make man too passive, naturism makes him too active, as if he had to save himself by his own efforts. He worries terrifically about his diet, goes through his exercises as if they were a solemn rite, and treats his 'controlled breathing' as a cure-all.

These two attitudes are not confined to healing, but can be seen in life in general. On the one hand there is the moralist, weighed down under his concern for perfection, obsessed by his fear of making a mistake, and always blaming himself even when he is the victim of the wrong. On the other hand there is the no less widespread attitude of the irresponsible person who expects everything to come from others, and especially from the State. He wants it to feed him, care for him and entertain him, to educate his children, to regulate his whole life and free him from

[1] Translated by Eithne Wilkins, Pilot Press, London, 1948

[2] S. C. F. Hahnemann, *The Homoeopathic Medical Doctrine or 'Organon of the Healing Art'; a New System of Physic*, translated by C. H. Devrient, with notes by S. Stratten, Dublin, 1833

the duties he undertook when he married, when these duties become irksome to him. I have shown that science is partly to blame for this passivity. I say partly, for the psychologist sees in it also a symptom of infantile regression. It is the attitude of the infant who cries when he is hungry, and waits for the maternal breast to be put into his mouth.

We see that there are two extreme and opposite positions, whose ultimate source is to be found in our conception of Nature. One view scorns Nature, the other over-estimates it; one boldly opposes and coerces it, the other slavishly submits to it; one prescribes innumerable medicaments, the other none at all; one deprives men of the benefits of healthy living, and the other those of medical science. We see, further, that these two views lead to a limitation of the fullness of human life and of human liberty. One makes men slaves of artificial and external processes from which they expect all help to come, and which they strive to multiply—think how many quite healthy people never go to sleep today without a sedative—and the other makes them slaves of their internal scruples.

7

THE BIBLICAL ATTITUDE

THE BIBLE, on the contrary, gives us a conception of
Nature and of man which alone can lead him to com-
pleteness. For such a man the whole of Nature is a gift of
God; it is a book in which he may learn from his Creator the
art of healthy living. But he has received from this same Creator
power over Nature, so that he is not its prisoner. In the Biblical
perspective he takes his place in Nature without being enslaved
by it. Such also is the best tradition of medicine, a tradition
which intoxication with modern discoveries is threatening to
obliterate. The best clinical practitioners of every century have
invariably drawn their inspiration from this tradition: careful
observers of Nature, always ready to be corrected by her,
judicious in their prescriptions, bold when necessary, but having
the patience of the peasant and no prejudices.

St. Paul also teaches this doctrine of liberty: 'prove all things;
hold fast that which is good' (I Thess. 5.21). 'All things are lawful
for me; but not all things are expedient. All things are lawful for
me; but I will not be brought under the power of any' (I Cor.
6.12).

For the Bible, Nature and Society have a meaning; they
are God's instruments, but still only instruments. They have a
meaning; that is to say, they are neither enemies nor values in
themselves. They are signs: their value, their meaning, lies in the
fact that they speak to us of God and lead us to Him. That is the
way in which all the men of the Bible regard Nature: they seek
in it always the voice of God.

For them, for example, the Flood has a meaning (Gen. 7.4);
it is sent by God, who engulfs in its waters a humanity that has
roused His wrath by its infidelities; whereas in Noah, who is
obedient to His as yet incomprehensible command, God prepares
a new human race with which He will be able to make a covenant. Similarly, the flowing back of the Red Sea (Ex. 14.21) or of

54

Jordan (Josh. 3.16) have a meaning. They have certainly a natural cause, in the great wind that drove back the waters. But in that wind the Biblical writer sees at work God's will to save His people from the Egyptians, or to bring them into the Promised Land. Here are some more examples. The prophet Isaiah watches the rain falling on the fields and making them fruitful, and sees in it a wonderful message from God: 'So shall my word be that goeth forth out of my mouth: it shall not return unto me void' (Isa. 55.11).

The prophet Elijah has performed miracles in God's service; in His name he has prophesied the drought and then the rain; he has revived a child in a state of asphyxia. This great fighter has stood up to King Ahab and to Jezebel, his sinister partner. Alone, faced by the 450 prophets of Baal and the 400 prophets of Astarte, he has called upon the Lord; he has confounded them, with God's help, and led the people to slay them.

But at the height of his triumph he is overcome with chagrin at Jezebel's inveterate hatred of him; he flees to the desert and begs for death; he begins to doubt himself: 'I am not better than my fathers' (I Kings 19.4). Then comes the storm, then an earthquake, then a fire; finally a 'still small voice' (I Kings 19.12), and it is in this soft breath of the breeze that Elijah hears God's voice. Something like Elijah's great experience has also been granted to me. After I had for years, in the bosom of my Church, put all my ardour into violent but practically fruitless arguments, God called me to myself and showed me that charity is more fruitful than strife, and entrusted me with a veritable spiritual ministry.

Very different was the case of Job, who heard God's voice in the tempest. An upright and God-fearing man, he had lost one after another, without complaining, his cattle and asses, his servants, his sheep and camels, and then his sons and daughters. Thereupon he fell sick with 'sore boils from the sole of his foot unto his crown' (Job 2.7). Lying on his mean pallet, he had to put up with the sarcasms of his wife and the self-satisfied discourses of his friends! How vividly the Book of Job warns us against those unfitting and complacent sermons preached at the sick person's bedside; they make even Biblical truths oppressive. Well might Job be roused to cry out in rebellion against God. But amid the roar of the storm Job heard the voice of God; beside His majesty he saw how small man is: 'Behold, I am of small account; what shall I answer thee? I lay my hand upon my mouth' (Job 40.4).

These men of the Bible, always listening to God, hear Him in Nature. They see His will, His command, His sign in the wind that drives away the clouds of the Deluge (Gen. 8.1), in the rainbow set in the sky (Gen. 9.13), in the fire that strikes the mountain (Deut. 4.36), in the varying dewfall (Judg. 9.15-23), and in the star that the Magi followed (Matt. 2.9).

To all these examples, which relate to people of widely differing types, I must now add that of Jesus Christ Himself. Everything in Nature speaks to His heart, attentive always to the voice of God. He looks at the birds flying above Him and the flowers in the fields around Him, and sees in them God's mighty care for each one of His creatures (Matt. 6.26). For Him there is no such thing as chance: 'The very hairs of your head are all numbered,' He says (Matt. 10.30). With His disciples He watches the sky reddening in the sunset, and teaches them to discern 'the signs of the times' (Matt. 16.2-3), the meaning of things, the meaning of History along with the meaning of Nature. He sees the sower in his field; He sees the parched grain that has fallen by the roadside and the wheat growing in the good ground (Luke 8.5); the flock of sheep that passes, following the voice of the shepherd (John 10.4); the weeds which grow in the cornfield, and which must be accepted and put up with until the harvest (Matt. 13.29); the fig-tree that bears no fruit because it has not been properly looked after (Luke 13.6); the yeast that the baker puts in his dough to make it rise (Luke 13.21); the husbandman pruning his vine (John 15.2). Everything speaks to Him of God, everything is an image of the spiritual world, from the smallest grain of mustard-seed (Mark 4.31) to the wind that blows where it lists without our knowing whence it comes or whither it goes (John 3.8). I could give many more examples; no one has ever seen the meaning of Nature better than He.

Our own bodies are also a part of Nature. 'Our brother the body,' Professor Delore calls it.[1] If we look upon Nature as an enemy, we must also regard as hostile our own bodies and their reactions. The import of such an attitude in medicine will be readily understood: it would entail a battle against oneself, a

[1] Pierre Delore, *Notre frère corps*, Paris, 1938

sort of internal civil war. Sick people have often expressed to me their irritation and resentment against their bodies. It is very understandable, when their bodies cause them great pain or seriously shorten their lives. Nevertheless, all bodily suffering and limitation has its meaning. We can learn much from our bodies. Some of my patients, filled with high ideals and fine ambitions, resent the way their bodies hold them back. Perhaps they ought to be thankful for this check on their over-impulsive natures.

Very often the protests of the body are alarm-signals. Last year my wife suddenly fell while running down the garden, and broke her leg. An absurd accident—pure 'chance', to use again the word I have had such frequent occasion to write in the previous chapters. But this accident had its meaning; we realized that God had a message for us. We were trying to do too much; we had allowed our lives to become too full. My patients lean on me, and I in my turn lean on my wife; too much on my wife and not enough on God. I had leant so hard that the support had snapped. God was calling us in that accident; calling us to reflect on the conduct of our lives and to check the headlong rush that they had become. My wife had been stricken by a succession of bereavements; and so as not to upset my work she had postponed the holiday that would have given her a chance of recuperation.

In disease also, many symptoms are signals. When the body creaks, it is not mere chance. The warning should be heeded. How often, for example, a 'nervous depression' is seen to be a sort of winter of the soul, in which Nature is resting and silently preparing for a new spring. Doubtless we may also see the merciful hand of God in the powerful drugs with which we may ease pain, arrest diarrhoea, stimulate a faltering heart, or procure a little sleep. But we must also be on our guard lest these aids drug the patient's conscience as well, blinding him to the need for reforming his way of life.

The Bible teaches that misfortune, accidents and disease have a meaning. Here are a few examples. Firstly, there is the well-known account of the Ten Plagues of Egypt (Ex. 7-11); and then the leprosy of Miriam, Moses' sister, which was a punishment for having spoken ill of her sister-in-law (Num. 12.10); the enteritis which struck down King Jehoram because of his unfaithfulness to God (II Chron. 21.18); the leprosy which fell upon

Gehazi, Elisha's servant, guilty of deceit and cupidity (II Kings 5.27); the death of the child whom David had by the wife of Uriah (II Sam. 12.18), and that of the two sons of Eli, both on the same day, in which the unhappy father sees a 'sign' of God's displeasure (I Sam. 2.34).

Everywhere the men of the Bible feel God at work in natural events, and they seek to discover in them His purpose and His message.

The Bible does not despise the body. It calls it the temple of the Holy Ghost (I Cor. 6.19). 'I will give thanks unto thee; for I am fearfully and wonderfully made,' cries the psalmist (Ps. 139.14). The supreme witness of God's love—we may say, therefore, His most 'spiritual' act—the Bible sees to be in the incarnation of Jesus Christ, in his taking the 'likeness and fashion' of a man, with all the consequences that are involved, including suffering and death (Phil. 2.6-7). Elsewhere St. Paul compares the love of a man for his wife with that of Christ for His Church (Eph. 5.25); and in the realism of the Bible that means an all-embracing love, carnal as well as spiritual. Similarly the physiological harmony of the body, the working together of all its organs, is presented as the image of the accord that should reign in the Church through charity (I Cor. 12.12-30). Thus, in the Biblical perspective, God's purpose is manifested in the harmony of Nature as well as in the spiritual communion of souls.

As Dr. Théo Bovet has pointed out,[1] the two passages just quoted show how mistaken is the distinction made by some theologians between ερος and αγαπη, carnal and spiritual love. The Song of Songs, the great love-poem of the Bible, exalts the passion which draws man towards woman (Song of S. 4.1), and the impatience of the woman as she waits for him on whom her heart is set (Song of S. 3.1), just as humanity seeks the love of God. Here also one might point to all the passages in the prophets, where they compare the love of God for His people with that of the man for the woman, and the unfaithfulness of this people with that of an adulterous wife (Ezek. 16.6-43).

The Platonic idea of spirit is not found in the Bible, unless it be in the case of God Himself before the Creation (Gen. 1.2; John 1.1). But it is quite clear that in these two passages the

[1] Théodore Bovet, *Die Ehe, ihre Krise und Neuwerdung*, Haupt, Berne

emphasis is on the Creation and the Incarnation. The Bible considers the Creation and the Incarnation to be of the very essence of God's plan, whereas Plato regarded matter as a temporary accident in the destiny of pure spirit. Evidence of the Biblical view is given by the strong insistence of the Gospel on the corporeal existence of the resurrected Christ (John 20.27). Similarly, the resurrection promised us by the Bible is not the immortality of the soul or its absorption into a great universal whole, but rather a personal resurrection, a resurrection of the whole person with a body as well as a soul (Phil. 3.21). The truth compels me to quote also from Ecclesiastes: '. . . and the dust return to the earth as it was, and the spirit return unto God who gave it' (12.7), a text often quoted at the grave-side in funeral services, and usually understood in the Platonic sense referred to above. I believe it must be interpreted otherwise, in the light of Christ's cry from the Cross: 'Father, into thy hands I commend my spirit' (Luke 23.46). As I have pointed out, that agony was followed by a resurrection of the body. Clearly it was a body of a kind quite different from that which we study in medicine, since the resurrected Christ was able to enter the room in which His disciples were gathered, in spite of the door being securely locked. It was what St. Paul was later to describe as 'raised in incorruption' (I Cor. 15.42). The 'dust' of Ecclesiastes would seem, then, to be the physico-chemical world which science knows, this corruptible world in which we are now living, with its perpetual cycles of anabolism and catabolism. We are none the less promised an incorruptible body after death—not, therefore, a pure spirit, but an incarnate spirit.

I have dealt with this subject at some length because of its extreme importance in medicine. The body is like a dog: if it is treated as an enemy, it snarls. To live in contempt of one's body, heaping it with abuse and vexation, is to wage a sort of civil war within oneself and to endanger one's health. We constantly meet patients who profess contempt of the body and at the same time an attachment to the things of the spirit. It is the cause of much neglect in the matter of hygiene and proper feeding. I have seen men and women, victims of narrow sectarianism, actually imposing under-nourishment on their wives or husbands and even on their children, on the plea of living a more Christian life.

I am not, of course, now advocating immoderation in food or drink. But such abuse itself is not unconnected, paradoxical though it may seem, with this idea that the soul and the body are opposed. A careful analysis of the mentality of the glutton will show that it is through his having lost the sense of the holiness of the body, of food or of drink (Ps. 104.10-15), that he treats them as inferior things that he may misuse as he likes.

We must also in this connection look at what St. Paul says to the Christians in Corinth: 'I buffet my body, and bring it into bondage: lest by any means, after that I have preached unto others, I myself should be rejected' (I Cor. 9.27). This text might be taken as an excuse for a negative attitude towards the body, and an appeal to an ascetic mortification of the flesh. I do not think it can be so interpreted. The Apostle has just alluded to the athlete who submits in order to 'keep fit' to a rigorous self-discipline. In his mind this severe training is not for a moment considered as an end, but as a means; not a redemptive mortification, but a proper mastery of the body for a particular purpose —the purpose of God in which this body has its proper role to perform. It is not a matter of treating the body as an enemy and raining blows upon it, but rather as a friend whom one helps to play his part correctly. As many doctors say nowadays, there is a hierarchy of the person, in which the body is not opposed to the spirit, but subjected to it, just as a good coachman holds his horse's reins firmly, not in order to maltreat it and paralyse it, but in order to put it on its mettle and to guide it.

I have known, for example, many young people obsessed with their fight against masturbation or lust. They often try desperately to mortify the body, either under the influence of the tendentious interpretation of the Bible which I am now condemning, or even influenced by a quite secular morality more akin to Hindu thought than to that of the Bible. Far from securing victory, this mistaken asceticism nearly always makes it more difficult. They exhaust their bodies in physical exercise, sleep on the floor, and cut down their food, and the only result is that their obsession is worse than ever. They lose that sense of direction and balance in their lives which is the prerequisite of victory.

It is to the point here to quote another of St. Paul's sayings, in his letter to the Christians in Rome, devoted entirely to the problems of immorality, of mistaken moral effort, and of grace: 'Overcome evil with good' (Rom. 12.21). That is to say, do not exhaust your strength in vain struggles, but adopt the positive attitude which is that of the whole Bible, in spite of certain strong traditions to the contrary in our Churches. 'Gospel' means 'Good news'; the good news of an active power, stronger than evil, disease and death, which is given us through Jesus Christ (John 16.33; Rom. 8.37; I Cor. 15.25-6). To overcome evil with good is to turn one's attention away from those besetting temptations, and to look towards Jesus Christ (Heb. 12.2), giving oneself up to Him body and soul, identifying oneself with Him (Gal. 2.20).

THE MEANING OF THE
INSTINCT OF SEX

JESUS CHRIST did not marry, it is true. But we find in
Him none of the symptoms of infantile regression which are
to the psychologist the distinctive marks of a repression of
instinct. On the contrary, He shows astonishing virility. For
those men are not the most virile who are weak enough to let
themselves be driven this way and that by every instinctive
impulse. The same can be said of most of the men of the Bible,
in whom one hardly ever finds repression of virility, and of the
women, too—they do not repress their femininity.

In the privacy of my consulting-room men and women of all
ages have often told me that they believe in God's forgiveness
for any sin except their sexual ones. For such sins they feel
God can never forgive them, but only despise them for ever. In
saying this they are projecting on to God their own contempt
of themselves, and proving that this contempt is not due to
the fact that they have sinned, but to the fact that the sin is a
sexual one. How different is Christ's attitude! His greatest
severity is reserved for those virtuous people the Pharisees.
He openly defends before them the woman taken in adultery
(John 8.3-11), and the challenge He throws out at them: 'He
that is without sin among you, let him first cast a stone at her'
(John 8.7), shows how well He knows the human heart. Those
are not the words of a man who has repressed his instincts into
the subconscious!

The gentleness and confidence with which He speaks to this
woman, as to the woman of Samaria (John 4.7-26), and to the
harlot (Luke 7.36-50) whose kisses He accepts, to the indignation
of Simon, show that His attitude is very far removed from that
puritanical contempt of sex which is only too often thought to

be Biblical. Elsewhere we read how He frequented the haunts of the more dubious characters, without a thought for His own reputation (Matt. 9.10).

With regard to the harlot, Jesus said to His host, Simon the Pharisee: 'Her sins, which are many, are forgiven; for she loved much' (Luke 7.47). He does not deny her sins, but unlike my patients of whom I spoke just now, He does not in the least consider them unforgivable. Further, His attitude towards the woman is in marked contrast with the attitude He adopts towards Simon. The scene made a great impression on our colleague, St. Luke—St. Paul calls him the beloved physician (Col. 4.14)—a keen observer of his fellow men.

Naturally, in saying 'she loved much', Jesus is not referring to the love that has become her profession, but to that quite disinterested love which she has just shown in the tears shed on His feet, in wiping them with her hair, and kissing and anointing them with perfume. To Jesus, this impulse of love is nothing less than faith: 'Thy faith hath saved thee; go in peace,' He says to her at the end.

But if it is really the Biblical attitude to sex that we are studying, we must not avoid seeing things as they are. Jesus, as this account shows, saw that people of loose morals—in spite of their misconduct and, of course, not justifying it—have very often more charity in their hearts than austere puritans like Simon, and they are more open to the impulses of faith. We too may observe the same thing. Jesus' own example shows us that we need not for that reason imitate their behaviour, but His attitude neverthe-less reveals the true Biblical meaning of the sex instinct.

I do not think that the Bible contradicts the theories of those psychoanalysts who have more or less identified the sex instinct, under the name of 'libido', with the life force and the need for love on the highest level. To Freud, the latter is but a sublimation of the former; to Jung, the sex instinct is an incarnate form of spiritual love. But both agree that there is a connection between the two, and this is in conformity with the Biblical view. I have already mentioned above, in quoting Dr. Théo Bovet, numerous Bible passages which clearly present the one as an image of the other.

The Bible honours sexual love; the Genesis account presents

the establishment of sexuality by God as His crowning act of creation (Gen. 1.27; 2.18-24). After creating the heaven and the earth, then the animals, and finally man—'male and female', that is to say, undifferentiated—God invented sexuality, sexual differentiation. A theologian once explained to me that the rib of Adam mentioned in this well-known story (my brother doctors will note that what took place was a surgical operation under anaesthesia!) could also mean 'side' in its abstract sense; and that what happened was the separation of the masculine and the feminine principles, whose instinctive mutual search to reunite was to become a most fruitful source of spiritual development.

The sex instinct in the Bible is not, therefore, a vulgar accident, but an element in God's scheme of things. By bringing man and woman together, and making their encounter a genuine communion in which each possesses the other, body and soul, it leads them to the discovery of the profoundest spiritual realities. This gives the marriage bond a character quite different from that of all other links between human beings; it is the only bond to which the Bible compares the communion between Jesus Christ and His Church. It explains why the saints, describing their deepest experiences of faith, have used an expression such as the 'mystic marriage' with Jesus Christ—an expression which has often shocked people who regard the instinct with disdain. This also explains the fact that psychoanalysis always reveals a deep-rooted mental association between the two spheres of sex and religion, being as they are the two spheres most heavily charged with emotion, reserve, and mystery.

However intimate we are with a friend, or however close our spiritual communion with a fellow Christian, there always remains a last barrier of reserve, which falls only in the marriage-bond. The giving of the body in conjugal love is forcefully described by that bachelor, St. Paul: 'The wife hath not power over her own body, but the husband; and likewise also the husband hath not power over his own body, but the wife' (I Cor. 7.4). In the Biblical perspective, this giving of the body in the marriage relationship, this tearing down of the last barrier of reserve, is the symbol of the giving of the whole being, and, finally, the symbol of the utter abandon of the self to God in faith. In speaking of the sex relationship, the Bible uses the word 'know'. 'And the man knew Eve, his wife' (Gen. 4.1). 'Joseph knew not Mary till she had brought forth a son: and he called his name Jesus' (Matt. 1.25). Now, the Bible uses the same word for the supreme bond of faith which binds man to God: 'And there hath not arisen a prophet since in Israel like unto Moses, whom the Lord knew face to face' (Deut. 34.10).

I remember a certain German-Swiss business-man whose French was more picturesque than scholarly. To describe his recent conversion he used to repeat: 'I dropped my dignity! I dropped my dignity!' The fact that the sex relationship demands this complete giving of the self led the men of the Bible gradually to a realization of the divine law of monogamous marriage. In fact, in the earliest Biblical times, polygamy was still customary. As far as I know, no later text expressly excludes either polygamy or free love, except perhaps St. Paul's admonitions on the private lives of bishops and deacons (I Tim. 3.2, 12). They are, however, foreign to the perspective of the Bible, which, in addition, severely condemns adultery. We may conclude, then, that they are inferior forms of sexual love. The Bible repeatedly asserts, on the other hand, the divine value, one may even say the holiness, of sexual love.

An element in God's purpose, an image of the complete self-giving and trust of faith, and a training for them: this is the place held by the sex instinct in the Bible. Here, then, is the answer the Bible gives to those who come to consult us about nervous or psychological troubles rooted in a conception of the body as opposed to the spirit; its answer to every neurosis due to repression of the sex instinct, and to contempt and—they always go together—fear of it; conditions such as infantile regression, and frustration of the vital impulse in melancholy, impotence, and frigidity. Here too is the answer to many marital conflicts apparently caused by what is claimed to be 'incompatibility of temperament', but whose real cause is sexual in that one of the partners, as a result either of upbringing, or of a sexual shock suffered in early childhood, has taken up a false, negative attitude to sex. As a consequence, he cannot enter the sexual life whole-heartedly. Almost always he comes to look down on his partner, as if he were superior, more spiritual because less attached to the things of the body; this is, of course, rationalization—that is to say, a false explanation of a state due in reality to unconscious emotional causes. This particular rationalization receives support from a prejudiced view of sex, based on a false interpretation of the Bible, and very common among religious people. Such people 'make a virtue of necessity', as the saying is, and pride themselves on what is in reality a pathological illness, of which they can be cured only by becoming aware of it through a genuinely Biblical interpretation of sexual life. Dr. Biot's Groupe Lyonnais, which studies problems of medicine, philosophy, and biology, has devoted one of its always remarkable annual sessions to these questions.[1]

It is a problem of considerable importance, since a number of psychoanalysts accuse Christianity of being the cause of many neuroses; for that reason they set up their 'principle of pleasure' in opposition to Christianity, and the idea is gaining ground among the public that one must choose either Christian faith or marital happiness, on the grounds that they are incompatible! This is the opposite of the truth. But we must recognize that there is some excuse for the line taken by these psychoanalysts, since even enlightened people too often confuse a more or less conscious contempt of sex with Christian faith.

I saw recently a woman who wished dearly to bring into being in her own marriage this harmonious fusion of spiritual and sexual love. She had discussed it at length with her husband, who, like her, was a practising Christian. They had therefore decided, to this end, to pray together before each act of sexual intercourse. My first reaction to this was most favourable. But after thinking about it, I put this question to her: 'Do you think that in your heart of hearts this prayer is really a sort of exorcism, as if sexual love were inferior, and needed to be as it were purified by prayer?' After a moment she replied: 'Yes. I think that what you say is true.' And I could see from her expression that she was making a discovery inside herself, that she could see an unsuspected contempt of sex lurking behind her wish to fuse spiritual and sexual love together in her religion.

The reader will understand that I was not criticizing the decision taken by this young couple, or wishing to stop them saying

[1] A. Godin, S.J., *Les journées d'études du Groupe Lyonnais*, Saint-Luc Médical, 1947, published by 'Nova et Vetera', Louvain

their prayers together as often as possible. I was concerned with the unconscious basis of their conscious decision. It was a matter of a false scale of values which considered fellowship in prayer to be holier than carnal fellowship, whereas both are the gifts of God.

This same Biblical view is also the answer to those who indulge in sensual excesses. We have here again the paradox which I spoke of in connection with contempt of the body. Having lost the sense of the holiness of sex, they indulge themselves in it as if it were something inferior and unworthy of any respect. Often, for example, a man who is being unfaithful to his wife has told me that he does it with a clear conscience, because, as he says, it is to him nothing more than a little sensual adventure which, he claims, has nothing to do with his spiritual love, which remains fixed upon his wife. The explanation of this, and of many other cases, for instance, of persistent masturbation, lies in a dissociation of the two elements of love—the genital, bodily element and the emotional, spiritual element. I should say 'non-fusion' rather than dissociation, since this fusion comes later in man's psychological development.

This fusion is part of God's purpose, as all the passages just quoted show. In the account of the institution of marriage, the Bible says: 'A man . . . shall cleave unto his wife: and they shall be one flesh' (Gen. 2.24); an evident allusion to the sexual union, but also an allusion to the total union of both body and soul that that implies. St. Paul is referring to this when he writes that the man who joins himself with a prostitute is one body with her; that he is therefore committing his whole person (I Cor. 6.16).

Looked at in this way, every act of sexual intercourse is a marriage, an act of God as well as of man, according to the well-known Biblical injunction: 'What therefore God hath joined together, let not man put asunder' (Matt. 19.6).

To sum up, there are four principal attitudes that are adopted towards sexual love: firstly, the attitude of 'devaluation,' which sees in it merely a physiological reflex—a view which serves as an excuse for amorous adventures either before or during marriage; secondly, the 'deifying' attitude which, by overestimating sexual love, consequently devalues everything that is specifically human in man, art, culture, the moral conscience, and faith;

thirdly, the attitude of contempt, which sees it as a degrading function. Now these first three attitudes show a remarkable affinity, in that they are all based on the non-fusion of carnal and spiritual love, the frequency and the evil consequences of which have been revealed by psychoanalysis. The fourth attitude, that of the Bible, is that in which spiritual and carnal love *are* fused, the attitude in which sex has a divine meaning. It is the great answer—I might say the great remedy—for all our patients' psycho-sexual troubles. To those who devalue the sex act, it reveals its true grandeur, which they have failed to recognize; it liberates those who have made a god of sex from the slavery in which they are held by it; and finally it reconciles with sex those who despise it, giving back to them the joy in it that God Himself meant them to have.

It may be objected that there are many Bible passages which speak of the incompatibility of flesh and spirit: 'the mind of the flesh is death; but the mind of the spirit is life and peace' (Rom. 8.6; see also Rom. 8.5-8; John 6.63; Matt. 16.17; Rom. 13.4; Gal. 5.16-20, 24-5; I Tim. 4.8, etc.). I have already dealt with this subject, but I must return to it here, to avoid a misunderstanding that has serious consequences in many cases of psychological disease. As Dr. A. Schlemmer has explained,[1] the word σαρξ (flesh) which is used here does not mean the body (for which the Greek word is σωμα), but natural man in the totality of his person, body, mind, and soul. In the account of the Fall it is the whole man who cuts himself off from God by his sin. His physical disobedience (eating the fruit) and his mental disobedience (the woman incited by the serpent, and the man by the woman), are but the symbols of his spiritual disobedience, his claim to independence of his Creator. Similarly, in the passages quoted, the word spirit means the new man, regenerated by Christ, by the baptism of the Holy Ghost.

Note, for example, that when St. Paul enumerates the 'works of the flesh' (Gal. 5.19-21) he includes not only what concerns the body (fornication, uncleanness, drunkenness, revellings) but also what concerns the soul and the mind: lasciviousness, idolatry, sorcery, enmities, strife, jealousies, wraths, factions, divisions,

[1] André Schlemmer: 'La foi chrétienne et le corps,' in *Les deux Cités*, Cahiers des Associations professionnelles protestantes, No. 4, Paris, 5 rue Cermeschi

heresies, envyings. Note also that though uncleanness is con-summated in the body, it has obviously its origin in the soul and mind. Similarly, in the 'fruit of the Spirit' which the Apostle then sets over against the works of the flesh, he adds temperance, which has a direct bearing on the physical, to love, joy, peace, longsuffering, kindness, goodness, faithfulness, and meekness.

We ought perhaps here to examine that well-known passage in the Sermon on the Mount in which Jesus says: 'Every one that looketh on a woman to lust after her hath committed adultery with her already in his heart' (Matt. 5.28). I have often given talks to young people on the Bible and love, seeking to awaken in them this high conception of the sex instinct. It has frequently happened that one of them in the discussion that followed has quoted this passage as forbidding his casting a desiring glance at an attractive girl. I have pointed out to him the obvious fact that this text did not apply to him, since he was a bachelor, or at least did not apply to him unless his glance led him to covet a woman he knew to be married. Our Lord is in fact here speak-ing of adultery, and His words are an eloquent confirmation of the demand of total self-giving made by marriage.

In this pronouncement, and in the succeeding verses, Jesus is also concerned to denounce the hypocrisy of a certain legalistic morality that is quite contrary to the spirit of the Gospel, the vainglory of those who consider themselves better than others because they abstain from certain actions, whereas the truth is that all men equally are sinners before God. For God looks into the hearts of men. Thus, a young man may see from this text that he is no purer than some comrade of his whose conduct he con-demns, and that he is himself in as much need of God's forgiveness.

It was, after all, God who put into the young man's heart the desire which attracts him towards the woman, the tendency to let himself be drawn by her beauty, and who put into the heart of the girl that desire to be desired, who gave her her beauty as a talent to be cultivated. The Bible does not condemn that. It shows us Jacob preferring Rachel to Leah because of her beauty (Gen. 29.17); it shows us Boaz conquered by the charm of Ruth the Moabitess, knowing nevertheless how to subordinate his desire to the removal of every obstacle to his legal marriage with her (Ruth 4.1-13).

9

THE MEANING OF DREAMS

IN STUDYING the Biblical significance of Nature, the body and the sex instinct, we must touch also on the significance of dreams, which have an important place in the Bible. The principal dreams recorded are: the dream of Abimelech, King of Gerar (Gen. 20.3); Jacob's two dreams, of the ladder between heaven and earth (Gen. 28.12), and of the 'ringstraked, speckled, and grisled' goats (Gen. 31.10); Laban's dream as he pursued Jacob (Gen. 31.24); the well-known dreams of Joseph, in which sheaves and stars personified his brothers prostrating themselves before him (Gen. 37.5, 9); the dreams of the King of Egypt's butler and baker, interpreted by Joseph (Gen. 40.5-22); Pharaoh's two dreams, of the seven fat and the seven lean cows, and of the seven fat and good ears of corn, and the seven thin and blasted ears, also interpreted by Joseph (Gen. 41.1-7), for which service he was elevated to the highest political office, a success not yet achieved by any modern psychoanalyst!

Then there is the enemy soldier's dream, in which Gideon sees the prophecy of his victory (Judg. 7.13); the dream of King Solomon (I Kings 3.5-9), in which he asks God to give him 'an understanding heart to judge thy people, that I may discern between good and evil'; the prophet Ezekiel's dream of the dry bones which came alive, and which represented Israel in exile (Ezek. 37.1-10); the two dreams of Nebuchadnezzar, that of the great statue (Dan. 2.31-5), and that of the great tree (Dan. 4.10-17) which were explained to him by the prophet Daniel.

In the New Testament, there are the two dreams of Joseph, that in which an angel tells him that the child conceived by the Virgin Mary is of the Holy Ghost (Matt. 1.20), and that in which another angel charges him to flee into Egypt (Matt. 2.13); then there is St. Peter's dream of the great sheet (Acts 10.9-23) by which God led him to see that the good news brought by Jesus Christ was meant for all nations and not only the Jews; St. Paul's dream (Acts 16.9), which started him on his missionary journeys to Europe. Finally, there is the whole Book of the Revelation of St. John. However, this last was rather a matter of visions than of dreams; but the frontier between the two is not clearly definable. For this reason I have not included the account of Christ's Transfiguration (Luke 9.28-36), for although the Evangelist says that Peter and his companions were heavy with sleep, he at once adds that they remained awake. It is generally admitted that the dreams we remember occur as sleep is ending, as we cross the indefinite boundary between sleeping and waking.

I strongly urge doctors to re-read all these documents in the light of modern psychoanalysis. Here, in the light of the Bible, we may examine the divergences of view between the School of Freud and that of Jung. As is well-known, Freud[1] and his disciples, true to their purely mechanicalist and causal conception of the human person, see in dreams only the expression of instinctive drives, 'the fulfilment of a repressed desire'. For Maeder,[2] on the contrary, the dream is 'an illustration of the dreamer's situation', and Jung,[3] who has adopted this definition, has shown more and more clearly in his numerous studies that it leads us to a purposive, spiritual conception of the person. For, seen in this light, the dream translates not only drives, but also the aspirations of the soul towards a goal.

My daily work permits me constantly to verify what there is of truth in the teachings of the two schools. The Freudian interpretation of our patients' dreams tells us a great deal about their repressed desires and their unconscious instinctive drives, and among the Biblical dreams I have quoted, those of Joseph, for example, fit exactly Freud's definition. Joseph, without daring to confess it, without even being aware of it, desires to dominate his brothers, and to see them bowing at his feet; and this desire finds fulfilment in his dreams.

But there is much more in it than that, and it is worth while,

[1] S. Freud, *A General Introduction to Psychoanalysis*, translated by G. S. Hall, Boni and Liveright, New York, 1920

[2] Alphonse Maeder, *Guérison et évolution dans la vie de l'âme. La psychanalyse et son importance dans la vie contemporaine*, Rascher, Zurich, 1918

[3] C. G. Jung, *Modern Man in Search of a Soul*, translated by W. S. Dell and C. F. Baynes, Harcourt, Brace, New York, 1933

for doctors who have but a hazy recollection of these old accounts, to tell the story in greater detail. Joseph is, in fact, the victim of what we now call a mother fixation. His desire to dominate is in reality his mother Rachel's desire, suggested by her to his subconscious. Its origin was as follows: as a result of the events related in Gen. 29.15-30, Jacob had become the husband of two wives, Leah and Rachel, the daughters of Laban. Jacob loved the younger, Rachel, who was 'beautiful and well-favoured' (Gen. 29.17), but barren, while Leah had given Jacob his first four sons, Reuben, Simeon, Levi, and Judah (Gen. 29.31-5).

One can well understand Rachel's brooding jealousy. She resorts to a proceeding which seems to us strange, but which is explained in Lévy-Brühl's study[1] of 'mystical identification'. She sends her maid-servant Bilhah to lie with her husband; and when Bilhah has reached her time, she is delivered on Rachel's knees; Rachel, by mystical identification with her, considers as hers the two sons, Dan and Naphtali, thus born (Gen. 30.1-8).

But Leah in her turn becomes barren, or more probably is forsaken by Jacob (Gen. 30.9-13). As a result, a similar jealousy awakens in her, and she has recourse to the same measures with her servant Zilpah, by whom Jacob has two more sons, Gad and Asher. Then follows a story of some mandrakes, the cause of a dispute between Leah and Rachel, which is no doubt why this plant was for centuries considered by doctors to have fertilizing virtues (Song of S. 7.13). It was not, however, she who got the mandrakes who became fruitful. Leah actually handed them over to her sister against the right to lie in her stead with Jacob; thus she gave birth to two more sons, Issachar and Zebulun (Gen. 30.14-21). The Bible cedes nothing to the Freudians in the matter of realism about the impulses of instinct!

This is how the story ends: Rachel at last became pregnant herself, and gave Jacob his eleventh son, Joseph (Gen. 30.22-4). The Bible, in its psychological realism, hints clearly at the result: Rachel's marked preference for this son of her own womb. Away with the consolations of mystical identification! Rachel projects on to Joseph all her jealousies and all her long-disappointed ambitions. She suggests to him the desire to dominate

[1] Lévy-Brühl, *Primitive Mentality*, translated by L. A. Clare, G. Allen and Unwin, London, 1923

which his dreams express. Later, the last tragic act of this passionate drama was to be played out. It is a *dénouement* that will surely be of interest to doctors. Rachel, that woman with an insatiable hunger for motherhood, was to die giving Jacob his twelfth son, Benjamin (Gen. 35.19).

But let us return to our dreams, and to the psychoanalysts. The Freudian interpretation of dreams is invalidated neither by our professional experience nor by the Bible. But it remains a limited, partial explanation, revealing only one aspect of the soul. The Zurich school has opened up quite new lines of thought, to which the Freudians have remained curiously blind. And here once more the agreement with the Bible is striking. The dream of Jacob's ladder, for example, answers exactly to Maeder's definition. But especially does the Bible confirm Jung's studies on the purposive nature of dreams, taking them as an expression of the aspirations of men's souls, and of the Spirit's call to them, an expression, in short, of that Word which God addresses to men through natural phenomena. There can, for example, scarcely be any question of a Freudian interpretation of the dreams of Joseph (Mary's husband), or of that of St. Peter; and St. Paul saw in his dream God's call to set sail for Europe, a call which had singularly fruitful results.

I feel that passions have clouded the issue between the two schools of thought. Both have taught us much. Each has thrown light on one of the two different aspects of the soul, without being for that reason as contradictory as is generally thought. The Bible also shows us these two aspects.

But I shall go further: dreams cannot be divided into two distinct types, Freudian and Jungian. In respect of each dream we may legitimately give both a Freudian and a Jungian interpretation. It is a proceeding which I often follow, finding that each interpretation makes a distinct and valuable contribution to the patient's self-knowledge. A simple example will suffice to illustrate this. A patient describes to me a dream in which she saw herself naked in front of me. The Freudian interpretation is not hard to guess, and the difficulty which she has experienced in bringing herself to tell me her dream derives from the fact that she herself is well aware of it.

But nakedness does not bring to mind sexuality only. We

speak of the 'naked truth'. To show oneself naked is to show oneself as one really is, without pretence or reserve, in absolute honesty; it is also to hand oneself over with complete confidence, every defence cast aside. I tried to explain this to my patient, and she said at once: 'That reminds me! I had been worried after our last talk because there was one point on which I hadn't been quite frank with you.'

It is clear that the same dream may have different meanings in different people; it is even susceptible of several distinct interpretations in the same person. We are so impregnated with rationalism that we are always tempted to ask: Which interpretation is true? Who is right—Freud, Adler, Maeder, Jung, or someone else? It was a great relief to me the day I realized that rationalism has nothing to do with these matters. Rationalism raises dilemmas and contradictions. Here, on the other hand, we are in the realm of concordance. Notice, for example, that the two distinct meanings of nakedness mentioned above are not without a link between them; and this link is the one I spoke of earlier with regard to sex, when I showed that the casting away of reserve in sexual love is a symbol of the aspiration of the soul towards total self-giving, a value of a spiritual order.

Let me give in conclusion a simple illustration of the Biblical view. Some cars are driven by their rear wheels, but others have a front-wheel drive. The instinctive drives of Freud are to the soul what a back-wheel drive is to the car; whereas the spiritual aspirations of the soul, as outlined by Jung, are comparable with the front-wheel drive.

But the soul, as described in the Bible, is a four-wheel-drive vehicle—they also exist! In the Biblical perspective a single engine, the living soul which God gives to man, sets in motion both the instincts of Freud, thrusting from behind, and the aspirations of Jung, pulling from in front. According to the Bible, it is God who endowed man with his instincts, who acts and speaks in Nature; and it is God also who calls man to Him and awakens in him a sense of vocation.

Man shares with the animals this propulsion of instinct; what is peculiar to him is the traction from in front, his spiritual life. But in the Biblical view he is identified neither with the animals nor yet with the angels, whom one might compare with the car driven only by its front wheels. He is moved simultaneously by the two forces perfectly wedded together because they both derive their power from the one source, God.

It is worth noting that in this image of rear propulsion and forward traction we may perceive Bergson's 'two sources of morality and religion',[1] social pressure and prophetic appeal. Note also that they correspond to what Odier calls 'functions' and 'values', and to the two distinct standpoints we investigated at the beginning of this book in speaking of the two diagnoses.

Finally, I cannot end this study without drawing the attention of my brother psychoanalysts, often embarrassed by patients who enjoy having their dreams analysed so much that their treatment drags endlessly on, to the words of Ecclesiastes: 'For in the multitude of dreams there are vanities, and in many words' (Eccl. 5.7, R.V. marg.).

All this has considerable practical application to our daily dealings with our patients. The materialist, organicist, Freudian doctor, who sees only rear propulsion, does not recognize the spiritual needs of the soul, and the role they play in disease and in healing. He thus often provokes a kind of tearing apart of the person, sending the rear wheels in a different direction from that of the front wheels, when he unleashes the instincts, freed from the constraints of the spirit. But the idealistic doctor, who sees only the front-wheel drive, who does not recognize the divine character of instinct, also risks this rending of the person, by encouraging outbursts of enthusiasm that do not take into account the demands of Nature.

[1] Henri Bergson, *The Two Sources of Morality and Religion*, Macmillan & Co., London, 1935

10

THE MEANING OF EVENTS

I HAVE QUOTED this passage where Jesus is speaking to His opponents: 'When it is evening, ye say, It will be fair weather: for the heaven is red. And in the morning, It will be foul weather today: for the heaven is red and lowring. Ye know how to discern the face of the heaven; but ye cannot discern the signs of the times' (Matt. 16.2-3). The signs of the times, and other analogous expressions, 'When the fulness of the time came' (Gal. 4.4), 'The hour is come' (John 17.1), etc., occur frequently in the Bible. They imply that events do not come to pass by chance, that God has a purpose, that History has a meaning. And Jesus is here linking this meaning of History with the meaning of Nature.

For if Nature has a meaning, it follows that the world has a meaning and that the history of the world has a meaning. And it is God's purpose which gives to the history of the world its meaning, as also to the history of peoples and of individuals. This conception runs through the whole Bible.

However strange it may seem to us, the covenant made by God of His own free will with a particular people, the Israelites (Ex. 34.17), dominates the thought of all the Biblical writers. This covenant meant the intervention of God in History, and it is this intervention which gives a meaning to History. This meaning becomes deeper with the New Covenant in Jesus Christ (Heb. 12.24), in which the multitude of believers takes the place of the restricted company of the chosen people, as was foreshadowed from the beginning in the covenant made with Abraham (Gen. 17.4).

In the Bible political history has a meaning: Jesus says to Pilate: 'Thou wouldest have no power against me, except it were given thee from above' (John 19.11); wars have a meaning: 'Thus saith the Lord of Hosts, the God of Israel: Behold, I will send

and take Nebuchadrezzar the King of Babylon, my servant . . .
he shall smite the land of Egypt' (Jer. 43.10, 11); victories have a
meaning: 'The Lord said unto Gideon, The people that are with
thee are too many for me to give the Midianites into their hand,
lest Israel vaunt themselves against me, saying, mine own hand
hath saved me' (Judg. 7.2); defeats have a meaning: 'The anger
of the Lord was kindled against Israel, and he delivered them into
the hand of Hazael, king of Syria' (II Kings 13.3); revolutions
have a meaning: 'He removeth kings, and setteth up kings'
(Dan. 2.21); peace has a meaning: Solomon 'had peace on all
sides round about him. And Judah and Israel dwelt safely, every
man under his vine and under his fig tree . . . all the days of
Solomon' (I Kings 4.24-5).

I have mentioned here only a few verses, but really I ought
to quote the entire Bible. Since we are here studying the Bible
not for its own sake but for its message to us as doctors, it is
less important to multiply examples than to understand their
spirit. For every person who comes into our consulting-rooms,
whether he be ill or well, whether the consultation he is asking
for be physical, psychological or spiritual, is concerned with
what is happening to him—a disease, an anxiety, a grief, a
problem; he has something to learn from this event, and a decision to make. Where is he to find help? In a short-sighted,
scientific pragmatism? In the principle of pleasure of the psychoanalysts? Or in seeking God's will?

To my list just now of politics, peace and war, I was going to
add that in the Bible law has a meaning; and this assertion will
help us to make clear the message the Bible has for medicine.
I am thinking now of that passage in Deuteronomy (6.20-5):
'When thy son asketh thee in time to come, saying, What mean
the testimonies, and the statutes, and the judgements, which the
Lord our God hath commanded you? Then thou shalt say unto
thy son, We were Pharaoh's bondmen in Egypt; and the Lord
brought us out of Egypt with a mighty hand: and the Lord
shewed signs and wonders, great and sore, upon Egypt, upon
Pharaoh, and upon all his house, before our eyes: and he brought
us out from thence, that he might bring us in, to give us the
land which he sware unto our fathers. And the Lord commanded us to do all these statutes, to fear the Lord our God, for

our good always, that he might preserve us alive, as at this day. And it shall be righteousness unto us, if we observe to do all this commandment before the Lord our God, as he hath commanded us.'

It is, then, God who acts first. It is His intervention in History which gives its true meaning to the law which He thereafter lays down for His people. The Ten Commandments in the twentieth chapter of Exodus have the following preamble: 'I am the Lord thy God, which brought thee out of the land of Egypt, out of the house of bondage' (Ex. 20.2). God gives commandments to His people, but first He has shown His love for them by intervening in their history. In the Decalogue, as in the text quoted above, the reader will note the allusions to what may properly be termed the medical significance of the law: 'that thy days may be long', 'that he might preserve us alive'. God intervenes in History because He has a purpose; we seek to obey His Revelation so that we in our turn may enter into this divine plan; and that plan is the very law of life.

In the New Covenant, under which we now are, the salvation wrought by Jesus Christ corresponds to the deliverance from Egypt in the Old Covenant. The Biblical perspective widens thus to include the whole of humanity, but it remains the same in this, that it is because God 'first loved us' (I John 4.19) that He demands our love; He, having acted first, requires our obedience in response to His love, and our co-operation in His purpose.

Seen from this angle, the law of God is divested of all 'legalistic' meaning. I insist on this, for doctors know well the stifling effect of a legalistic interpretation of the Bible, an interpretation repeatedly condemned by Jesus Christ in His debates with the Pharisees. As scientists we may say, 'You must take digitalis,' but if, as doctors of the soul, we say 'You must' to our patient we are departing from the Biblical perspective; we are becoming mere moralists, trampling on our patient, treating him as a child rather than as a person. The Bible would have us help him to discern for himself what God has done for him, what God is saying to him through events, so that his decision and his obedience may be free and spontaneous.

Here I must make an important observation on this word 'meaning' which I am constantly using in this book. The reader

her intuition had not erred. The idea that God has a purpose for
the world and that it is in relation to this purpose that every
event of our lives has meaning is the very axis of the Bible. It is
also what makes the Bible so important to us doctors. Medicine
really consists in helping men to conduct their lives healthily:
it seeks also to repair to the best of its ability the damage they
suffer as a result of the discord which has broken in upon the
primitive harmony of Nature.

The men of the Bible see every event as a sign from God.
Here I ought to quote the whole of the prophets; for them,
God speaks and acts in every circumstance of the national life,
in the disasters of political life as well as through the blessings
of peace and justice. They seek to communicate to their people
this spiritual understanding of History.

They try to let themselves be led by God. God's command
may come to them as they meditate: 'Get thee out of thy
country . . .' (Gen. 12.1); 'Go in, speak unto Pharaoh . . .' (Ex.
6.11); 'Go in this thy might, and save Israel . . .' (Judg. 6.14);
'Go, and tell this people . . .' (Isa. 6.9); 'Arise, and go toward
the south unto the way that goeth down from Jerusalem to
Gaza . . .' (Acts 8.26). But they also seek God's commandments
in events. It is in this perspective that they consider everything
that happens to them in their own lives.

When Jeremiah goes down to the potter's house, it is to seek
there a message from God as he watches the potter fashioning
his vessel as it seems good to him to make it (Jer. 18.1-10); when
he is arrested, cast first into prison, then into a pit, then delivered,
and then taken into Egypt, he is seeking all the time to know
what this means in God's purpose (Jer. 37, 38, 40, 43). The train
of events that brought Joseph to Egypt is well known; when he
sees his brothers again, he tells them that God sent him there;
it is clear that for him this unfolding of his own destiny is part
of God's purpose for his family and his people: 'God sent me
before you to preserve you a remnant in the earth, and to save
you alive by a great deliverance' (Gen. 47.7).

David is pursued by Saul, who hates him because God has
chosen him to become king in his stead. For the second time
David succeeds in penetrating unseen into the heart of the camp,
where the sleeping king lies. His companion Abishai whispers:

'God hath delivered up thine enemy into thine hand this day' (I Sam. 26.8). But to David this is a God-given opportunity to show his magnanimity, and he contents himself with removing the king's spear and his cruse of water (I Sam. 26.12). When Samson falls in love with a beautiful foreign woman he astonishes his parents, for, the account adds, they 'knew not that it was of the Lord' (Judg. 14.4).

When Jesus learns of the illness of His friend Lazarus, discerning by faith all that God wishes to show by raising him, He says to His disciples: 'This sickness is not unto death, but for the glory of God' (John 11.4). When St. Paul is arrested and carried off as a prisoner to Rome, he sees in it the will of God, permitting him to spread the gospel (Phil. 1.12-14).

I could add many more examples. I ought to quote all the Psalms, in which the poet turns over in his heart the mysterious problems raised by History: the injustice of the world, the triumph of the wicked, the misfortunes that befall the innocent; and he confesses: 'When I thought how I might know this, it was too painful for me' (Ps. 73.16). And yet, a little farther on, the Psalmist in a wider view of History, discerns God's righteous purpose, and asks Him to lead him (Ps. 73.24). In the same spirit, St. Paul exclaims: 'To them that love God all things work together for good' (Rom. 8.28).

This desire to be led by God always dominates the men of the Bible. Abraham in exile wants for his son Isaac a wife from the land of his fathers. He sends his servant to seek her. It is a delicate mission: the wife whom God destines for Isaac must be found. So the servant says to God (Gen. 24.14): 'Let it come to pass, that the damsel to whom I shall say, Let down thy pitcher, I pray thee, that I may drink; and she shall say, Drink, and I will give thy camels drink also: let the same be she that thou hast appointed for thy servant Isaac.' Then 'before he had done speaking' Rebecca came out with her pitcher upon her shoulder, and used those very words. The man stared in astonishment at her, the account adds, 'holding his peace, to know whether the Lord had made his journey prosperous or not' (Gen. 24.21).

In saying that the men of the Bible try constantly to let themselves be led by God through what happens to them, I do not claim that they are never mistaken in their interpretation of events. That would be too much to expect. This would be Heaven, not the earth. We have already seen the difference of opinion between David and Abishai beside the sleeping Saul. And now a last example will show the problem in all its seriousness.

If there is no such thing as chance, and if one may ask God for signs, is it not permissible to try to discover His will by using 'chance' itself? The primitive Church thought so, the idea being undoubtedly prompted by faith. Judas had betrayed Christ. By whom should he be replaced? The concern of the Church was to choose the new Apostle properly, not according to human opinions, but according to the will of God. Two men seemed qualified to be Apostles. They were Joseph, surnamed Justus, and Matthias. 'And they prayed and said, Thou, Lord, which knowest the hearts of all men, show of these two the one whom thou hast chosen. . . . And they gave lots for them, and the lot fell upon Matthias; and he was numbered with the eleven apostles' (Acts 1.24, 26).

We know how God Himself chose a twelfth Apostle, in the person of St. Paul, the great persecutor of the Church, whom He overwhelmed on the Damascus road (Acts 9). When we think of the fruits of Paul's ministry, we see how far the mind of God was above the narrow views of the primitive Church. God was not to be caught in a dilemma created by men, however faithfully they sought His guidance. God is not at our service. He keeps His secrets. We may look for signs, but His sovereign majesty escapes our grasp. He remains a God who hides Himself (Isa. 45.15); a God who reveals Himself as He wills, who requires of men that they strive to 'feel after him, and find him' (Acts 17.27).

PART TWO

THE PROBLEM OF MAGIC

11

BELIEF IN MAGIC

GOD IS NOT at our service. To claim to penetrate His secrets, know His signs, and have His power at our beck and call is not faith, but magic. This is a great problem, which we must now examine. Doubtless many of my readers have had it in mind during the preceding chapters. They will have realized that I was concerned first to show the broad outlines of the Biblical perspective, in which all Nature and all History have a meaning.

Is not that also what primitive savages believe? Is it not the superstition that is characteristic of them? Lévy-Brühl, whose work is well known among doctors, is quite definite on this point. In the primitive mind, he writes, 'there is no such thing as chance. The idea of accident does not even occur to a native's mind, while on the contrary the idea of witchcraft is always present.'[1]

It is true that for primitive man everything has meaning. Our scientific thought is completely unknown and inaccessible to him. In order to understand his mentality and his reactions, we must divest ourselves of the scientific view of the world. The idea of a rigid succession of cause and effect governed by natural laws is quite foreign to the savage: if civilized men tell him there is going to be an eclipse, he is convinced, when it happens, that they themselves have produced it by magical power; for how could they foresee it if they did not themselves engineer it? If the doctor has cured a sick person with a dose of medicine, the doctor and the medicine have magical power. And if the doctor refuses to give the same medicine to another sick person with a different disease, it is because he is evilly disposed towards him. Even worse: when the doctor has administered a dose of medicine, the savages come back next day to complain if the patient

[1] *Op. cit.*, p. 50.

has not yet been cured! (Has that never happened to you among civilized people, my friends?) For if this medicine has a magical power of healing, why the delay? Primitive people frequently claim presents from the doctor who has cured them: they consider him indebted to them, since they have consented to enter his hospital, eat his peculiar food, swallow his potions, pass in front of his X-ray screen—to submit, in short, to his every caprice. But if the sojourn in hospital is prolonged, then he seems altogether suspect: 'What can he be up to, this white doctor, this great magician, keeping them like that? What is he going to practise on them?' My colleagues are aware that such suspicions can be harboured in the civilized mind as well!

The world, then, appears to the savage to be the constant playground of divine forces, now benevolent, now malevolent, whose intentions must be guessed, whose favours must be won, and whose evils must be warded off. This must be done by sorcery, which reigns supreme in primitive society. Thus a savage cannot imagine a death from natural causes. If someone has died, it is because he had to die, a lot had fallen on him. The same sorcerer who was consulted with religious awe is now hated for his magical power. If he can control occult forces for good, he can use them also to bring about evils which nothing could avert. Lévy-Brühl tells of a woman who 'had nursed very carefully, and cured, a certain disease. It had been concluded that it was she who had caused it. How could she have known how to make it disappear, if she had not been the one to make it come?' The spirits of the dead too are particularly feared; they come unseen to dwell among the living. They are invoked to protect the tribe or to give it victory over its enemies, but they can also wreak terrible vengeance on the living, mysteriously venting their spite.

With such a conception of the world, everything has its significance, and may help to reveal the secrets of Fate. For example, the flight and the cry of birds are considered to be unmistakable omens. Upon them the savage builds a whole system of beliefs whose authority is unquestionable. Experience can never disprove it, for the faith in omens is so strong that the savage will undertake nothing if they are unfavourable, and so he has no opportunity of giving the lie to them.

An important point is made here by Lévy-Brühl. In the primitive mind, the sacred birds do 'not only announce events, but also . . . bring them about. As the mouth-piece of invisible beings they predict; as these invisible beings themselves, they operate.'[1] They are, then, much more than symbols in the accepted meaning of this word. Modern thought has preserved the notion of symbol, but restricts its meaning to that of a mere poetic image. Thus, for us, primroses and snowdrops are symbols of spring. But for the savage, the wagtails have 'the power to produce the spring they announce,' just as Edmond Rostand's celebrated poem *Chantecler* shows us the proud cock convinced that he causes the sun to rise by filling the sleeping countryside with his frenzied 'Cock-a-doodle-doo'!

The psychoanalysts have shown that although our modern conscious thought is purely rational, dominated by the scientific idea of cause and effect, the whole network of our subconscious mind is on the contrary dominated, like the savages, by the symbolic significance of things. Read again Dalbiez's masterly study[2] of Freud, especially the pages devoted to what he calls the 'effect-sign'. A dream is the 'effect-sign' of a repression, a dream symbol is the 'effect-sign' of the thing repressed. Dalbiez demonstrates how far removed is Freudian from scientific determinism. The effect-sign does not translate a causal link in the scientific meaning of the term; nor is it concerned, consequently, with inverted causality, that is, with prevision. But at the same time it may be concluded from Dalbiez's exposition that the effect-sign is much more than a symbol in the poetic sense. It is more than an image of the thing symbolized; it has with it an intimate relationship which corresponds to a psychological reality. Hence, it is not to be ascribed to poetic fancy, but to a rigorous determinism.

Jung goes considerably further. In his 'archetypes' he has raised symbols to the status of permanent, active spiritual powers, common to all men. To the modern who smiles at the magical medicine of the Egyptians he boldly asserts the soundness of its basis and the validity of its practice. 'An ancient Egyptian . . .

[1] *Op. cit.*, p. 131

[2] Roland Dalbiez, *Psychoanalytical Method and the Doctrine of Freud*, translated by T. F. Lindsay, Longmans, Green & Co., New York, 1949

was bitten by a snake', writes Jung.[1] 'The Egyptian doctor tried
to fit this particular accident into the scheme of mythology,
referring to some sacred text which told how the great Sun-god
was bitten by the reptile. . . . The telling of this story was nothing more or less than a process of therapy. . . . Its images took
such a hold on the whole person of the patient that his vascular
system and his glandular reactions re-established the threatened
equilibrium.'

I shall return later to this interesting topic. For the moment
all I wish to do is to point out to the reader the discovery of
the psychoanalysts that the primitive mind seems strange to us
moderns only because we have pushed it down into the subconscious; but it is still there, and it even reigns there supreme.
It is not, therefore, foreign to us; it has not been superseded;
hidden off-stage, behind the visible scenes of our conscious
rationality, it goes on working in secret.

Let us deal now with one final point made by Lévy-Brühl,
a detail which I shall have occasion to mention again later in
connection with children and with civilized neurotics. Let us
suppose that some members of a primitive tribe embark in a
canoe; if they notice certain birds on their left, they conclude
that the omens are against them, and abandon their voyage. But
if their voyage has already lasted several days, and is nearly over,
it would be too irksome to interrupt it. So these men turn
their canoe round: the birds are on the right, the omens are
favourable, and the situation is saved! They disembark on the
bank and light the ritual fire to render thanks to the spirits who
have thus so clearly shown their benevolence.

Lévy-Brühl gives another example. The savages go to the spot
where they are to build a hut. Nothing will make them begin
the work so long as they hear the cries of certain birds of ill
omen. Suddenly these birds give way to others, whose cries are
a pledge of success. Construction begins at once. Now it would
be most regrettable if, during the operations, the birds of ill
omen were to be heard again. So a band of musicians is set to
work beating loudly on their drums to drown the sound of
any birds.

[1] C. G. Jung, *L'homme à la découverte de son âme*, Mont-Blanc Publications,
Geneva, 1944

The attitude of primitive peoples towards the spiritual powers to whom they attribute every happening is seen to be an odd mixture of religious awe and airy disrespect. They are like children.

Indeed, we find the same mentality in the children of civilized people. The child finds himself in a situation rather like that of the savage: everything seems mysterious to him; he cannot grasp the rational causes of things, and so he imagines irrational causes for them. His parents appear to him to be all-powerful divinities of whose protection and favour he must make sure. Without them, he is afraid of everything; with them, he is afraid of nothing. He venerates them and fears them, and when necessary he plays mischievous tricks on them like the savages. We noted a certain logic in the savage, as, for example, in the story of the eclipse. We find the same sort of reasoning in the child. I shall refer here to the authoritative work of J. Piaget.[1] He has carefully studied this childish logic, which he has called 'prelogic'. Like the savage, the child personifies the favourable and unfavourable forces which he feels around him. If he bumps his head on a table, he attributes an evil intention to the table, and hits it to punish it, saying, 'Naughty table!'

Piaget has also noted in children behaviour which recalls that of the savages with their canoe. Take, for instance, the child's attitude to the rules of the game he is playing. When he is small, he considers the rules to be sacred and untouchable—magical, in short. Later, when he is bigger, he will consider them as no more than a social convention which the players can alter by common consent. Now, the interesting thing, which reminds us of the savage, is that the small child, with his magical conception of the rule, willingly cheats if occasion so demands, while the older child respects it much more loyally.

Think also of the enormous part played by symbols in the life of the child. When he plays with an up-turned chair, seated between its legs and whipping up an imaginary horse, the chair does not, as the adult thinks, merely symbolize a cart: it *is* a cart. In the same way the father does not symbolize authority: he is the unquestionable authority himself, even if he behaves

[1] J. Piaget, *The Child's Conception of the World*, translated by J. and A. Tomlinson, Kegan Paul & Co., London, 1929

towards the child in a manner unworthy of any true authority.

Similarly, the mother's good-night kiss does not only symbolize maternal love; it is itself that love, without which the child cannot live. Several of my patients, in their childhood memories, have told me of how they lay awake in mortal anguish when this kiss had been withheld. In the eyes of the adult it was a simple punishment or a way of exerting moral pressure, but to the child this deprivation took on unsuspected proportions, and left an indelible scar.

Consider, too, the magical power of the mother: her child has fallen down and hurt himself; she takes him on her lap, kisses the sore place and says: 'There. Mummy's kissed it better. It doesn't hurt any more.' And true enough—the tears dry up; it stops hurting, because Mummy has said so. The mother would be quite indignant if someone spoke to *her* like that when she hurt herself.

Very often the parents of young children abuse this magical power. Exposed to all kinds of humiliations in their own lives, they enjoy the flattering feeling of mastery that it gives them. 'If you don't do what Mummy tells you, something terrible will happen to you,' or else: 'The Black Man'll get you,' or, worse: 'You'll make Mummy die.'

And when the child grows older and casts off this primitive mentality, when he becomes capable of objective judgment and discovers that his parents tell lies and are imperfect, their resentment is very great, even though it may be unconscious. Their very useful magical prestige disappears. Then often, in an attempt to preserve it, they make grave mistakes, resorting to more and more threats, dictatorial commands, and claims to 'respect'.

As well as in savages and children, we always find the magical mentality in neurotics and people with mental disease. I shall not spend much time on the latter, for everyone can easily see the part played by the idea of magic in the ravings of a paranoiac who accuses the Freemasons or other occult powers of exercising an all-powerful, evil influence over him by means of electric rays.

I shall always remember a mental patient who was sent to me by a psychiatrist in the belief that she was a neurotic. It was soon after I had been led enthusiastically to take up psychotherapy. These sufferers can show implacable logic. This woman spotted and denounced with a knowing smile the slightest slip in my explanations, or my most secret reactions of annoyance. Nevertheless, in the end my honesty and goodwill won her over, and she had an experience which I at first thought to be authentic: she seemed really to have been converted. The tenacious hostility which she had shown towards me was replaced by complete adherence to what I represented for her: faith and the realization of the significance of things. But as regards the 'meaning of things' she went too far. Discussion became impossible: everything had a message for her over-excited soul—a pebble, by its odd shape, a wisp of straw by the way it lay at my garden gate, and the clouds, the wind, everything. I was faced with a case of acute mania.

But what is much more important for us doctors is the more subtle part played by the idea of magic in neuroses. Dr. Charles Odier gives an excellent description of this in his book, *L'angoisse et la pensée magique*.[1] Since reading it I have had daily occasion to prove the truth of this interpretation of neurosis. It is, of course, no more than a further confirmation of what we had already learned, that neurosis is a syndrome of infantile regression.

This is particularly marked in serious cases of neurotic obsessions, in which the subject is the slave of complicated rituals. We find unhappy people who feel compelled to wash their hands a hundred times a day, however much their reason tells them it is unnecessary. Others cannot get into bed without having made repeated careful checks of the lock, the gas-tap and many other such minor arrangements in the bedroom, although they have no rational motive for so doing. Another of my patients felt he had to wrap up his Bible in a specified number of pieces of paper, and could take it out again only after going through a complicated rite of exorcism.

But even in mild cases of nervous illness we always find traces of belief in magic. There is always in some degree a feeling of 'possession', a predilection for mystery, for the occult, for astrology, and astonishing credulity as regards quacks, clairvoyants and experts in personal radiations.

There was the case of a sensitive person who suffered from a functional disorder which was started off by the slightest emotion,

[1] Published by Delachaux and Niestlé, Neuchâtel and Paris, 1947

even a pleasant one; he got very worked up about it, and imagined fantastic explanations, which naturally further aggravated his sensitiveness, and concentrated all his attention upon himself and his feelings. He was irritated with all the doctors he had consulted, and who had told him not to worry himself so much about it. Finally, he went to a noted herbalist who understood him at once. 'You have some putrefying matter inside you,' he told him. After that his visit to me was bound to fail. It was useless for me to explain to him that there is putrefying matter inside everybody. I could not assail the prestige of that magic word.

Many people with nervous disorders are full of bitter complaints and criticism against everyone around them. If I ask one of them, 'Have you any real friends?' he answers warmly: 'Oh! Don't talk to me about friends! I've been disappointed in every one of them! I'd rather not have any more, than have it happen again.' And he adds, with sincerity: 'The fact is, I'm not fitted for this wicked world; I can't stand hypocrisy; if once I find a friend out in a lie, it's all over, I can never trust him again. I have too high ideals for a world that hasn't got any at all!'

A little thought will show that this is a magical attitude, a nostalgia for the fairy-tale. This wretched individual is carrying over into adult life the childhood dream of meeting a fairy, wonderfully beautiful, good, and wise and powerful. This image is projected on to the friend he meets, or, worse still, on to the person he is engaged to. He finds in them every good quality, and gives himself over to boundless admiration; but the moment he finds a failing, the whole edifice crumbles and leaves nothing but bitterness. Here we have again that sudden change from veneration to hostility that the savage feels for the sorcerer.

Dr. Odier has described in detail[1] the magical role played by the 'object' in 'surrender neuroses'—that is to say, the person who in these states occupies the emotional centre of the invalid, the person from whom the patient believes all his ills to come, and from whom alone he expects salvation.

This is one of the greatest dangers in psychotherapy. All our patients are terribly inclined to see us as magicians. That can be a factor working towards success, but it is very treacherous when

[1] *Op. cit.*

this magical mechanism is itself at issue. For my part, I distrust it and fight it with all my strength. If we fail, the same patient heaps reproaches on us and sincerely holds us responsible for all his misfortunes.

The reader will note that we have come back here, paradoxically, to the attitude I earlier described, of the modern man whom a scientific view of the world renders passive, who sees only external causes for his ills, and so expects help also only from outside.

12

SCIENCE AND MAGIC

ALL THAT I have said in the last chapter is already well
known to doctors. It is not surprising then that when we
speak to them of the Biblical view of the world, of the
meaning of things, of signs from God which a patient may
discern in his disease, many doctors think that this is a throwback
to a primitive stage of development, that the primitive mentality
is fighting to regain its position.

Is it not precisely because he fails to study Nature scientifically
that primitive man gives it a magical interpretation? To many
doctors, human history appears as a slow process of emancipation from primitive magical anxiety. This process, they believe,
is the work of science. These doctors are serious men, sincerely
concerned with human well-being. They are honest believers in
the messianic mission of science in the world. I am going into
great detail in this matter of magic, because it is a big problem
which must be faced, and because I wish to discuss it frankly with
opponents whose point of view I fully understand. Let us therefore
look more closely at the reasoning of those who hold that science,
and science alone, can deliver humanity from the primitive
mentality.

What is common, they say, to the savage, the child and the
neurotic is fear. 'The starting-point of belief in magic is fear',
writes Dr. Odier.[1] Surrounded by natural phenomena, often
harmful, whose mechanism he does not understand, the savage is
afraid. From this fear arises his magical interpretation. He personifies the forces with which he feels himself to be surrounded, and
attributes evil or good intentions to them. He tries to anticipate
their caprices, to discover signs from them. He finds a meaning in
things.

[1] *Op. cit.*

The child feels himself in the same situation, equally powerless. He needs the protection of his parents, and the food and care they give him. He makes gods of them.

The neurotic is the victim of subconscious forces which control his behaviour, his feelings, and every motion of his being. He, also, feels powerless in the face of these dark incomprehensible forces. He too anxiously looks for protection.

Now science, they continue, by explaining the mechanism of things, divests them of their disturbing mystery. At the same time it shows men how to protect themselves efficiently by tackling the causes of phenomena. The storm that bursts, the lightning that strikes the earth with its fire, the terrible rattling of the thunder, which ancient mythologies attributed to Zeus or Jupiter, in which Job believed he heard the mighty voice of God, in which a savage sees the vengeance of a spirit from the dead, and which makes the child or the neurotic tremble in their beds, are all explained by science. Science measures the electricity in the atmosphere and forecasts a storm. Further, it studies the laws of electricity, its affinity for the earth, and the attraction exercised by metallic points connected with the earth. The lightning conductor is invented; many disasters are avoided; men are freed from fear.

The rainbow whose splendour you see after a shower, in which Noah believed he saw a sign of divine mercy, is but the effect of the refraction of light in the prism of rain-drops; it can be reproduced with a piece of crystal. A sign from God—a fine poetic idea! Let the poets go on talking about it like that, and see as many symbols in it as they like. But we shall take their words for poetry and not for truth. It is science that tells the truth, that every effect has its cause, that nothing has a hidden meaning, that fear is the result of ignorance.

Our opponents' conclusions are now clear: impart to the savage our scientific understanding of the world, send the child to school, and the belief in magic will vanish, and with it the heavy burden of anxiety that it laid upon them. And in the case of the neurotic, we shall show him the psychological mechanisms at work in his subconscious, which give him the uneasy feeling of being in the grip of occult forces. Are men still afraid? There persist threats of calamities and wars? But science is only in its infancy. We are going to study sociology and political economy, organize society scientifically, invent hundreds of new techniques!

The Bible, they think, with its meanings for everything, its Creation by God, its divine purpose and its signs from God in natural phenomena and in events, belongs to an outmoded age from which humanity is being liberated by scientific progress.

In medicine, too, we study the mechanisms of the body and the mind, and into this sphere also science brings its twofold benefit. Firstly, by discovering the true causes of disease, it is able to find efficient remedies: *Sublata causa, tollitur effectus.* The great epidemics that were the curse of the Middle Ages have disappeared; antiseptics have freed childbirth from the puerperal fevers that beset it; they have opened the way for unbelievable progress in surgery; and so on. Against the few miserable cases in which fervent believers, without, of course, any proof, attribute a cure to miraculous intervention by God, scientific medicine can point proudly, and justly, to countless successes. The believers are scarcely in a position to preach to the scientist.

Secondly, science delivers the sick from the magical interpretations which make them think they see a spiritual meaning in their illness. All such ideas are pure imagination, and most pernicious in the distress they cause. If they are ill, it is simply the result of a chain of phenomena which are investigated and explained by science. All the rest is just a fairy tale. There is no mystery in it, or if there is still something unexplained, science will one day make it plain.

Do not missionaries report that disease is a defilement in the eyes of the savage? Even converts to Christianity do not dare to go to Communion when they are ill, because they consider themselves to be spurned by God.[1] When the men of the Bible, or modern Christians, think they can see their sickness as a divine punishment, it is merely a survival of this magical preconception. This is the cause underlying the false shame about their sickness that we find in so many of our patients, especially those with nervous complaints. It compromises their moral resistance and makes a cure more difficult.

Religion, then, in the eyes of these doctors who argue the case for salvation by science, was only an attempt at consolation

[1] Lévy-Brühl, *op. cit.*

98

—a quite touching one, it is true, but quite ineffective—in the days when other remedies for disease and social injustice did not yet exist. It can be explained historically by the belief in magic of primitive man, a belief from which science is happily emancipating him. The Biblical interpretation of the world, the rites of the Churches and their belief in invisible realities, in a 'beyond'—all this is but a survival of the idea of magic.

It must be frankly admitted that much that has been said on the Christian side has been such that it might well confirm the scientist in this view, giving him the impression that Christian experience is nothing but magic. Since I took a stand openly for the spiritual renewal of medical thought, I have frequently received letters which though touching, have made me stop to think: 'I, too', I read in one of these, 'have had a miraculous experience; I had cancer and was cured of it by prayer; I told my doctor about it; but he is so incredulous that he smiled and asked me if I were really sure it was a cancer.' The medical commission at Lourdes is clearly right to be as severe as it is before it endorses a cure as a miracle.

The attitude I have described is shared to some extent by most civilized people today, whether or not they are aware of it. They believe that only science can deliver humanity from the ancient magical and religious interpretations of life. We have all imbibed this view of history at school, where it is officially taught, implicitly if not explicitly. Agnostics profess it openly, and it spurs them on in their scientific work. Thus do physicists, doctors, lawyers and economists think they are making a greater contribution to the well-being of mankind than the dreamers, the poets, the philosophers and the preachers.

But what of believers? Do they not also often share these views, without daring to acknowledge the fact? Does not this explain a certain hesitancy shown in face of their antagonists? For in their hearts this doctrine hardly fits in with the faith they have received either by up-bringing or by personal experience. Their reaction is to restrict the application of their faith to the sphere of the feelings, where it will be spared all conflict with reason. There it blossoms forth in an inner contemplative life, carefully shielded from all contact with the active life outside. In their intimate spiritual life such believers commune with Almighty God; but in the realm of action they have recourse, just as do unbelievers, only to the positive and objective data of science and technology.

Thus many Christian doctors are sincerely convinced of the necessity of keeping their religious life separate from their professional life, believing that neither the one nor the other has anything to gain from mixing them together. Medicine is a technical matter. Its scientific attainments are objective and equally valid for all doctors: their religion has nothing to do with it. On the other hand, in his feelings towards his patients, the Christian doctor allows himself to be inspired by the ideal of love of the gospel. Of course! But many non-believing doctors show as much love and devotion towards their patients as he does. They show themselves to have, like him, a professional conscience and respect for the patient.

Clearly, reduced to this narrow province of the feelings, faith has no longer very much to give to medicine. Medicine is left to the undisputed sway of science. As regards the object of our study, the Bible, the doctor who adopts this conception sees nothing more in it than a handbook of piety; a valuable book, which he reads, and upon which he meditates in his private devotions, but which remains outside his professional activity. It is for him a collection of edifying stories and poetic symbols. What such a doctor no longer sees in it is just what we have called the Biblical perspective. For the idea that everything has a meaning and that God intervenes in events is, according to him, but a relic of the old magical conception of the world, now happily superseded by the scientific conception of a rigorously determined mechanism.

In this doctor's eyes, the Israelites, in believing that God intervened to dry up the Red Sea, and Job, in believing he heard the voice of God in the thunder, were following their own lights. Let us preserve their writings, he says; they are beautiful, and speak to our hearts without our minds having necessarily to believe every word of them. We read the old fairy tales, and Greek mythology, as well. They too contain profound truths, although they are no more than poetic images. The reader will observe that we are coming back here to the remark we made just now about the meaning of symbols. The Biblical writings are still considered to be priceless, but they come to be thought of only as poetic symbols. The Exodus from Egypt, the conversation between God and Moses on Sinai, the miraculous birth of Jesus Christ, His acts of healing, His death and Resurrection, the grace attached to Communion—they all become symbolic, in the modern sense of being mere images.

If anything is mythical, it is just this very doctrine of the liberation of man by science. It will not stand up for a moment to objective examination.

In the first place, science most certainly does not free man from fear. Modern man is as full of fear as was his primitive ancestor. On this all the psychologists are agreed. Dr. Oscar Forel, whom nobody can accuse of having a Christian bias, declares roundly that 'metaphysical anguish' remains the fundamental human problem.[1] The scientists are as much afraid as the rest. I have already referred to a remark made by Harold Urey,[2] Nobel Prize-winner for Physics, one of the inventors of the atomic bomb: 'I write in order to make you afraid. I am myself a man who is afraid. All the scientists I know are afraid.' The men of science, whose numbers are increasing today, are clearly becoming conscious of the limitations of science: that it is no more than a representation of things—a representation that is most fruitful in practical deductions—but that it tells us nothing of things themselves, not even of matter or energy, which it has made the chief objects of its study. It can never, then, have an answer for the problems that haunt the heart of man.

And those problems—the meaning of things, the meaning of Creation, of Nature, of life, of death, and of eternity—are declared by the psychoanalysts to be tormenting their patients' souls today, in the midst of our scientific civilization, every bit as much as they torment the soul of the savage. This is a fact observed not only by psychoanalysts who openly profess the Christian faith; C. G. Jung[3] affirms that religion, in its widest sense, of course, is still the dominant preoccupation of all his patients.

[1] Oscar Forel, 'Psychologie de l'insécurité: peur, panique et politique', in *Revue suisse de psychologie*, 1942, Nos. 1-2

[2] Quoted by André George, 'L'humanisme scientifique', in *Les grands appels de l'homme contemporain*, Editions du Temps présent, Paris, 1946

[3] C. G. Jung, *Psychology and Religion*, Yale University Press, New Haven, 1938

The only difference is that in modern man this preoccupation is usually unconscious, whereas in the savage it fills his conscious thoughts. Thus this so-called liberation of man from his 'metaphysical anguish' by science is only the repression of the anguish into the subconscious. And anyone who has studied psychology knows that an idea thus repressed is much more dangerous.

Even the reader who has not made a special study of the psychology of the deeps of the mind will, if he is honest, grant that science is very far from having freed man from belief in magic. Proof is not far to seek. Go to the nearest newsagent's shop; you will find there astrological magazines with enormous circulations; you will find columns devoted to the same sort of thing in respectable daily newspapers and in the most genuine family weeklies. If you visit a fortune-teller, you will find in the ante-room serious-minded people who will be the first to tell you that science has got rid of old-fashioned prejudices. A university lecturer once came to consult me armed with his horoscope to facilitate my work.

I was talking once with an engineer. The conversation happened to turn to man's lack of objectivity; I told him I was convinced that nobody, myself no more than anyone else, is objective. He at once replied: 'There is only one class of men who are objective: engineers; because their job keeps reminding them that two and two make four.' But a moment later he told me that having been unfaithful to his wife he went to see a friend of his who was a clairvoyant, and she predicted the early death of his wife, which would straighten everything out. He had believed her implicitly. Although the prediction had not been fulfilled, he continued avidly to read books on astrology.

Going a step further, consider the great rise in popularity everywhere of national lotteries.[1] The State knows how to cash in on the belief in magic. Look at the four-leaved clovers, the black cats and other magic symbols that figure so largely in the lottery advertisements. The whole publicity industry itself, with its slogans, uses the technique of the magic formula. Think again of how contemporary humanity is dominated by the magic of the

---

[1] Translator's note: This Continental custom is comparable to the 'investment' by millions in British football pools

printed word, the magic of the machine, the magic of the State, the magic of revolutions. It is impossible to gainsay the fact that it is belief in magic which subjugates whole peoples, muzzles the critical spirit, crushes independent thought, unleashes the partisan passions of mobs, their delirious enthusiasm, their wild acclamation of a dictator whom they deify, which implants in whole sections of humanity such prejudices with regard to each other, that all objective discussion becomes impossible.

And the final odd paradox is that science itself takes on a magical prestige. Agnostics can be heard speaking with satisfaction of the 'miracles of science'. The whole idea of the messianic mission of science, to which I have referred above, is, in spite of its apparent rationalism, only the result of man's longing for magic, of his hunger for the marvellous, of his thirst for salvation.

Nor has science in medicine removed from men's hearts their questions about the meaning of disease, of life, and of death. But scientific medicine, by resolutely shutting out this aspect of things, leaves the sufferer still more lonely and defenceless before these mysteries. Remember my sick colleague, in his hospital bed, alone with his distress, while devoted doctors were thinking about blood-cultures.

THE BIBLE AND MAGIC

I T BECOMES CLEAR that modern man, despite appearances, is less aware of his own nature and motives, and is lonelier as he faces them. We pity the savage amid his mysterious, menacing spirits, but at least he shares his fears with all his tribe, and does not have to bear the awful spiritual solitude which is so striking among civilized people. And the primitive tribe does at least lay down a certain magical interpretation, which, however mistaken, is satisfying because it is unquestioned. In the same way, the modern fanatic, who unhesitatingly accepts all the dialectic and the slogans of his party, is happier than the sceptic. And this explains the strange resurgence of the primitive mentality which we are witnessing today.

Uncertainty is harder to bear than error. Now, science, by claiming to do away with the problems to which it has no answer, has left men alone in their grip. It leaves man in complete uncertainty as to the meaning of things, and the question still haunts him. That nothing should have meaning in this world is so contrary to that common sense which Descartes prized so highly, that man will simply refuse to believe it, in spite of all the theories of science. Men stricken by disease will never be prevented from asking whether their sickness has a meaning, and what that meaning is.

And as we have seen, modern man is left to shift for himself in this matter, constructing his own interpretations and never knowing whether they are right or wrong. Every one of my colleagues will doubtless, like me, have heard some quite fantastic explanations of diseases. It is, of course, the 'taboo' subjects, those most highly charged with emotion, which control these interpretative mechanisms. Masturbation, for example, is considered by countless invalids to be the true cause of their condition, which seems to them to be a divine punishment for the self-abuse to which they succumbed in their youth. I have lately received yet another letter from a patient suffering from dilatation of the heart, in which she thus attributes her malady to her former habit of masturbation; she asks for my opinion on this because she does not dare to ask her own doctor. No one will be surprised when I assert that such ideas sap the patient's own powers of recovery. The same is true of the frequent notion of an implacable curse, an idea often provoked by an actual suggestion: there are, for instance, mothers who, in a moment of aberration may say to their children: 'Curse you!' But I have also seen a fair number of patients who have become the victims of quacks who having failed to effect a cure have covered up their own failure by declaring that the patient was under a curse or possessed by a devil.

At this point an explanation is necessary. It will perhaps be objected that the idea of devils is in fact Biblical. In the Bible, at least in the New Testament, they are often mentioned: to 'heal a sick person' and to 'cast out a devil' are synonymous expressions (Matt. 9.33). We are even shown Jesus speaking to the devil (Matt. 17.18). In the thought of the Bible, evil—for the devils represent the source of moral evil as well as sickness (Rev. 18.2)—is not the absence of good, or some simple, natural failing; it is an active personal power, with its order of battle and its strategy. Doubtless there are many doctors who in their struggle against disease have had, like me, the feeling that they were confronting, not something passive, but a clever and cunningly resourceful enemy.

But it should be noted that the word 'devil', used frequently in Jesus Christ's day in connection with any kind of disease, had by no means the same significance then as it has today when used by the chagrined charlatans I mentioned just now. When they said to the patient, 'You are possessed by a devil,' that patient went away feeling he was quite different from other patients, that he was under a special curse. I have noticed also that the patients who questioned me about references in the Bible to devils were always nerve cases, and that they were thinking of devils only in connection with nervous complaints, an attitude which corresponds to the common idea that there is something wicked about such conditions. The Bible attributes physical as well as psychological ailments to devils.

But in speaking of the unconquerable need of man to find a meaning for his ills, I have mentioned only a subjective aspect of the problem. Objective, scientific observations in increasing numbers set before us the problem of the inner meaning of disease. I have already referred to the work of Freud on conversion hysteria. I might quote the entire work of the American psychosomatic school, that of the French school, and lastly the work of Professor V. von Weizsäcker[1] in Germany—one of the most original clinical specialists of our day—and of his pupils, including Drs. Mitscherlich and Huebschmann.

Take, for instance, a study[2] by the last-named on the pathogenesis of tuberculosis. He carefully examines four cases, the probable circumstances of contamination and of the weakening of the 'terrain'; but he notes also a certain delay between these original circumstances and the appearance of the disease, which only breaks out at the very time when the subject is suffering from a serious psychological conflict, torn between a conscious desire and an unconscious resistance. And the physical malady, or even in one case the death of a child, resolves the psychological drama, as if 'the price of psychological equilibrium were the health of the body,' as if 'one condition of psychological healing were the loss (the sacrifice!) of a part of the body, whether it be a matter of cells, tissues, organs, or—a child'.

This is a mode of thought that is as yet unfamiliar to most of my colleagues, but which opens important horizons capable of leading medicine to new discoveries. Every doctor has, of course, known cases where diseases follow each other in succession, alternating perhaps between psychological and physical disturbances like those described by Dr. Huebschmann, or else confined to a series of varied physical ailments. In such cases the idea of a 'meaning' forcibly impresses itself upon us; it is difficult to attribute them to pure coincidence.

Whatever the explanation, it will be clear to the reader that even in the case of organic diseases the problem is not so simple as a mechanicalist doctrine of medicine would have us believe.

[1] Viktor von Weizsäcker, *Grundfragen Medizinischer Anthropologie*, Furche-Verlag, Tübingen, 1948

[2] Heinrich Huebschmann, 'Über die Pathogenese der Tuberkulose', in *Psyche*, No. 10, 1950, Verl. Lambert Schneider, Heidelberg

As regards the psychological aspect, I return now to Dr. Charles Odier's study[1] of anxiety and the belief in magic. Having demonstrated the role of the magical mentality in neuroses, and shown the complete uselessness of rational discussion with such patients, he draws this practical conclusion: 'One magic can be combated successfully only by another.'

The reader will doubtless understand the implication of this affirmation. In fact it denies the claim of science to liberate humanity by its rational explanations of the world from the magical mentality. We have seen the burden of suffering that the magical mentality has laid upon man since the beginning. We have seen that science, in simply denying the meaning of things, does not ease man of this burden; that the worst ills of our time, both neuroses and political troubles, stem from the persistence of this very mentality, in spite of all the progress of science. Another remedy is therefore needed. We need 'another magic', as Dr. Odier says. That is to say, something which answers the magical mentality on its own ground—that of the meaning of things, with which science does not deal.

Might there be a good magic?

I have heard this expression from the lips of another psychoanalyst, Dr. Maeder. What then could this 'good magic' be? It would be a true answer about the meaning of things, which could replace the false answers represented by the fantastic interpretations of the primitive mentality.

And this is just the answer that the Bible gives us!

All the arguments of the scientific rationalists set out in the preceding chapter are based on a serious misunderstanding—namely, the confusion of magic with the Bible, between the superstition of primitive man and the Biblical revelation. Because both seek to give meaning to things, countless people of good faith today confuse them, classifying them together in the category of outmoded magical prejudices from which science must free the human race.

The Bible and magic are not to be confused. On the contrary, they are most strikingly antagonistic. Re-read the whole Bible on the subject: you will find that there is not a single page which does not bear witness to the same implacable conflict between

[1] *Op. cit.*

the attitude of primitive magic and that of the true faith granted through revelation.

The Israelites leave Egypt, a country completely permeated by the belief in magic; they take up their abode in Palestine amidst superstitious pagan peoples among whom diviners, sorcerers, and astrologers abound.

The flight from Egypt is already considered as a symbol of the liberation of God's chosen people, snatched by Him from their unhealthy surroundings. The years in the desert seem like a period of quarantine—the word means 'forty'—in the course of which, by many trials, through many struggles, and in many devious ways, God leads them to the discovery of the true faith, the true meaning of things, which the Sinaitic law begins to reveal.

Then all the wars against the indigenous peoples of Palestine, all the prohibitions of marriage with pagans, all the fierce struggles of the prophets against the worship of false gods which foreign influence kept bringing into Israel—all this too is part of the unending war of the true faith against magic.

'Ye shall not use enchantments, nor practise augury. . . . Ye shall not make any cuttings in your flesh for the dead, nor print any marks upon you. . . . Turn ye not unto them that have familiar spirits, nor unto the wizards; seek them not out, to be defiled by them' (Lev. 19.26, 28, 31). 'And the soul that turneth unto them that have familiar spirits, and unto the wizards, to go a whoring after them, I will even set my face against that soul . . . for I am the Lord your God' (Lev. 20.6). 'A man also or a woman that hath a familiar spirit, or that is a wizard, shall surely be put to death' (Lev. 20.27). 'When thou art come into the land which the Lord thy God giveth thee, thou shalt not learn to do after the abominations of those nations. There shall not be found with thee any one that maketh his son or his daughter to pass through the fire, one that useth divination, one that practiseth augury, or an enchanter, or a sorcerer, or a charmer, or a consulter with a familiar spirit, or a wizard, or a necromancer. For whosoever doeth these things is an abomination unto the Lord' (Deut. 18.9-12).

The whole of the history of the people of Israel is full of the great struggle of the prophets of the true God against the magical practices into which the people constantly fall back. 'And when they shall say unto you, Seek unto them that have familiar spirits and unto the wizards, that chirp and that mutter: should not a people seek unto their God? on behalf of the living should they seek unto the dead?' (Isa. 8.19). In the Bible there is no difference between the fight against magic and the fight against false gods. King Manasseh, along with many other kings, is reproved for having done 'that which was evil in the sight of the Lord . . . he practised augury, and used enchantments, and practised sorcery, and dealt with them that had familiar spirits, and with wizards' (II Chron. 33.2, 6).

To have recourse to magic is to turn away from the true God, to seek other help than His. King Saul, suffering from a mental disease, finds God silent, and consults 'a woman that hath a familiar spirit' (I Sam. 28.7). A passage in the Book of the Chronicles that is hardly flattering to doctors is to be taken in the same sense: 'and in the thirty and ninth year of his reign Asa was diseased of his feet; his disease was exceeding great: yet in his disease he sought not unto the Lord, but to the physicians. And Asa slept with his fathers, and died' (II Chron. 16.12-13). As Dr. Kressmann has remarked,[1] the physicians mentioned here are the magicians of that time. Once again, to have recourse to them is considered the same as turning away from the true God. This text therefore does not condemn medicine. It condemns a medicine that is separate from God and opposed to Him, a medicine whose benefits turn people away from God: in short, a deified medicine. Dr. Kressmann calls it 'magical medicine', and he distinguishes it from 'prophetic medicine', which is under God's authority, and which as an instrument of grace leads the patient to God. Clearly, the struggle goes on in every age, in the time of Asa and in our own time; whether it is the art of the magicians or of modern science, the Bible condemns a medicine which claims to replace God, to relieve men of the necessity of seeking Him.

The New Testament echoes the Old: it shows the same opposition between the true God and magic. I have already quoted St. Paul's words on the subject (Gal. 5.19). Annoyed by a clairvoyant, even though she is singing his praises, he turns to her and casts the magical spirit out of her, to the great anger of her masters who were exploiting her (Acts 16.16-19). We see

[1] *Op. cit.*

him at grips with the magician Bar-Jesus, who was opposing his preaching for fear of losing his influence over the Proconsul, Sergius Paulus (Acts 13.6-12). St. Paul strikes him with blindness, a symbolic enough infirmity for a seer! To the Christians in Corinth he writes: 'Ye cannot drink the cup of the Lord, and the cup of devils' (I Cor. 10.21). He writes this to those who in that church were taking part now in the Holy Communion and now in the pagan ceremonies in which was eaten meat sacrificed to idols.

It is a striking passage. The reader will remember what we have said about 'good magic', if we may so call the true, the Biblical, reply to what there is of good in man's need of magic, which is none other than his need of communion with God. That is what the Sacrament gives: identification with Jesus Christ, and so, real communion with God. We can see why Paul declares this communion to be incompatible with pagan magic. St. Paul has elsewhere vividly expressed this identification with Jesus Christ: 'Christ liveth in me' (Gal. 2.20). This is no mere poetic symbol as the rationalists claim; it is a living reality nourishing the soul. Rationalism leaves unsatisfied this mystic hunger of man, driving him into every kind of false magic, conscious and unconscious, including—and beginning with—the magic of rationalism.

14

THE TEMPTATION
OF MAGIC

THE OPENING WORDS of the Ten Commandments are well known: 'Thou shalt have none other gods but me. Thou shalt not make to thyself any graven image, nor the likeness of any thing that is in heaven above, or in the earth beneath, or in the waters under the earth. Thou shalt not bow down to them nor worship them' (Ex. 20.3-5, B.C.P. Version). The lure of magic is then in the first place the temptation to follow false gods, to deify creatures in the place of God the Creator. We are constantly coming upon examples of it in medical practice. It happens in every case of 'mother fixation', in which the infant's deification of the mother is prolonged into adult life. The mother is thought of as the embodiment of every virtue, and retains her attributes of supreme authority. On every subject her opinions remain the norm. This son (or sometimes daughter) who 'adores' his mother cannot have any real opinions of his own, nor can he really control his own life. Many men deify their wives, and *vice versa*. I have just received a touching letter from a widow in the grip of the blackest despair; but already her trial is bearing fruit, and making her examine her own conscience: 'I had made a god of my husband', she writes. She is seeing a priest now; and has gone back to the Church. She wants to find God again, after having let her husband take His place. We very often meet cases where parents have made a god of their child—to his harm, as well as their own, you may be sure.

We see eminent men deifying a master, slavishly accepting all his ideas. More often still we see people depending on the person who has led them to faith, so that they run the risk of losing it if ever some conflict should separate them from him. I knew a young man who was cured of a mother fixation and brought to

faith by a woman psychotherapist; it was a tremendous liberation; but he soon saw that that woman—his doctor and his
prophet—had taken the same exaggerated position that his
mother had occupied; he felt himself dependent on her, and
came to see me because he wished to hand over this bond to God,
to depend for the future only on Him.

There is another of my own patients, a woman whom I have
not often seen. But I have helped her at certain decisive moments
in her life, and we have always kept in touch. She used to come
and see me from time to time, and letters were exchanged. In
everything she felt, in every department of her life, she thought
constantly of me, she loved to tell me all about it, to know that I
was interested, and to have my advice. Then one day as she
thought about it, she realized that she had concentrated too much
on me. She came to see me for the last time, to make a full and
frank confession; and a few days later I received her last letter:
she had decided not to see me again, or to ring me up, or to write;
she was going to burn all my letters. Good! She would be able
to be fully herself, a real person.

Every light casts a shadow; in everything we do for the good
of a person's soul we run in some degree the risk of taking God's
place there. I have often had to take over the treatment of patients
who have become so dependent on their doctors that a brutal
separation has become essential. But in such cases I am courting
the same danger as my colleague unless I can succeed in bringing
the patient to the true faith, whereby he will depend on God
alone. There is no other way; either we find the true God, or
else we go from one false god to another.

I do not need to dwell upon the other false gods that we meet
daily in our medical work, and that have always a disturbing
effect psychologically: money, love, science, the State, instinct,
art, work, morality—or oneself. This is the whole Biblical perspective: the Bible presents all these things as gifts from God, and
it forbids us to give them in our hearts the place that belongs to
God. 'No servant can serve two masters', says our Lord (Luke
16.13).

In this connection there is a noteworthy passage in Deuteronomy: 'If there arise in the midst of thee a prophet, or a dreamer
of dreams, and he give thee a sign or a wonder, and the sign or

the wonder come to pass, whereof he spake unto thee, saying, Let us go after other gods, which thou hast not known, and let us serve them; thou shalt not hearken unto the words of that prophet, or that dreamer of dreams: for the Lord your God proveth you, to know whether ye love the Lord your God with all your heart and with all your soul' (Deut. 13.1-3). Thus the Bible will not accept success, even when it is miraculous, as convincing proof against the Word of God. Reading this text, I am reminded of the worship of science, of those who argue from its 'wonders' that in it is to be found the salvation of mankind.

But making to oneself false gods is only a very ordinary magical temptation, if I may put it so. There is a much more subtle one. The story of Christ's Temptation will serve to make it clear. At the age of thirty, Jesus is on the threshold of His ministry. He knows He is the Messiah; He knows that His people expect of their Messiah resounding deeds which will rally all the Israelites to His authority, ready to shake off the Roman yoke. He feels Himself clothed with divine power. How shall He use it?

He repairs to the desert, there to fast and to meditate (Matt. 4.1-11). But when one goes aside to meditate, one meets not only God, but also the Devil. How are their voices to be distinguished? Especially when the Devil quotes the Bible to support his temptations, and when his advice seems aimed at the success of God's own cause. Satan, in fact, suggests to our Lord that He should throw Himself from the top of the Temple, relying on God's protection, so that everyone may recognize that He is His Son; he reminds Him of a passage in one of the Psalms: 'For he shall give his angels charge over thee, to keep thee in all thy ways. They shall bear thee up in their hands' (Ps. 91.11-12).

It is clear that this is not a question of the struggle between the true God and the false gods of magic; it is a question of how Jesus Christ is to accomplish His divine ministry. It is the most subtle temptation, to have recourse to magical methods, to aim at magical successes, in God's own cause. Jesus resists it, and replies to the the tempter: 'It is written, Thou shalt not tempt the Lord thy God' (Deut. 6.16).

We may say, then, that magic exercises a twofold temptation; one sort is crude, the other subtle. The latter consists in trying to use magically the gifts of God Himself, His own promises, the faith He has given us, the experiences He has granted us, the Bible He has inspired, the dogma He has revealed. In the account to which I have just referred it is God's promises that are used. The Devil quotes the Scriptures in an attempt to awaken in Jesus the apparently legitimate ambition to demonstrate in some striking way the power He possesses, in order to sway the multitudes. And Jesus replies that this would be to tempt God.

I spoke just now of the opening words of the Ten Commandments. Now we can place Christ's words beside the next words of the Decalogue: 'Thou shalt not take the name of the Lord thy God in vain' (Ex. 20.7). This is generally understood as forbidding oaths. I think it goes further. It puts us on our guard against this subtle temptation of magic, that of giving way to magic in the name of God Himself.

In the Acts of the Apostles we see exorcists confounded for having imitated St. Paul and called on the name of Jesus Christ, instead of using their cabalistic formulae, in their magical rites (Acts 19.13-16).

Returning to the account of the Temptation of Jesus Christ, we may say that on that day, even before His ministry had begun, He had chosen the way of faith that must lead Him to the Cross, and had rejected magic. On the night of His arrest in the Garden of Gethsemane, Simon Peter, His most impetuous disciple, draws his sword and strikes the High Priest's servant (John 18.10); Jesus heals the man and reproves His Apostle, adding: 'thinkest thou that I cannot beseech my Father, and he shall even now send me more than twelve legions of angels?' (Matt. 26.53).

I remember as a child regretting with all my heart that He had not done so, and confounded the traitor who had just laid hold on Him. I was at the age of magic! I dreamt of a magical triumph for Jesus Christ. But the fact is that Jesus rejected it. Instead of calling upon God to ensure His magical triumph, He bowed to His will, even to the death of the Cross. There is no better evidence of the deep cleavage between magic and true faith.

What is magic, in its essence? It is the desire to control spiritual powers, an impure mixture of heaven and earth, as Théo Spoerri writes;[1] it is the desire to use the power of God, His promises, His grace, magically, and even in His own cause; it is claiming to have God at one's service, instead of putting oneself under His authority; it is the claim to penetrate His secrets. This was clear enough in the account of the choosing by lot of the Apostle Matthias, which led us to this study of magic.

Christ always resisted this temptation. He did not hesitate to use His supernatural power in miracles, in healing, in sensational raisings from the dead. Even further, He openly invoked these things as proofs of His divine sonship. When John the Baptist sends to ask Him if He is really the Messiah, He replies to John's disciples: 'Go your way and tell John the things which ye do hear and see: the blind receive their sight, and the lame walk, the lepers are cleansed, and the deaf hear, and the dead are raised up, and the poor have good tidings preached to them' (Matt. 11.4-5). At the disparaging Pharisees He hurls this reproof: 'though ye believe not me, believe the works: that ye may know and understand that the Father is in me, and I in the Father' (John 10.38).

But when the multitude becomes enthusiastic about these miracles, and, excited by the idea of magic, wishes to 'take him by force, to make him king' (John 6.15), He escapes from them and withdraws into solitude. And when some of the scribes and Pharisees come to ask Him for a miracle, He refuses (Matt. 12.38-9). It is in examining these and many other texts that we realize that the solution of the problem of magic lies in complete obedience to God. When Jesus feels Himself led by God to work miracles, He works them; when He feels they are not in accordance with God's will, He refuses.

There is another Biblical story that is interesting in this connection. Eli, the Judge, was ninety-eight years old, and idolatry was everywhere in Israel, and with it had come social disintegration. The result was military defeat. The Philistines had vanquished Israel at Eben-ezer and slain four thousand men (I Sam. 4.2). Then came the temptation of magic: they went to get the Ark that Moses had made as a symbol of God's covenant with His people. When it appeared, 'all Israel shouted with a great shout, so that the earth rang again' (I Sam. 4.5), because they

[1] Théophile Spoerri, *Notre Père*, P. Mottu, Lausanne, 1943

now took victory for granted, thanks to the magical power of the Ark. That is magic—that claim to possess God's power, that easy popular enthusiasm, without penitence or amendment of life, costing nothing; it reminds us of the outbursts of the crowd when Jesus entered Jerusalem on Palm Sunday (Luke 19.37).

But the shouts of the Israelites excited the Philistines; they marched against Israel and inflicted on them an even greater defeat; thirty thousand men were slain, and the Ark itself taken (I Sam. 4.10-11). On hearing the news of it, old Eli 'fell from off his seat backward . . . and his neck brake, and he died' (I Sam. 4.18).

Nevertheless God had not abandoned His people. As often happens in history, the victory brought no advantage to the Philistines. From the time that they captured the Ark (I Sam. 5.6), they were visited by diseases and misfortunes so great that in the end they themselves brought it back, with gifts, to the Israelites (I Sam. 6.10-16). Then the young prophet Samuel helped his people to turn from easy enthusiasm to true repentance: 'If ye do return unto the Lord with all your heart, then put away the strange gods and the Ashtaroth from among you, and prepare your hearts unto the Lord, to serve him only' (I Sam. 7.3). And then Israel defeated the Philistines at Mizpah (I Sam. 7.11).

There are then two contrary errors: to refrain, for fear of magic, from every kind of bold and sensational act, even when God requires it of us; this course has been all too common in the Church, and is what has made it as poor as it is today in manifestations of God's power. And, on the other hand, through zeal to demonstrate that power, to run after the sensational, even when God does not will it, and so fall into magic; certain religious sects are guilty of this. In the Gospel, the sceptics sneered at the miracles in Galilee and at the Cross: 'He saved others; let him save himself, if this is the Christ of God, his chosen' (Luke 23.35). Neither the miracles nor the Cross can be taken out of the Gospel without distorting it.

It is clear that the conduct of the doctor must, by analogy, be the same: he must beware of faint-heartedness as much as of recklessness; he must know how to take a bold technical risk when he feels it is in keeping with God's purpose, but at the same time he must not let himself be tempted by all the audacious powers his skill confers on him. Which means to say that he must let himself be led by God in his choice of the technical means put at his disposal by science.

Our trouble is that we are less certain of God's will than Jesus Christ was. And the danger of being mistaken is always greatest at the moment when we flatter ourselves that we know His will. At that point we are already falling into the error of magic, claiming to penetrate the secrets of God. But without ever being sure that we know in advance what God requires of us, we may never stop humbly seeking His will. This is the first necessity in the exercise of our vocation.

We saw this in connection with the meaning of Nature: all the men of the Bible are constantly listening-in to God. They seek His guidance, not only through inspired meditation, but also in the events of Nature. For us doctors these 'events', in the exercise of our profession, are the objective examination of the patient, the history of his disease, the information contained in a detailed anamnesis, and everything that a profound understanding of his state of mind can tell us.

But with us, as with Jesus Christ in the desert, the authentic voice of God and the tempting voice of magic are always together, side by side, yet diametrically opposed. Here I should like to borrow an excellent illustration used in one of his books[1] by Dr. Théodore Bovet. It is like a wireless set, in which the slightest rotation of the variable condensers takes us in an instant from one concert to another. This is especially true of the short wave bands, where the tuning is of the finest. We must admit that we very often get the wrong wavelength.

In one case, for example, I know that I was guided by God to put a certain apparently trivial question to the patient, and it struck home; light broke in upon his understanding of the meaning of his illness, and of a personal problem that was tied up with it; he was able to solve it. But then in a similar case I was tempted to reproduce the same experience artificially; to repeat my question, not now in a moment of inspiration, but coldly and calculatingly. I was succumbing to magic: I was treating the question that God had suggested to me in a specific case, as

[1] Théodore Bovet, *Sur la terre comme au ciel*, J. H. Jeheber, Geneva, 1944

if it were a magic formula by which I could at will switch on the divine power.

What I wish the reader to understand is that by 'twiddling the knob' of my receiver I went from one concert to another, from the free and authentic inspiration of God to the magical attitude which tries to exploit God instead of submitting to Him.

In the same way, a certain theologian was suddenly enlightened while reading Karl Barth: he received a new vision of the greatness of God and the littleness of man, of which the theology he had been taught knew nothing. He realized that the greatest event in history was the unbelievable fact of God speaking to men, and that this 'Word of God' is as high above human speech as the heavens are above the earth. But at once he was in danger of using the expression 'the Word of God' on the slightest pretext, as if it were a magic formula that would resolve all problems, whereas Barth was stressing the very fact of our inability to resolve them.

Or take the woman who, in a moment of perplexity, opens her Bible at random, and happens to light upon a passage which exactly meets her need; she sees in it a direct personal message from God. She too is in danger of magic if on another occasion she uses the same means and imagines that she is certain to find God's reply to her new problem in some verse thus chosen.

While attending an 'Oxford Group' meeting, a certain young man realized the importance of writing down his meditations. He tried it and found it most valuable: he carried out the orders thus written, and his life was transformed. But he would be in danger of attaching a magical value to this kind of meditation if he claimed by means of it to penetrate the secrets of God.

Another man goes to a Pentecostal Movement meeting, and realizes that the Church has neglected the 'gifts of the Spirit' (I Cor. 12.1-11), and in particular the gift of healing. He engages actively in prayer for the sick, and lays his hands on them as the early Christians did. The temptation of magic is the greater for this new adept the more eager he is to heal sick people.

We see now the way belief in magic insinuates itself into our hearts, coming in the wake of even our most authentic spiritual experiences. It rears its head the moment we make generalizations based on a particular experience, as soon as we claim that

that experience is the necessary condition that inevitably leads to true faith. We see that the indefinable frontier between faith and magic is the frontier between humility and pride, between the humble search for God and the proud claim to possess Him. This is the psychological cause of all the quarrels that divide Christians. Such disputes are tragic and fruitless, for each invokes in support of his own system the living experience on which it was based, without seeing that between the experience and the system there has been a subtle switch from one wavelength to another, from faith to magic.

Every one of these systems comes under the heading of the 'graven images' of the Ten Commandments, in that it substitutes a truth received from God for God Himself. We often hear Protestants reproaching Catholicism for conferring a magical value on the sacraments, on the priesthood, on dogma, or on the Church. But there again they are confusing the systematization with the authentic experience on which it is based, and from which too many Protestants are cut off by their fear of magic. The psychologist can see quite as many magical deviations—many of them less consciously realized—in Protestantism, where they abound among the various sects, among the pietist movements, and even among the rationalists, who do homage to the magic of Reason. The spirit of magic lies in wait for the Christians as much as for the agnostics and the pagans. It arises, in fact, from an inherent tendency in human nature, and none of us can boast of being proof against its wiles. It is the longing for the fairy tale, for the magic wand that will charm away the difficulties of life, the suffering, the limitations, and the uncertainties of our human condition.

Recently I read a pamphlet[1] denouncing modern superstition. It contained an impressive list of the fabulous beliefs current today, even among those who affect not to hold them. But the author had added an equally lengthy list of the superstitions of Christians. The reader must realize the extreme importance of this problem. Each time that we Christians cross, without noticing it, the frontier between true faith and magic, we are helping to give colour to the widespread error that I am here pointing out —the identification of true faith with magic, and the setting of

[1] E. Kremer, *Les yeux ouverts sur la ruse de Satan*, Le Réveil, Mulhouse

both over against the rationalist view of the world, whereas the truth is that true faith and science are in complete accord, and ought to be joining forces to deliver man from the temptation of magic.

Man finds himself in an impossible dilemma as long as he thinks he must choose either reason or magic and faith confused together: he has to repress one or the other of the two, to become either a rationalist, stifling his mystical longings, or a mystic, stifling the voice of his reason. The integration of his person, the harmonious marriage of his deductive and inductive functions, is possible only if he accepts the true dilemma: the choice between magic and true faith, faith in the one true God.

It seems that the human mind is too small to grasp God in His fullness; so it clings to one of His attributes, one of His gifts, exaggerating its importance, and basing a system of life on it. The Bible, the Church, dogma, experience, meditation, ceremonies, spiritual gifts, or natural gifts—all have their true value, but we end up by claiming to confine God in them.

'I shall never believe it possible to monopolize Christ', wrote Mauriac.

15

THE PERSONALISM OF
THE BIBLE

THE READER may now pass from these religious examples
to those to be found in his own profession. In medicine
the idea of magic enters into the exaggerated vogue of
some remedy or other, either among the public or in the medical
profession, or perhaps in the mind of one doctor who has had
wonderful results with it in particular cases, and who thereupon
prescribes it for everything. There is the magic of the laboratory,
of X-rays, and of various theories of dieting. There is the magic
of chiropractic, of psychoanalysis, of vitamins, and of shock-
treatment. All such crazes have their roots in the longings of
primitive man that still persist in us in the form of a desire to
find an effective panacea, a certain and generally applicable line
of action that would bring us out of the darkness in which we
are stumbling.

My old professor, Dr. Roch, to whom I owe so much, spoke
of this modern paradox in his inaugural speech[1] at the Twenty-
seventh French Medical Congress: 'Never before have diagnostic
methods been so perfect and so abundant; never have their results
been so sure and so clear; never have we possessed so many and
such effective techniques of healing; never has compulsory state
education been so widespread in our respective countries; and
yet, to our sorrowful astonishment and sometimes our vehement
indignation, there has never been a time when quacks, and all
the foolish practices of modern witchcraft, have been so popular.
A short while ago, in Geneva, the seat of a faculty of medicine,
and the headquarters of the World Health Organization, I saw
a young diabetic mother who allowed herself to die through

[1] M. Roch, 'Discours prononcé à la séance inaugurale du XXVIIᵉ Congrès
français de médecine tenu à Genève le 29 septembre 1949', in the *Revue
médicale de la Suisse romande*, 25 October, 1949

having given up receiving insulin injections. Instead, she had buried at the bottom of a garden a piece of string knotted in accordance with some rite or other. . . . It must be concluded that the scientific spirit has brought little enlightenment to the mass of our fellow citizens, and also that the patient needs to enter into a sympathetic and even a mystical relationship with the person from whom he expects a cure. He needs to be treated with friendliness, as a person, and not merely as a number on a card.'

But let us beware: there may be a magic of the quack, and science may be regarded as having a magical virtue, but the same danger threatens the doctor who seeks inspiration in religion to help him in his work. Many of my patients begin by saying to me: 'I've come to see you because I can have confidence only in a Christian doctor like you.' Flattering, isn't it? But it is utterly mistaken, and it falsifies our relationship right from the start unless I can manage to undeceive them by showing them that in their minds this idea of a 'Christian medicine' has a magical attraction.

In fact these people expect me to be a magician. They think that I 'possess', in virtue of my religion, insight or powers which would be lacking in a non-Christian colleague. This notion of 'possessing' spiritual power is the mark of belief in magic. These patients imagine that I am going to tell them what is God's purpose for them, that I am going to sweep away their difficulties, free them from their bonds without much effort on their part, save them from error, from stumbling, from the suffering and darkness which are still part of human life.

We have here, as we saw in Chapter 11, an infantile attitude, the persistence in modern man, even in the believer, of the primitive mentality described by Lévy-Bruhl. Now the doctor's first task is to help men to fulfil their destiny, and that means helping them to become men in every sense of the word—that is to say, persons.

What is the person? It is man in so far as he becomes adult, freed from himself because dependent on God, assuming full responsibility for himself before God. Such is man as the Bible presents him; and this is what I now wish to show, emphasizing what it means for medicine.

In the Biblical view, man is not the most highly evolved of

the animals; he is a special creation of God. He is not merely a physical and mental machine; he is 'spirit and soul and body' (I Thess. 5.23), for he has been created in the image and likeness of God (Gen. 1.26). And also, what distinguishes the God of the Bible from the divinities of every other religion is that He is a personal God, who speaks personally to man, who calls upon him (Gen. 3.9-10). I have already quoted Professor Siebeck's remark: 'It is the calling that creates the person.' Throughout the Bible we see God calling men, and drawing them thus out of the primitive mentality in which they were wallowing. It is a fact that the savage has no consciousness of himself as a person: he identifies himself with his tribe; he identifies himself also with Nature, by mystical participation; for him the microcosm that is himself, and the macrocosm that is the world, are confused.

'The Lord said unto Abram, Get thee out of thy country, and from thy kindred, and from thy father's house' (Gen. 12.1). God takes him out of his tribe, out of his impersonal existence, conditioned by his environment; He makes a person of him through his personal obedience to a personal command. The personal God makes man into a person. In the view of the Bible, the link between God and man is a link between persons; it is this that makes man a complete being, responsible for himself before God. Right up to the last page of the Bible you will find men called by God out of the prejudices of their tribe, away from the impulses of their own instincts, so that they no longer live the automatic life of animals, but become persons and prophets —prophets in the Biblical sense, but also prophets in the philosophical sense of which Bergson speaks—that is to say, emancipated, adult, creative men, discerning the true meaning of things and teaching it to others.

God says to Moses: 'I know thee by name' (Ex. 33.17). He says to Cyrus: 'I am the Lord, which call thee by thy name' (Isa. 45.3). These texts express the essence of the personalism of the Bible. One is struck, on reading the Bible, by the importance in it of proper names. Whole chapters are devoted to long genealogies. When I was young I used to think that they could well have been dropped from the Biblical Canon. But I have since realized that these series of proper names bear witness to the fact that, in the Biblical perspective, man is neither a thing nor an abstraction, neither a species nor an idea, that he is not a fraction of the mass, as the Marxists see him, but that he is a person.

The proper name is the symbol of the person. If I forget my patients' names, if I say to myself, 'Ah! There's that gall-bladder type or that consumptive that I saw the other day', I am interesting myself more in their gall-bladders or their lungs than in themselves as persons. The patient is at once aware of this. He realizes, of course, that the human memory has its limits; and if I have forgotten his name it is better simply to ask him what it is than to employ subterfuges in order to find him on my list. What matters is my real attitude towards him; if I am really interested in him as a person, his name will become important, just as the proper names in the Bible are important.

He will then be no longer merely a case to me—that is to say, a combination of physical and psychological phenomena—but a person. By treating him as a person, I help him to become one. This aspect of the doctor's task seems to me to have particular importance today, when man finds himself so gravely depersonalized by the mechanization of life and the 'massification' of society.

But medicine itself has become frighteningly mechanized today. We will be able to heal others only if we cure ourselves of the feverish haste in which we live. Real personal contact with the patient requires calmness and time. How many doctors there are who see a patient ten, twenty, or more times for a few minutes at a time, without ever finding time for a conversation on any but a superficial level. Such an exchange, on a deeper level, might bring them to quite a new understanding of their patient. If the doctor during one of those innumerable visits makes, say, an intravenous injection, he gets a larger fee from the social insurance funds than if he undertakes an extensive clinical examination or has a long talk with his patient to help him govern his life better. I am of the opinion that in all countries medical associations ought to claim from social insurance funds a scale of fees based on the time devoted to each consultation.[1]

[1] Translator's note: Dr. Tournier is, of course, speaking here in terms of the situation in his own country, but the point of his remarks will not be lost on doctors in the United States and Britain

I am speaking here in particular to my colleagues engaged in 'social medicine'. Men pass hurriedly through their hands one after another, as if on a mass-production belt, coming from their factories, where they are merely anonymous tools of production, or from the impersonal masses, conditioned by the collective ideas of the cinema, the radio, and politics: they are no longer men; they above all need to be made persons again.

As they come for a consultation, they are received by officials who take their cards from immense filing-cabinets, or, if they are there for the first time, ask them the mechanical questions that officials always ask: 'Single? Married? Father not known, eight children. . . .' It all goes down automatically, as if all that mattered was to fill all the blanks in the index card.

When the patient's turn comes, the card is passed to the doctor, who often will not even read the surname inscribed on it. He too runs the risk, in the monotony and rush of his work, of giving way to the spirit of the impersonal administrator. And then all his scientific training tends to concentrate his attention on the case rather than on the person. And yet this may be the only opportunity the patient has had for a long time of talking with someone as man to man, of being treated as a person and not as a thing. Professor P. Delore, of Lyons, is concerned with the same problem in making his plea for a 'hospital on a human scale',[1] for when the number of beds in each ward exceeds a certain figure, the relationship between doctor and patient must suffer.

Of course, a social insurance doctor, like a general practitioner or a surgeon, cannot spend as long with each of his patients as does the psychotherapist. But even a few words will be enough to show that the doctor is treating his patient as a person, and the atmosphere of the consultation will be transformed. 'You have a North-country name; have you been in the South long?' By such a simple question may the whole personal life of the patient be brought into the consultation. So in the Bible one word from God transforms a life, creating a person in that life, and opening in it the way to service.

[1] Pierre Delore, 'L'hôpital à l'échelle humaine', in *Personne humaine et organisation hospitalière*, 'Pages documentaires', No. 6, August-September, 1949, Paris

St. Paul, the great theologian, does not address the churches as if they were anonymous congregations. In his letters, the most abstruse arguments are followed by news of this person and that (I Cor. 16.12-20), by special greetings to this person or that (Col. 4.10-17). He signs his letter in his own hand to make it more personal (Col. 4.18). That ambassador of impersonality, the typewriter, did not then exist, but Paul probably suffered from weak eyesight and usually had to dictate his letters.

In the same way, the Gospels contain no general and abstract theory. They are full of the personal encounters of Jesus with beings of flesh and blood, clearly-depicted individuals, each with his own character. Almost always the Evangelist is careful to record their names. The changes in names—Abram to Abraham (Gen. 17.5), Jacob to Israel (Gen. 32.28), Simon to Peter (Matt. 16.17-18), Saul to Paul (Acts 13.9), etc.—have also an important place in the Bible, and have to do with the symbolic meanings of proper names, which are often explained.

This fact of the proper name symbolizing the person shows us clearly that the latter is not to be considered as a body with a soul and a mind added to it, but as a complete entity in itself. At this point the Biblical view differs radically from existentialist philosophy. I have already quoted the passage in Genesis where God invites man to give names to all the creatures (Gen. 2.19). We said it was the founding of science, but it also shows the creative power of man: things become a reality, they can be distinguished, only in so far as man gives them individual names.

Here is a very eloquent story on this subject. In Switzerland the Federal Penal Code permits therapeutic abortion in exceptional cases and under strict medical control. For this purpose experts are appointed in each canton. One of these, my friend Dr. Plattner, a psychiatrist who lives near Berne, told us of a recent experience of his. A certain pregnant woman, who was trying to get his consent to an abortion, often referred to the child she had conceived as a 'little collection of cells'. Such is the conception that science gives us of man—a 'little collection of cells', or, for an adult, a 'big collection of cells'. Instinctively, this woman turned to science when she wished to devalue the life that was at stake. One day Dr. Plattner had the idea of putting to the woman this question: 'What name would you give to this child if it were to be born?' At once the atmosphere of the conversation changed. The woman was silent: one felt that the child, as soon as she gave him a name in her own mind, was ceasing to be a 'little collection of cells' in order to become a person. 'It was staggering', concluded Dr. Plattner. 'I felt as if I had been present at an act of creation.'

Thus the doctor who puts himself inside the Biblical perspective, who absorbs the Biblical conception of man, becomes as a result a doctor of the person. He can no longer see man as a collection of cells, but as a spiritual being, called to a personal destiny and endowed by God Himself with priceless value. The parables of the Lost Sheep (Luke 15.3-7), of the Prodigal Son (Luke 15.11-32), and of the Good Samaritan (Luke 10.30-7), bear particular witness to God's personal care for every man, but the entire Bible is the reflection of it.

16

THE INTEGRATION OF
THE PERSON

WHAT, THEN, is the medicine of the person? It is a
two-dimensional medicine, the two dimensions being
those of which we spoke at the beginning of this book
in connection with the 'two diagnoses'. It is the medicine which,
at the same time as it tries to cure the disease by all the technical
means that science puts at our disposal, tries to create in man that
full harmonious development which will make him a person.
On several occasions I have seen sick people get better only after
they have been helped to have sufficient confidence in themselves
to accomplish some creative act. Now all lack of development,
every inner disharmony, endangers health; it follows that these
two aspects of the medicine of the person, these two dimensions,
although distinct, are intimately bound up with each other, and
are complementary. And as man truly becomes a person only
when he comes in contact with God, doctors who profess the
medicine of the person know that they are bound to the Biblical
revelation, as Professor R. Siebeck of Heidelberg writes. 'The
key to a truly integrated medicine', writes Professor Pouyanne of
Bordeaux, 'is to be found in Christian doctrine.'[1]

Perhaps I ought rather to have said a three-dimensional
medicine; for there is a further difference, between the development of a man, as described for example by Jung under the
term 'integration', and the birth of the person, which implies the
intervention of a force unknown to Jung's psychology: the Holy
Spirit. In fact, I believe the birth of the person to be none other
than that new birth 'of water and the Spirit' of which Jesus spoke
to the learned Nicodemus (John 3.5). I used to wonder why Jesus

[1] Louis Pouyanne, 'Le médecin et la vie chrétienne', in *Les deux Cités*, No. 4,
loc. cit.

had said 'of water and the Spirit' rather than 'of the Spirit' only. Is it not a proof that even in the new birth which we have traditionally considered to be a purely 'spiritual' birth, the Biblical perspective still remains, on the contrary, that of incarnation? Water is the chemical compound *par excellence*, the symbol of matter. The new birth, the integration of the person, is not only a spiritual, but also a physical and psychological regeneration; and the medicine of the person is not a 'spiritual medicine', but three-dimensional: physical, psychological, and spiritual.

So that the reader may the better understand what I mean by the integration of the person, and in order at the same time to draw some general conclusions from our lengthy study of the problem of magic, I wish to make here a brief exposition of the views of Dr. Aloys von Orelli, of Zurich.[1]

In Chapter 12 I gave an account of the doctrine, very prevalent among modern intellectuals, which sees human history as divided into two great periods: the first, primitive and magical; the second, modern and scientific. In the human soul there are on the one hand inductive and intuitive functions, and on the other functions that are deductive and rational. The first refer to the inward feelings, the second to intellectual knowledge. The former are subjective, the latter objective. The first discern what philosophers call 'first causes'; the others what they call 'secondary causes'.

Lacking an intellectual culture, which evolves but slowly, primitive man tries to comprehend the world through his inductive, intuitive, and magical functions. Lacking a divine revelation, which he cannot find for himself, he strays into false interpretations and into the casuistry of omens of which we spoke in Chapter 11, on the belief in magic.

Now, we saw also that the intuitive, magical function, that which seeks the meaning of things, does not disappear from the human mind in the scientific period; it is only repressed into the unconscious or at least into the subconscious, where it remains a source of distress to which science has no answer. There is, then, no solution in the eclipsing of the magical function in favour of the

[1] In an unpublished paper given at Bossey in 1948, under the title *Die Entwicklung der ärztlichen Anthropologie*

rational function. It enriches man with vast intellectual know-ledge, but impoverishes him in his inner life through the repression of his intuitive faculty. His poverty is the greater in that it is the latter which is truly creative, as Bergson has shown: man becomes a technician rather than a creator.

Therefore the true solution of man's problem will be found only in the 'integration' of the two basic functions. Such is von Orelli's theory. To the two historical periods of which we have spoken he adds a third, on the threshold of which he claims we now stand.

The first he calls the period of mystical participation; the second, the period of the scientific picture of the world; and the third, the period of the spiritual vision of the world.

The savage has not yet become conscious of self. He is fused with the world, whose forces he feels at work in himself; he is in a state of mystical participation in the tribe and in Nature. In the second period, becoming conscious of self, man detaches himself from Nature. He becomes an observer, and Nature an external object which he observes. He himself becomes an object to himself. The world becomes a picture which he contemplates at a distance: the scientific picture of the world, the huge, impersonal mechanism we have described. Man thus loses consciousness of the link which binds him to Nature and to the community, and becomes an individual. This evolution was perfected in the Renaissance and in the great scientific advance which followed it.

But modern man, fashioned by this evolution, stands alone and in distress; distressed by the inner disharmony brought about by the repression of his magical function; alone, tortured by an imperious longing to find once again the sense of community. The third period will be that of the integration of the person—that is to say, the amalgamation of the two fundamental functions, the inductive and the deductive, the consciousness of the meaning of things and of the link that binds us to society and to Nature, and the consciousness of the self and of the mechanism of things.

It will therefore not be a regression towards the primitive mentality, but a more complete and harmonious development of the person, leading to a spiritual vision of the world: a vision, no longer a picture, for the picture is detached from the observer and external to him, whereas he is personally engaged in his vision; and, finally, spiritual, for this integration cannot be achieved by man himself: he needs an integrating force, the Holy Spirit, and a supernatural guide, the Biblical revelation.

In the natural state, dependent on his own strength, man must give free rein either to his magical function or to his rational function. He falls back either on mystical participation or on the impersonal picture of the world. These two concepts are irreducible, irreconcilable, impossible to integrate. Man represses one or the other, and cannot attain to fulfilment.

The reader will perhaps object that he does not yet see clearly what this 'spiritual vision of the world' can be, how it will reconcile what science and religion teach us, what we know intellectually of the mechanism of things and what we feel intuitively of their meaning. I admit it willingly. We have developed our two faculties separately; we have scarcely yet begun to think of the whole man. But we are aware of the urgency of the search; we are aware that this discovery of a true conception of the human person is the great problem of today. And we also feel that we cannot undertake the search without a sure guide.

We have come back, in fact, to the distinction made earlier between false and good magic. False magic consists in the false interpretations of the meaning of things that man, like the savage, imagines of his own accord. The good magic is the purpose of God, the true meaning of things, which man can only discover as it is revealed to him by God. As Jung says, we must re-awaken the primitive man that is in us, instead of repressing him. But what he does not tell us is how to re-awaken him without falling back again into false interpretations like those of the savage and of our modern neurotics. For my part, I can see no other solution than to ask God Himself to bring about this synthesis in us.

We should bear in mind that not all the intuitions of the savage were mistaken, mixed up though they were with the false ideas of his magical mentality. I believe that in the search for integration that we must now undertake, men of the coloured races, enlightened by the Biblical revelation, will have a useful contribution to make. They are less deformed by the secular intellectualism which we of the white races have inherited.

Recently I gave two talks to a world conference of delegates of the Y.W.C.A. I was struck by the preponderant part played in this assembly by representatives of the black races of Africa, the yellow races of Asia, and many others from distant places, including the island of Trinidad. A Negro girl from the Gold Coast, speaking with great authority, asserted that missions had made grave mistakes in approaching the natives in an attitude of disdain, as if the missionaries had everything to teach them and nothing to learn from them. She added that on the contrary many converted Africans were discovering in the light of the Bible the true meaning of some of the customs and intuitions handed down by tradition in their tribes.

But let us return to medicine. Dr. von Orelli is fond of quoting the great figure of Paracelsus, who is considered the pioneer of scientific medicine. Medicine too had been magical up to then. But in him there were two men: the alchemist, carrying on the ancient tradition of the intuitive search for the symbolic meaning of things, and the scientist, inaugurating a new era. Since then, orthodox medicine has not been able to conduct these two kinds of research together. It has become exclusively scientific, and magical medicine has taken refuge in all the paramedical schools of thought.

The reader will note, in support of the thesis I am here defending, that it is especially in the United States, a country where technical civilization has had its greatest triumph, that these magical beliefs have prospered.

The reader will understand that I am not urging either a return to the alchemy of Paracelsus or the adoption of one of those modern magical systems alongside our scientific methods; nor do I even wish, following the example of some doctors— Dr. Bircher-Benner, for instance—to attempt the acclimatization in our own medicine of certain spiritual ideas originating in India.

The true integration of the magical function into medicine will not be an intellectual operation only; it will not be taught theoretically, or learnt pragmatically, any more than it will be an appeal to the ideas of the charlatans. It implies of necessity for us doctors an integration of our own persons. When we studied the temptation of magic with reference to the Temptation of Jesus Christ in the wilderness, we saw how difficult it is for us to distinguish the authentic voice of God from the voice of false magic. We remarked that they are always side by side. There is no objective criterion, outside of Revelation, by which they may be separated. But even in interpreting Revelation we hesitate constantly. How could we help our patients to acquire, as far as possible, this true sense of the meaning of things, if we were not seeking it ourselves in our own lives?

Only Jesus Christ always distinguished the voice of God from the temptation of magic. We can approach this true spiritual vision of the world and of things only in so far as we enter into communion with Christ. This is why Dr. Plattner has written[1] that the medicine of the person is concerned first of all with the person of the doctor. We do not have access to it by adopting some doctrine of man, even a Biblical one, but through personal experience of Jesus Christ, and a strenuous seeking after His inspiration. It is not what we say to our patients, it is not talking to them about God, it is not even praying with them that makes us doctors of the person; it is what is happening in our own lives, it is the solving of our own life's problems, the integration of our own persons. Sick people are not to be helped to find the true meaning of life by exhortations, but by the contagion of our own experience.

Following then the example of our Lord, let us give a big place in our lives to intimate and private communion with God. For both the doctor and the patient, the integration of the person is accomplished essentially in meditation; for to meditate is to be led by God to the discovery of ourselves. It takes time. That is not easy in the harassed life of the doctor. But we always find time for the things we judge to be the most important. Nothing makes our lives so worth while as this faithful seeking after God's purpose in order to find the solutions of our own problems and of those that our patients bring to us as soon as they feel us to be attentive and understanding. But I should be the last to say it is easy.

Here again the Bible is realistic. It shows us men filled with

[1] Paul Plattner, 'Médecine de la personne', in *Die neue Sendung des Arztes*, *loc. cit.*

boldness when God has spoken clearly to them. But it also often shows them hesitating and perplexed when God is silent. 'Verily thou art a God that hidest thyself', cries Isaiah (Isa. 45.15). It shows us how much it cost Moses, Gideon, Isaiah, or Jeremiah to make certain of God's call. Jesus Himself, in order to see clearly what was God's will for His ministry, spent forty days in the wilderness (Luke 4.2). St. Paul, after his conversion, went away for three years (Gal. 1.18). He confesses that he really believed he was obeying God in persecuting the Church (Acts 26.9). The Bible reports his disagreement with the Church in Jerusalem (Acts 15.6) on the interpretation of God's will concerning converted Gentiles, and his difference of opinion with his old comrade Barnabas (Acts 15.39). And, finally, he confesses his hesitations (I Thess. 2.18), and the trouble he has in choosing from among all the calls that are made on him (Rom. 1.13-15). At the moment of Christ's Transfiguration we find Peter, giving way to the temptation of magic, making an absurd proposal for, the account adds, 'he did not know what he said' (Luke 9. 33).

But once again it is the Bible as a whole that I should call to witness, rather than this example or that. The Bible shows us inspired men, passionately seeking to understand God's purpose, but discovering it only slowly and laboriously, as if feeling their way, and at the cost of making many mistakes. They suffer because of it; and in their suffering they cry out to God: 'Oh that thou wouldest rend the heavens, that thou wouldest come down . . .' (Isa. 64.1). And when in Bethlehem God did come down, the form He took was so different from what believers expected that He was recognized only by those who, as the Scriptures repeat several times, had eyes that could see Him and ears that could hear Him (Matt. 13.14-16).

It is also important not to seek on one's own, but to study the Bible with others, meditating with them and praying with them (Matt. 18.20). Thus, at the outset of St. Paul's great missionary work we see the Church in Antioch, at prayer, receive this command from the Holy Spirit: 'Separate me Barnabas and Saul for the work whereunto I have called them' (Acts 13.1-3). And thus we see Moses, wonderfully inspired as he was, listening to the wise counsel of his father-in-law (Ex. 18.24). Many doctors, in danger like him of letting themselves be crushed under the weight of the responsibilities they have assumed, also hear their wives say: 'The thing that thou doest is not good. Thou wilt surely wear away' (Ex. 18.17-18); but they do not always accept their advice with as much humility as Moses showed in taking that of his father-in-law.

But what the Bible shows us above all is that if we are to understand God better, we must obey Him. It presents the long and troublous wanderings of the Israelites in the wilderness as the consequence of their rebellious complaints and their disobedience. Jesus said: 'If any man willeth to do his will, he shall know . . .' (John 7.17). We intellectuals are always wanting to know, to be sure, before we obey; the Biblical view is the opposite. First let us put order into our own life, let us answer what our Lord requires of us: 'Be ye therefore perfect, even as your Father which is in heaven is perfect' (Matt. 5.48, A.V.). We shall indeed never attain to it in this world; but in so far as we strive resolutely towards perfection, we become free men, persons.

'What is the aim of medicine?' asks Dr. Kressmann;[1] he goes on: 'In order that our activity should be fully effective, it is necessary . . . that it be liberating; it must free the life of the individual from all the chains that hamper it.' That means freeing men, as far as in us lies, from suffering; but it also means freeing them from their loneliness, from their anxieties, their remorse, from their rebelliousness, and from all the enslavements that compromise their physical, psychological, and spiritual health.

And then Dr. Baruk sees in this passage from Isaiah the whole vocation of the doctor:[2] 'The spirit of the Lord God is upon me; because the Lord hath anointed me to preach good tidings unto the meek; he hath sent me to bind up the brokenhearted, to proclaim liberty to the captives, and the opening of the prison to them that are bound' (Isa. 61.1). And at the recent Protestant Medico-Social Congress at Lyons Professor Mouriquand called doctors the 'removers of distress'.

This distress, as we have seen, arises out of the disturbing

[1] *Op. cit.*

[2] H. Baruk, *Psychiatrie morale expérimentale, individuelle et sociale*, Presses Universitaires de France, Paris, 1945

The Problem of Magic

mystery which hangs over the meaning of things, over the meaning of life and death, of sickness and of all that happens to us. It suggests to men's minds all the delusive answers of magic, a new slavery from which also they must be liberated. That liberation is to be found in the integration of the person, of our own persons as doctors, and of the persons of our patients; it means liberation from every false belief, from every kind of infantile regression, from fleeing away from life and self-responsibility. Then let us continue now our study of the Bible, in order to seek in it the true meaning of life and death, of disease and of healing.

PART THREE

LIFE, DEATH, DISEASE AND HEALING

17

THE MEANING OF LIFE

'GOD LIKES LIFE; He invented it!' I well remember these words, spoken by my friend Roger Fauré, who gave his life for France while leading his battery in June, 1940. He often repeated it, with that warm smile that used to light up his face. His very death confirms the truth of what he said; for war, bringing so much death in its train, is the result of all man's disobedience to the will of God.

Yes, God likes life; He invented it. Throughout the Bible, the idea of life is connected with God. It is portrayed as a force proceeding from the Creator and animating creatures. Life awakens at God's call. All through the story of the Creation we find the words: 'God said . . . God said . . .'; it is the Word of God which gives life and existence to every single thing (Gen. 1.3).

Note that the fundamental distinction made by us between the organic world and the inorganic world is scarcely present in the Bible. In the Bible there is but one world. The rhythmic repetition of the same formulae in the account of the Creation brings out the essential unity of the world in the Biblical perspective.

Every differentiation is a manifestation of life as understood by the Bible, right from the first separation of light from darkness (Gen. 1.4). Without God, all is nothingness, 'waste and void' (Gen. 1.2); at God's call, everything takes on movement and life. It is God who moves the stars; their infinite motions show forth the power of the life of God. I have no doubt that had the Biblical writers been aware of Brownian movement, chemical affinity, cosmic rays, radioactive bodies, electrons, neutrons, protons and all that physics has still to discover, they would have seen in them also the effects of the power of the life that proceeds from God.

The Bible lays great stress on the superabundance of the life which God pours into the whole universe, and which has made such a deep impression on biologists that they have spoken of the wastefulness of Nature: 'Thou openest thy hand, and satisfiest the desire of every living thing', cries the Psalmist (Ps. 145.16). But, as we see in the account of the Creation, there is a gradation; there is one life, but there are degrees of it, leading to that of man created 'in the image of God' (Gen. 1.27)—that is to say, the life of man endowed through self-consciousness with a quality akin to that of God. And complete and total life is incarnate in Jesus Christ: 'For it was the good pleasure of the Father that in him should all the fulness dwell' (Col. 1.19).

But observe men, consider that half-formulated subconscious thought which is as it were of the very texture of their souls: you will see that frequently, even in the case of believers, it is permeated by the idea of an opposition between God and life, so that God appears to be a sort of brake, a barrier, limiting life. Men claim the right to 'live their own lives', and in the name of that right they protest against the restrictive authority of God. As if God prevented us from living our lives, when all the time it is only by Him that we can live them to the full!

This same idea leads many believers to see God as the sort of father who systematically forbids his children everything that gives them pleasure and increases the joy of life. Often has some believer told me, in the privacy of my consulting-room: 'I don't think that it is God's will that I should have such and such a thing, because it makes me envious.' Twisted ideas of that kind are usually the result of the negative education of which I have spoken elsewhere. One of my patients, the victim of such an education, exclaimed one day: 'I can see now that the fundamental slogan taught me by my parents was this: enjoyment of life prohibited. It was never actually put like that, but it has become part of me, and I am completely hamstrung by it.'

I am reminded of a young woman to whom I said at the door after one of our first discussions: 'Permission to live!' I felt her to be quite repressed and inhibited by her past; I fear I did not know to what an extent. Even now she has not yet succeeded in availing herself of her 'permission to live'; it is the most painful failure of my career. She always spoke of the armour she put on in order to come and see me; she explained once that it was not for protection against me, but against herself: a sort of padlock on her pent-up life, for fear of an explosion if it should happen to escape to freedom.

Truth to tell, we all know that fear of ourselves, that fear of the life-force which we feel in ourselves, that it might overflow. Each of us knows that such a bursting of the banks would be a breaking of the divine laws of life. And so we come near to thinking that the life-force is opposed to God, whereas it was He who gave it to us. It is clear that to put it under lock and key is no answer; the solution is to abandon our life to God and to ask Him to direct its powerful course.

Just as the Bible scarcely recognizes our distinction between the organic and the inorganic worlds, so also, as Professor Ellul points out,[1] it ignores the contrast which we make constantly between biological and spiritual life. As we have seen, according to the Bible life is a force which comes from God, animating the world and all living beings; this same force, this same Word of God, the Spirit, gives to man his moral conscience and wakes in him what we call his spiritual life. 'Thou hast granted me life and favour', says Job (Job 10.12).

'The Lord God formed man of the dust of the ground, and breathed into his nostrils the breath of life; and man became a living soul' (Gen. 2.7). A breath, let us note: the Bible gives us no static notion of life; it is presented as a compelling guiding force. The Bible does not consider spiritual life, any more than it does biological life, as having a separate existence of its own, like a sort of acquired capital. It is a motion from God animating and directing our souls.

Thus, Ezekiel, called by God, prophesies: 'Come from the four winds, O spirit, and breathe upon these slain, that they may live' (Ezek. 37.9, R.V. marg.). Jesus Himself likened the Spirit to the breath of the wind (John 3.8). After His Resurrection He breathed on His disciples, saying to them: 'Receive ye the Holy Ghost' (John 20.22). When telling how He brought back to life the daughter of Jairus, the evangelist writes: 'Her spirit returned'

[1] Jacques Ellul, 'Positions bibliques sur la médecine', in *Les deux Cités*, No. 4, *loc. cit.*

(Luke 8.55). In order to explain to the intellectual Athenians what God He is preaching, Paul says to them: 'in him we live, and move, and have our being' (Acts 17.28).

Professor von Weizsäcker writes[1] that we all feel intuitively that life is something more than what physiology has to show us. In this he rejoins that inspired founder of experimental medicine, Claude Bernard, whose aphorism, 'All we know of life is death', is well known. What does this mean but that in the laboratory, with our scientific methods, we cannot discover the mystery of life? But though Claude Bernard developed his deductive faculties in the laboratory in such a masterly fashion, he did not on that account repress his inductive faculties. In him, alongside the scientist, and without any conflict with science, we see the philosopher of life, who wrote: 'The life-force directs phenomena which it does not produce; physical agents produce phenomena which they do not direct.'

You can see how we have here exactly the idea of life which is to be found in the Bible, that of a guiding force. At the same time Claude Bernard's remark is an illuminating expression of the close relationship existing between the two aspects of living reality that we described at the beginning of this book in connection with the two diagnoses. So far from physico-chemical mechanisms creating life, it is actually life which directs these mechanisms and communicates to them their particular development to a definite end.

Claude Bernard, then, the perfect example of the scientist, is here upholding a purposive conception of life. He admits that a directing will, inaccessible to science, gives a meaning to the phenomena whose mechanism science studies. Professor Siebeck of Heidelberg has similarly pointed out the limitations of science and its incapacity to comprehend life: 'Its method is analytical; from the entirety of life it takes single processes, whose limits can, as it were, be taken in at a glance, in order to discover the laws that govern them. But the full depth of life cannot be plumbed thus, for under analysis its true essence vanishes.'[2]

---

[1] *Op. cit.*

[2] Richard Siebeck, *La vie, la maladie, le péché, la mort. Le point de vue du médecin*, an unpublished lecture given at Bossey in 1950. See also his *Die Medizin in Bewegung*, Georg Thieme Verlag, Stuttgart, 1949

The Meaning of Life

In his various works, Lecomte du Nouy[1] has developed similar views. He also has demonstrated the inability of scientific methods to reveal the essence of life, which, he says, resides in 'organization' —that is to say, in the harmonious working together of all the phenomena of an organism which suggests to our minds the notion of an 'anti-chance', of a guiding force.

Similarly, Dr. Jean de Rougemont has noted[2] that in the most elementary of biological phenomena, the cell feeding itself, there is an element of choice: the cell chooses from its surroundings what it is able to assimilate, and refuses the rest. Now choice implies purpose. Dr. Tzanck[3] uses this same word 'choice', without which life is incomprehensible; and he says that everything takes place in biology as if an Intelligence inaccessible to our science had, in the beginning, imparted an impulse in a certain direction to the vital phenomena, which have since been unfolding according to a predetermined plan. Dr. Maurice Vernet has recently put forward an analogous theory of life.[4] He gives the name 'organic sensitivity' to that fundamental faculty of all living matter by which it exercises control over the physico-chemical phenomena which occur in itself. What characterizes the living organism is, he says, its biological constants (such as, for instance, the composition of the blood, the temperature of warm-blooded animals, blood-pressure). With each of these constants there is a certain margin of normal oscillation, which may be compared to the slight deviation from its course of a ship, thrust now to port, now to starboard, by the action of the waves. But like an automatic pilot, correcting each deviation and bringing the ship back on to its course, this organic sensitivity ensures constant regulation. As for disease, it is an oscillation beyond the normal margin. Death is the loss of the regulator.

We see that the biologists' explanations of life are in complete agreement with the Biblical conception of it. Whether we speak in terms of a guiding force, of organization, of choice, of consciousness, or of organic sensitivity, we must imply a will, a purpose, a meaning; and this, as we have seen, is the central principle

avenir de l'esprit, N.R.F., Gallimard, Paris, 1941
[2] Jean de Rougemont, *Vie du corps et vie de l'esprit*, Paul Devain, Lyons, 1945
[3] *Op. cit.*
[4] Maurice Vernet, *Le problème de la vie*, Collection 'Présences', Plon, Paris, 1947

143

of the Biblical view. And since, in the Bible, biological and spiritual life are one, we shall naturally find that what Dr. Maurice Vernet has described in the case of biological life is also true of spiritual life.

Our spiritual life, too, does not follow a straight line; it also is made up of perpetual oscillations. I often meet Christians who find this hard to accept. But it too has its regulator. Here it is the voice of God that plays the part of organic sensitivity. This voice of God in us we might call 'spiritual sensitivity'. There are the normal oscillations of doubt and temptation. And there are the more violent oscillations of disobedience to God, of sin. These oscillations bring the regulator into action—the call of conscience, which brings us back to faith and to obedience. It is for this reason that the great tradition of belief has handed down to us the strange expression, *felix culpa*: the happy fault, which leads us to humility, which brings us back to God, and to our proper direction, which is the action in us of grace.

You see, we have come back to what we said about the Bible itself, of all the men of the Bible whom God guided, but who still erred, oscillated, but who learned, in spite of their errors—and sometimes through them—to know God.

This knowledge of God, this perpetual rediscovery of God with its new understanding of His will, even at the cost of our faults, is the meaning of life according to the Bible. There is no life without oscillations; this continual activity of deviation and correction maintains life. In the fallen world the spiritual life is a cycle of sin and grace, of doubt and faith, of turning away from God and rediscovering Him. As Calvin said:[1] 'What is the end of man? To know God.' And he added at once: 'What is his happiness? The same.' This life under God's guidance, of which we were speaking above, which does not preserve us from errors of direction, but in which these very errors help us to know God better, is the only life that has a meaning, and the only life that is truly happy. That is what gives its meaning to our life in general; but it is also what gives its meaning to each thought, each feeling, and particularly to each action, as St. Paul says: 'do all to the glory of God' (I Cor. 10.31).

'It is only God that makes sense of life,' said a patient to me

[1] *The Geneva Catechism*

once. Our 'spiritual sensitivity' is such that as soon as we disobey God, we find ourselves in doubt, hesitation, and suffering. 'If thou wilt not observe to do all the words of this law . . . thy life shall hang in doubt before thee' (Deut. 28.58 and 66). But as soon as we turn again towards God, joy springs up, confidence is born again. This is the source of all solid faith, and without faith there is no true life. 'Whatsoever is not of faith is sin', writes St. Paul (Rom. 14.23).

One of my patients used to say to me: 'Really, I'm not truly alive, because I don't allow myself to accept the demands that life makes.' To accept those demands is to accept responsibility for oneself, to seek God's will and to risk making mistakes about it; it is to accept humility and the grace that restores us to life.

18

VITALITY

THE LIVELY FORCE which sets in motion things, bodies and souls, and directs them on a fixed course is life; and the Bible tells us that all life comes from God. There was one patient of mine, the youngest daughter in a large family, which the father found it difficult to support. One day she heard him mutter despairingly, referring to her: 'We could well have done without that one!' You can guess the effect of such a remark—not wanted by her parents, not wanted in life. She was overwhelmed by bitter anguish. Some years later, when she was being prepared for Confirmation, she asked her pastor this question: 'Can a child come into the world without God willing it?' The pastor answered: 'You shouldn't be worrying about such things at your age. You run along and play with your friends.'

But that was precisely what she could not do, for she felt herself to be different from the others; she believed herself to be unwanted. There are many people who feel themselves to be more or less unwanted in the world. This is frequently the case, for example, with illegitimate children; it is the case with all those who, rightly or wrongly, believe themselves to have been loved less than their brothers or sisters by their parents; it is the case with those difficult children whose reactions, whose faults or whose failures exasperate their parents; and parents, even without saying so, often make children feel that they are a burden.

Our children are the fruit of the love which God has set in our hearts. The love we bear them is the reflection of the love that He bears them. That is our great responsibility. The child who doubts the love of his parents doubts the love of God. The child who thinks himself unwanted by his parents thinks himself unwanted by God.

It can readily be imagined what repercussions such a feeling may have on the life force, on that vital energy which psychologists call the libido. This is the underlying cause of those neuroses that have been described as 'surrender neuroses'. A young woman suffering from a neurosis of this type said to me recently: 'I can't read the Bible, because it is full of promises of life and of Eternal Life. I hate life, so the idea of Eternal Life is quite unbearable!' But I believe the consequences to be not only psychological; there is also inhibition of physical vitality.

The only answer is given by the Bible—that all life comes from God. Nothing gives such sufferers back their self-confidence and the feeling of their own infinite value better than the certainty that their life was willed by God, even if it is the fruit of some thoughtless sexual relationship between two strangers on a drunken night out. Their child is also a child of God; he does not owe his life only to his parents, but also to God, who imparts His own creative power to men; Jesus Christ died for him too; he is even the object of that special concern with which God favours the wretched; and the love he may find in a psychotherapist, even in a non-Christian one, will be the essential factor in his cure, for that love will be the reflection of the love which God has for him. Thus, just as a negative attitude to life entails a negative attitude towards God, so, inversely, a positive attitude towards God entails a positive attitude towards life.

All life comes from God, and it is this that makes it sacred and inviolable. Even atheists understand this, and that is why they set over the entrance to Buchenwald Concentration Camp this notice: 'Here there is no God.' After the very first murder God said to Cain: 'What hast thou done? the voice of thy brother's blood crieth unto me from the ground' (Gen. 4.10). To Noah God said: 'Whoso sheddeth man's blood, by man shall his blood be shed: for in the image of God made he man' (Gen. 9.6). God commended the Hebrew midwives who refused to obey the orders of the King of Egypt to kill the male infants (Ex. 1.15-17). And on Sinai God gave His law to Moses: 'Thou shalt do no murder' (Ex. 20.13), and Christ repeated this commandment, giving it its full meaning (Matt. 5.21-4): He denounced anger and hate as the primary source of murder, as contempt of a life given by God.

The Bible also shows us in the divine origin of human life the basis of social legislation: 'No man shall take the mill or the upper millstone to pledge: for he taketh a man's life to pledge' (Deut. 24.6). I might well quote here all the provisions by which the Mosaic law protected the weak and upheld the right to live. I shall mention in passing but one of them which will be of interest to doctors, for it lays down, even in those early times, the principle of civil responsibility and of indemnity against loss of earnings: Ex. 21.19. But now we must return to the Biblical meaning of life and its bearing on medicine.

In the Biblical perspective life is communion with God, and death is separation from Him. Take, for example, the words of the father to the elder brother in the parable of the Prodigal Son: 'This thy brother was dead, and is alive again' (Luke 15.32). Jesus said: 'He that heareth my word, and believeth him that sent me, hath eternal life . . .', he 'hath passed out of death into life' (John 5.24). The communion re-established with God by Jesus Christ is constantly called 'eternal life' in the Gospel: 'God so loved the world, that he gave his only begotten Son, that whosoever believeth on him should not perish, but have eternal life' (John 3.16). 'I am the way, the truth, and the life,' says our Lord (John 14.6).

I am concerned in this book with the medical rather than the spiritual significance of these affirmations. For this life that comes from God, which springs up when man is in communion—conscious or unconscious—with God, is his physical vitality and his mental energy as well as his spiritual life.

The notion of physical vitality is an exceedingly difficult one to grasp. It is too easily confused with the idea of temperament, which is but a superficial and visible manifestation of life. Every one of my brother doctors will be aware of the surprises we may have in medical practice: people who are apparently solid and overflowing with life can collapse completely in the course of some trifling ailment; they react to no treatment, and the doctor can only stand by with an awful sense of helplessness, watching their inexorable descent towards death. Others, on the contrary, seem fragile and puny; one feels that a breath of wind would blow them down; they are always ailing; and yet they show unsuspected powers of resistance.

Be that as it may, in the Biblical perspective we must consider that capacity of life to defend itself as proceeding from the will of God. I am not, of course, claiming that it is a measure of the faith of the patient. Faith is not an insurance against disease, or a guarantee of vitality; and faith is not essential to recovery; but there is no recovery apart from God's will. It frequently happens that the re-establishment of spiritual communion with God is made manifest in a recovery of physical vitality.

There was a case of a young woman who in her childhood had been a sort of Cinderella. While still at school she had had to slave away at all the housework as well. Serious psychological complications arose to sap still further her physical powers of resistance. The result was that she fell ill. But her parents, in the hardness of their hearts, paid no attention, and met her complaints with further reproaches, saying she was only trying to find excuses for her idleness. Finally, an outraged neighbour took her to see the doctor, who discovered her to be at an advanced stage of pulmonary tuberculosis.

When she arrived at the sanatorium she overheard the doctor in charge talking very pessimistically about her to his assistant. But that night, lying wide awake in bed, that child, in whose life religion had played but little part, suddenly and in a way which one would never have expected had an experience of God. The moon had just come out, its light streaming through the window opposite her. All at once she felt herself possessed by an over-whelming certainty: God loved her. This certainty was as it were doubled by another that was an integral part of it: she would get well. Early next morning she, who had not been hungry for months, was eating her breakfast with a hearty appetite. The doctor was astounded. She said to him: 'I heard what you said yesterday about my chances of recovery, but last night God made me quite certain that I am going to get better.' 'In that case,' replied the doctor, 'you must obey me to the letter!' Obedience was, indeed, not difficult for her, and she was soon making rapid progress.

Such occurrences are not rare. Since I first published an account of some of them, many of my colleagues have told me of things they themselves have observed. There was, for example, the girl whom one of my friends had been treating for several months for anaemia, without much success. As a last resort, my colleague decided to send her to the medical officer of the district in which she worked in order to get his permission to send her to a mountain sanatorium. A week later the patient brought word back from the medical officer. He proved to be a good fellow, and had granted the permit, but he added: 'On analysing the blood, however, I do not arrive at anything like the same figures as those you quote.'

My friend, somewhat put out, at once took a fresh sample of blood, and rushed to his laboratory. Sure enough, the blood-count had suddenly changed. 'If I had not been the sort of person who keeps carefully to laboratory routine', my friend's story went on, 'and if I had not previously checked my figures at each of my patient's visits, I might have thought that I had made a mistake.'

He returned to his patient and asked her:

'Has anything out of the ordinary happened in your life since your last visit?'

'Yes; something has happened,' she replied. 'I have suddenly been able to forgive someone against whom I bore a nasty grudge; and all at once I felt as if I could at last say "Yes" to life!'

Saying 'Yes' to life and saying 'Yes' to God are exactly alike. How many people really say 'Yes' to life? I leave the answer to my colleagues. But they will certainly realize that our private attitude to life, be it positive or negative, has an effect on our powers of resistance to disease. Psychoanalysts have produced a wealth of evidence of this in the case of neuroses. Dr. Maeder of Zurich has written a book[1] on the forces of healing, which are present more or less latently in every sick person, and which it is the task of the psychotherapist to awaken, so that they may play their decisive part in bringing about a successful cure.

But these forces are no less important in organic diseases. I am reminded of another tuberculosis patient who at the end of a costly confession said to me: 'For ten years now I have been afraid of living. How could I possibly have got better?' The will to live is a powerful ally whom the doctor must arouse with affection. At the medical conference at Annecy of which I have spoken, there was a former patient, M. Jean Gouzy, who told us movingly

[1] Alphonse Maeder, *Selbsterhaltung und Selbstheilung*, Rascher, Zurich

of his first interview with the doctor at the sanatorium he had just entered. This doctor had frankly told him that he must prepare for a long stay; but he found it possible to add a brief affectionate remark that made the patient exclaim within himself: 'Here at last is someone who realizes that I want to live!'

Quite often when a sick person, or one in good health, is telling me his life-history, I am led to ask myself the question: what, at bottom, is the motive force of his life? How many people really ask themselves this? Is the answer, without our knowing it, just the successive impulses of instinct? Is it often no more than a mechanical reaction of contradiction and revenge? Or is it merely the force of external circumstances, blowing us hither and thither like a rudderless ship? When we see how many people seem to need stimulants of all kinds, we have some measure of their lack of any real inner force.

A woman doctor writes me: 'From that moment' (when she found a living Christian faith) 'my hyperchlorhydria ceased completely, and I soon gained well over a stone in weight.' A woman who had been for years a sufferer from epileptic fits which had resisted every kind of treatment came to see me. We scarcely mentioned her fits: the nerve specialists who had examined her were far more competent than I to make a scientific diagnosis. She did, however, speak frankly to me about a certain problem which she had never dared to mention before: she was a member of a very strict religious sect, and had had a disagreement with the head of the community; out of Christian obedience, she had given way, but deep in her conscience there remained the feeling that she was disobeying God. A few months later she wrote to me: 'I had one or two more fits after my visit to you, but since then I have had no more. I can scarcely believe it is true.' A year after that she wrote to confirm that she was cured—and to announce that she was going to get married!

'Grace flows from the soul to the body', said St. Thomas Aquinas. Although vitality, the natural healing force, is never the measure of faith, it is undoubtedly strengthened in a great number of cases by the re-establishment of a positive relationship with God. As the wisdom of Solomon puts it:

Life, Death, Disease and Healing

> *My son, attend to my words;*
> *. . . For they are life unto those that find them,*
> *And health to all their flesh* (Prov. 4.20, 22).

One of Christ's acts of healing is of particular interest in this connection. I refer to the case of the woman with an issue of blood (Mark 5.25-34). She had come in the midst of the crowd to touch Jesus' garment from behind, saying to herself: 'If I touch but his garments, I shall be made whole.' At once she 'felt in her body that she was healed of her plague'. But Jesus must also have felt something, for He turned round, saying: 'Who touched my garments?' This account seems to indicate that there went out from Jesus a physical vitality, a healing force so concrete that He felt it go in the same way as the woman felt its effect.

Dr. Racanelli, of Florence, who has a gift of healing, and who practices the laying on of hands in all kinds of nervous affections, has said that he has a very strong sensation of this force working in him and passing out through his hands.[1] Whereas his patients are left with a sense of well-being and calm, he himself experiences such fatigue that he is compelled to observe a strict austerity of life when he is practising this type of treatment, so as not to become exhausted.

When we discussed this subject, another doctor from Florence told us that he had also practised this kind of healing with success; but, he said, he had had to give it up because he was himself too sensitive to it. 'Thus,' he told us, 'for example, my patient, suffering from angina, would find that his angina had suddenly gone; but I myself at once suffered a similar attack.' When I told my wife about this, we were reminded of a fact we had frequently observed: that we regularly had a quarrel ourselves during the evening of a day in which we had been able to help in the reconciliation of another married couple. One is reminded of the passage in the Gospel recalled by Carl Jung[2] after the collapse of the Nazi régime: that when a devil is cast out he goes somewhere else (Matt. 8.28-34).

These are things which will no doubt always be shrouded

[1] Francesco Racanelli, *Le don de la guérison*, Delachaux et Niestlé, Neuchâtel, 1951

[2] C. G. Jung, *Essays on Contemporary Events*, Kegan Paul, London, 1947

to some extent in mystery; but they fit in with the point I have made several times in this book—namely, that the Biblical perspective is that of incarnation, that grace does not belong solely to the realm of pure spirit, but that it is at work materially in Nature. Perhaps some day we shall possess some device which will be able to detect its physical emanations.

It is not my purpose to 'explain' all Christ's miracles. The raising of Lazarus, for example, in which an already putrefying corpse was brought back to life, goes against all that we know of Nature. But in many of the cases of healing, which could have been brought about also by natural means, we can as doctors try to understand what it was that happened. At one of our international conferences, one of my colleagues—I forget now who it was— put forward the theory that the life force which went forth from Jesus Christ was able to provoke an extreme acceleration of the normal biological processes of healing. Lecomte du Nouy has shown, for instance, that the speed of cicatrization obeys the same law as chemical reactions: that, at a given age, it doubles when the temperature of the body is raised by four degrees. It is conceivable that a spiritual force may provoke a similar and even greater acceleration. It may be noted here that several of the healings performed by Jesus were not instantaneous. This was the case with the ten lepers (Luke 17.12-14) and with the man born blind (John 9.6-7).

19

DIVINE BLESSING

LIFE IS A GIFT from God, a force proceeding from Him. It is also, in the thought of the Bible, a sign of benediction. The Bible, with a precision that may perhaps seem naïve, stresses the remarkable longevity of certain men blessed by God. We are told that Adam lived 930 years (Gen. 5.5), Abraham 175 (Gen. 25.7), Isaac 180 (Gen. 35.28), Jacob 147 (Gen. 47.28), Joseph 110 (Gen. 50.22), Joshuah also 110 (Josh. 24.29), that David died 'full of days' (I Chron. 29.28), and that Job lived for 140 years after he was healed (Job 42.16).

Very many passages represent long life as the reward of man's obedience to God's law: 'Hear, O my son, and receive my sayings; and the years of thy life shall be many' (Prov. 4.10). In the psalm I quoted in connection with the temptation of Christ, God says of him who loves Him: 'With long life will I satisfy him' (Psalm 91.16). To the list just given I ought to have added all the patriarchs enumerated in Chapter 5 of Genesis. I would call attention to the simple expression, 'and he died' (Gen. 5.5, etc.), repeated in respect of each one. One feels that these words call to mind the 'normal' death of the old man 'full of days', as the Bible also often puts it.

I have always liked old men, and I think that the psychological cause of this is that I am the son of an old man; my father was seventy when I was born, like the patriarch Kenan (Gen. 5.12), and like Terah, Abraham's father (Gen. 11.26). For many years I was the doctor of a Catholic institution for old women. I took a special pleasure in visiting the inmates. My doctor friends would say to me: 'I don't understand you; it isn't very interesting looking after old people; there isn't much more you can do for them.' I have no taste for action. I derive more pleasure from human relationships, and it is often with old people that they have been deepest. Old people seem to me to be nearer to God. At their age, companions are disappearing, worldly vanities are fading; they must grow in their inner lives, as St. Paul says: 'though our outward man is decaying, our inward man is renewed day by day' (II Cor. 4.16). In old age our own character is accentuated; the egotist becomes cantankerous, and the warm-hearted achieve serenity.

Professor Jung has written[1] about the art of growing old. He has shown how important it is to accept the change of objective which old age demands; how instead of placing the emphasis on what one does, one must gradually put it on what one is. But our modern world of the West sets more store by 'doing' than 'being'. Old people have often said to me, even without being ill or infirm: 'Life is a burden to me; my strength is gone; the world has no more use for me; I ask God to take me back.' To these old folk the Bible's reply, contradicting the false values suggested by civilization, is that a long old age is a blessing from God.

But even more than length of days, children are stated in the Bible to be a sign of God's blessing. It is easy to see the medical importance of this assertion, since there is bound up with it the great problem of birth-control. 'God blessed them: and God said unto them, Be fruitful, and multiply, and replenish the earth' (Gen. 1.28). Along with the entire ancient world, the Bible is full of the idea that there is a curse in sterility. It shows realistically to what extremes maternal hunger will carry a woman: the two daughters of Lot are so distraught at not being mothers that they make their father drunk in order to lie with him (Gen. 19.31-4). The Bible tells us of the opprobrium of Sarah, Abraham's wife, and how Hagar, her servant, finding herself pregnant, looked upon her with scorn (Gen. 16.4); and how God showed His blessing on Abraham and Sarah by bringing her barrenness to an end. As she was then ninety years old, Abraham burst out laughing when God told him that she was to bear him a son (Gen. 17.17). And it was on this son, Isaac, that the blessings and the promises of God rested.

This idea of the reproach of sterility lies behind certain provisions of the law of Moses (Deut. 25.5-6): 'If brethren dwell

[1] C. G. Jung, *Collected Papers on Analytical Psychology*, edited by Dr. Constance E. Long, 2nd edition, Baillière & Co., London, 1920

together, and one of them die, and have no son, the wife of the
dead shall not marry without unto a stranger: her husband's
brother shall go in unto her, and take her to him to wife, and
perform the duty of an husband's brother unto her. And it shall
be, that the firstborn which she beareth shall succeed in the name
of his brother which is dead, that his name be not blotted out of
Israel.' We see here again the importance of the name, which
I mentioned earlier. The custom already existed before being
codified in this law, and it was for trying to evade it that Onan
was severely punished (Gen. 38.9). It will be seen that the taking
of Onan's name to form the technical term 'onanism' was a
mistake, since masturbation is not alluded to here. The story
goes on to show how Judah, Onan's father, also recognizes his
own guilt in not having given his third son Shelah to his daughter-
in-law, Tamar (Gen. 38.26).

The first mention of disease and healing that occurs in the
Bible is that of the sterility visited by God upon the wife and
maidservants of Abimelech (Gen. 20.17-18). What is remarkable is that this curse is represented as punishment for an unconscious sin, and one that was not even consummated. Abimelech,
King of Gerar, had sent and taken Sarah, Abraham's wife. But
the blame really lay with Abraham, for he had passed her off as
his sister for fear of being murdered because of her. God Himself
warned Abimelech in a dream (Gen. 20.3), and Abimelech's
response was magnificent; not only did he restore Abraham's
wife to him, but he made him presents as well, and gave him
the right to settle wherever he liked in the country (Gen.
20.14-15).

Let us now look more closely at the important Biblical notion
of divine blessing. Although Abraham was the guilty one,
although Abimelech had not touched Sarah, and although he
had responded so loyally to God's warning, it was upon
Abraham's prayer that God healed his wife and his maidservants
of the sterility he had visited upon them. For Abraham had been
chosen by God, who had made a covenant with him. Upon him
there rests a blessing that is quite independent of his conduct:
Abraham may sin, and yet not cease to be blessed and to be
capable of passing on the blessing to others.

It is, of course, true that many Biblical passages present divine blessing as the reward of human obedience. 'Behold, I set before you this day a blessing . . . if ye shall hearken unto the commandments of the Lord your God, which I command you this day' (Deut. 11.26-7). But in the Bible this obedience is seen to be concerned more with faith than with morals. Because of his faith, Abraham answered God's call, and thus won God's blessing (Gen. 12.1-3), and even won also the power of passing on God's blessing, standing, as it were, proxy for Him; and this power he retains in spite of his shortcomings. But above all the Bible emphasizes, as we shall see later, the absolute sovereignty of God to choose those whom He will upon whom to set His blessing.

Whether we like it or not this Biblical idea of blessing and curse still remains deeply embedded in the human mind. In the absence of religious faith, it quickly comes to the surface in our patients in the guise of magic, bringing with it all the false interpretations of magical distortion. This often happens in neuroses, where the patients feel themselves to be possessed by hostile forces. 'I feel that I am making a mess of my life; I spoil everything I do,' they will say to us. 'What have I done to deserve such a curse?'

These are the people who, as a result of things that happened in their childhood, have that negative attitude to life of which we were speaking earlier, and who in turn attribute to God a hostile attitude towards them.

I am reminded of a young woman on whom I was moved to beseech God's blessing, laying my hands on her, so deep-rooted in her mind was this idea of being under a curse. She claimed that it was proved by the fact that she continually slipped back into wrongdoing, in spite of her good resolutions and her religion. As if we were not all in the same case! But when I asked her, 'This idea of a curse, weren't you rather fond of the idea even as a child?' she replied that that was true. It was a clear example of the part that psychological complexes play in the setting up of this notion of being under a curse.

These are grave and difficult problems, in which a person's whole life is involved. With these neurotics, disturbances that are psychological in origin are put down to religious causes. The patient believes himself to be under a divine curse, when really he is the victim of simple psychological traumas suffered during childhood. It is especially desirable in cases of this nature that the minister of religion should seek the collaboration of the doctor.

With regard to the procreation of children, the Biblical view that this is a sign of divine blessing is also deep-rooted in the human mind. I have known of many women who, having brought about an abortion in the case of a child conceived before marriage or shortly after it, have thereafter remained sterile in spite of every kind of treatment. There have been others who, not wanting children at the beginning of their married life, have used contraceptives, and then, finding later that they did not become pregnant, have wondered remorsefully if conception would have taken place before.

The distress of these women—and of their husbands—can be very great. Doctors cannot be too careful to put young newly-married couples on their guard against the dangers of avoiding, without good cause, the divine order of procreation.

Every abortion is a murder. This cannot be doubted. It is not only the law of the Bible and of the Church; it is written in the human heart itself. I have heard too many confessions on the subject, all of them too heavily burdened with emotion, not to affirm that no one has recourse to abortion with a clear conscience. This inner conflict, especially when repressed, may often bring severe psychological disturbances in its train. The medical section of the Protestant Study Centre in Geneva recently discussed thoroughly the question of therapeutic abortion, after hearing reports from a lawyer, a gynaecologist, a psychiatrist, and from both Roman Catholic and Protestant theologians. Certain resolutions were passed unanimously, and forwarded to the medical profession and to the civil authorities. The Government of the Republic and Canton of Geneva has in fact expressed its concern at the increase year by year of such abortions since they were legalized under the Federal Penal Code. 'In the Christian, and more particularly the Protestant, view', declares one of these resolutions, 'the child is the gift of God, and the Sixth Commandment expressly forbids murder (Ex. 20.13); thus every pregnancy must be respected. Now, the life of the child begins with conception; it is specious arbitrarily to fix its beginning at any particular month of pregnancy. Whenever it is practised, abortion is still a grave attack against life; it cannot therefore be considered otherwise than as a violation of God's will and commandment. The Protestant Church, however, makes a distinction between the strict discipline which the believer imposes on himself in order to remain true to his faith, a discipline which governs the whole of the sexual life, and the law which the State, recognizing its responsibilities, imposes on the whole of society in order to safeguard public health and preserve order. Though the Christian must reject abortion, except in quite exceptional cases, the Church admits that the State must legislate with less severity in regard to the whole of the population. The Church requests the authorities to promulgate decrees whose aim is the public weal, and which neither encourage laxity and immorality nor give rise to clandestine practices.'

Let us turn now to the question of the use of contraceptives, a subject of frequent debate among Christian doctors. According to the Bible, the chief aim of sexual intercourse is procreation; when God instituted marriage He said: 'Be fruitful, and multiply' (Gen. 1.28). As we saw in Chapter 8, the Bible considers sexual intercourse as being also the expression of the total union of man and wife: '. . . and they shall be one flesh' (Gen. 2.24). Finally, in I Cor. 7.5, St. Paul describes the sexual relationship in marriage as a safeguard against impure temptations: 'Defraud ye not one the other, except it be by consent for a season, that ye may give yourselves unto prayer, and may be together again, that Satan tempt you not because of your incontinency.'[1] This is a further example of Biblical realism, and it comes from the pen of the Apostle who was called by God to chastity, and who writes: 'Yet I would that all men were even as I myself' (I Cor. 7.7). To these words he adds, however; 'Howbeit each man hath his own gift from God, one after this manner, and another after that.' It could not be more clearly stated that each man and each couple must above all seek God's guidance in this matter, at the same time taking care not to judge others who may have been guided by God into a different course. The reader will have noted too that St. Paul says 'by consent'. This is of capital importance to the

[1] Translator's note: Or, more clearly, in Moffatt's translation: 'Do not withhold sexual intercourse from one another, unless you agree to do so for a time, in order to devote yourselves to prayer. Then come together again. You must not let Satan tempt you through incontinence'

husband and wife who are seeking God's will for their conduct. It is also emphasized in the passage I have previously quoted: 'The wife hath not power over her own body, but the husband: and likewise also the husband hath not power over his own body, but the wife' (I Cor. 7.4).

We may, then, on the basis of these texts, consider chastity as a vocation to which God calls certain people; and we should recognize that those whom God calls to marriage He may also call, for a time, and on condition that both parties are in full agreement, to abstain from sexual intercourse, bearing in mind the dangers and temptations that may accompany such abstinence. The Roman Catholic Church, which on principle and on the ground of the order 'be fruitful, and multiply', condemns birth-control, does, however, admit the application of Ogino's rule, which actually implies abstention 'for a season'.[1] Dr. Maget has given a clear exposition of Roman Catholic teaching on this subject.[2] He invites the believer who uses Ogino's method to consider seriously his motives. Protestants insist on this examination of the conscience whatever method of birth-control is contemplated. For all Christians, then, voluntary restriction of conception is in principle contrary to the spirit of God's law; in the light of the Bible, it is permissible only in exceptional circumstances, and for reasons of conscience, such as the safeguarding of the life of the mother, or the sense of responsibility of the parents with regard to the other children they have to bring up.

The delicate problem of eugenics has been studied from the point of view of the medicine of the person by Dr. Kressmann,[3] and by Drs. Hijmans and Waardenburg, whose work is as yet unpublished. The last-mentioned has made a special study of the Biblical foundations of eugenics.

I have seen sterilization result in serious psychological disturbance. I know of a woman whose husband had persuaded her to submit to it solely on the grounds that they were leaving together to go to the colonies, where he considered that pregnancy

[1] Kyusaku Ogino, *Conception Period of Women*, English translation by Dr. Yonezi Miyagawa, Medical Arts Publishing Co., Harrisburg, 1935

[2] A. Maget, *Médecine et Mariage*, University Press, Fribourg, 1943

[3] Philippe Kressmann, 'Le respect de la vie humaine: l'eugénisme', in the *Bulletin des Associations professionnelles protestantes*, January-April, 1949, Paris

would be inconvenient. She returned safely from the colonies, but she was the victim of that awful suffering which is always the lot of the woman who has been prevented from having children.

I cannot touch on this grave subject without saying a word to those unmarried women who often find it more difficult to accept not having children than not having a husband. The Bible speaks to them also in the words of St. Paul we read just now: that celibacy is to be considered a vocation, God's call to dedicate oneself to His service in a way that a married woman cannot: 'She that is unmarried', the Apostle writes, 'is careful for the things of the Lord, that she may be holy both in body and in spirit: but she that is married is careful of the things of the world, how she may please her husband' (I Cor. 7.34).

On these terms, the life of the celibate can be as fruitful as that of a mother, for the creative power that God gives to man is not limited to procreation: 'He that believeth on me', said Jesus, 'the works that I do shall he do also; and greater works than these shall he do' (John 14.12). At the cost, too, of this renunciation, she finds a real family; in fact, she may share in our Lord's promise: 'Every one that hath left houses, or brethren, or sisters, or father, or mother, or children, or lands, for my name's sake, shall receive a hundredfold, and shall inherit eternal life' (Mat. 19.29).

Consider with what fatherly care St. Paul, bachelor as he was, spoke of the churches he had established: 'There is that which presses on me daily, anxiety for all the churches. Who is weak, and I am not weak? Who is made to stumble, and I burn not?' (II Cor. 11.28-9). Consider with what tenderness he speaks to Timothy, calling him 'my beloved child' (II Tim. 1.2).

And so life, as shown to us in the Bible, in all its fullness and all its glory, is communion with God and fellowship with Jesus Christ through faith. 'O Lord', cries King Hezekiah after he is healed, 'by these things men live, and wholly therein is the life of my spirit: Wherefore recover thou me, and make me to live. . . . The living, the living, he shall praise thee' (Isa. 38.16, 19). I myself felt that very strongly once, after escaping death in a road accident: that if God was granting me my life, it was only so that I might dedicate it more completely to His service: 'The Lord is the strength of my life . . . I will sing, yea, I will sing praises unto the Lord' (Ps. 27.1, 6).

20

THE MEANING OF DEATH

JUST AS, in the Bible, life means communion with God, so death means separation from Him. And since the Bible does not set spiritual life over against physical life, or even distinguish them, it uses without discrimination the same word, 'death', for our spiritual separation from God by sin and our physiological death.

To the first meaning of death we shall return later. We shall confine ourselves for the moment to picking out, from among many passages, St. Paul's words to the Colossians: 'You, being dead through your trespasses . . . you, I say, did he quicken together with him' (Col. 2.13); and this text from the Revelation: 'Thou hast a name that thou livest, and thou art dead' (Rev. 3.1). So, for the Biblical writers, a man may be dead while still alive physically and mentally. This conception will not come as a surprise to doctors, who can often see even temperamentally exuberant people who seem to lack real creative life, who have become ossified and fossilized.

But it would be a mistake—the 'spiritualist' mistake already referred to—to think that the death spoken of by the Bible is this spiritual death only. It actually means physical death as well, the quite concrete death against which the doctor is fighting every day; the death which he tries to ward off in an urgent case of heart-failure; the death against which the surgeon races when operating in a case of extra-uterine pregnancy; the death against which the psychiatrist protects a melancholic obsessed with the idea of suicide. That is why the Bible is so important for us doctors.

The Bible does not minimize the importance of death, like the Stoics of antiquity or the Orientals of our own day. It takes death seriously; it describes with heart-rending realism the anguish that men experience in the presence of death, and the

overwhelming catastrophe of it. It does indeed bring us the
triumphal shout of faith, like that of St. Paul: 'For me to live is
Christ, and to die is gain' (Phil. 1.21). But even the most lively
faith does not spare man the anxiety of death.

Two years ago I lost a near relative, taken in the prime of life,
after only a few days' illness. An ordinary attack of influenza
had been rapidly complicated by congestion of the lungs, and
then by serious and unexpected cardiac failure. She was rushed
to hospital, where she was given injections of digoxin. A day or
two later, although her pulse was not yet normal, I was beginning
to hope that the danger had passed. It was then that she opened
her heart to me and told me of the inner crisis she had just lived
through. 'When I realized, when I felt that death was not far
off, I felt shattered and rebellious. I cried out inside of myself:
No, I won't die, it isn't fair at my age. . . . At the same time
I was reproaching myself for these interior explosions: a Christian
woman such as I ought to be accepting death quite differently.
But it was too strong for me; I was kicking against death with
everything I had.'

I replied to her what I maintain here: that the Bible is infinitely
human; that it understands and shares the natural horror of life
faced with death, and does not condemn it. The Bible calls death
'the king of terrors' (Job 18.14); it considers it to be the greatest
enemy, so great that it will be the last to be defeated (I Cor.
15.26). It shows us Christ Himself crying out from the Cross:
'My God, my God, why hast thou forsaken me?' (Matt. 27.46).

We had a long talk together about death, and about the realism
of the Bible, which brings us the certainties of faith, but does
not therefore claim to take away from us the awful pangs through
which we must pass. Fear of death is not lack of faith. I recieve
many letters from sick people on this subject. To keep one's
faith is not to be superhuman, to imagine that one is not subject
to fear; it means rather admitting one's natural rebelliousness and
confessing it, and receiving, thereafter, supernatural strength to
overcome it. My patient understood all this and drew immense
consolation from it.

And then, the day after this conversation, I was suddenly
recalled to the hospital: the heart was faltering again. I stayed
beside her bed for two hours, my fingers on her wrist, on the

look-out for a revival of the pulse, feeling moment by moment that it was becoming more unlikely. I made several injections. The ward-sister—I have often noticed that sisters are in this respect more realistic than doctors—whispered in my ear: 'Doctor, is it worth while going on torturing her?' I answered, a little curtly: 'We must always do everything we can!'

But at this stage my essential task was not in the sphere of therapeutics; it was not even to talk; during those two hours no word had passed between the patient and me. We looked into each other's eyes, and there passed between us, quite simply, a slow smile of understanding. She knew, with complete certainty, that I understood her. But there was much more, more than any conversation could ever say. In her eyes there was, as it were, an allusion to the terror of which she had spoken the day before; her look said: 'You see, Paul, death is there in front of me again.' There was in it a question to which I could not reply; but there was also, at the same time, a deep peace, which became ever more serene, until the moment when, suddenly, that look was lost in the beyond.

The fear of death is present in all of us. It was Pascal who said that we spend all our lives trying to take our minds off it. Sometimes men will manage more or less to repress it, to delude themselves. But the psychoanalysts, like Jung, tell us that they find it still there in the depths of our consciousness. *Media in vita in morte sumus*, said the ancients: in the midst of life we are in death. Every sick person who comes to see us is in process of becoming once more aware of it.

The fear of death plays a much larger part than we imagine in many of our patients, even in those who seem to be the strongest. How valuable it is for them to be able to speak to us about it! How valuable also for us to be able to speak about it to them! It happens only too seldom.

There is an old man, distressed and embittered, whom I have been seeing for several weeks, without being able to feel that my visits have done him any good. He always brings out the same bitter complaints about his loneliness and his failing faculties. And he himself adds tragically: 'I have always found fault with people; I have always wanted affection, but I repel everyone with my surliness.' On one occasion, after a long silence, he suddenly began to talk to me about his fear of death. 'I've been obsessed with it all my life,' he said. 'When I was just a child I used to hang about the cemetery; overcome with emotion, I used to hide when I saw a hearse pass by, and yet it fascinated me. Now that I am old the fear is worse than ever.'

As he spoke, a small voice deep inside of me was saying: 'You must pray with him today.' But I hesitated. How would he take my suggestion? Had he not just been regaling me with all his criticisms of the Church, of the pastors who had done him harm, and with all sorts of intellectual objections to faith? And then we always find it difficult to suggest to someone, quite simply, that he should say his prayers.

I made the suggestion, and he replied: 'I wanted it so badly, but I didn't dare to ask you; as I have told you, I am an unbeliever, but I am in torment. After your last visit I tried to open the Bible, but what I read repelled me; then, on Sunday, I wanted to listen to a sermon on the wireless; but what the preacher said disgusted me, and I switched off. Yes, thank you, will you pray with me?'

I write these lines with diffidence. On the subject of death, we should prefer to be silent. And even so we have not yet answered the title of this chapter: the meaning of death. Perhaps with death more than with anything else we feel that faith consists in respecting God's mysteries rather than in trying to explain them. And yet we may seek to let ourselves be taught by God in reading the Bible; for what we think about death is of great importance to our patients, even if we do not speak to them about it at all.

I must therefore attempt to set down here the Biblical view of death, and in doing so I follow Professor Jaques Courvoisier's study, 'Révélation chrétienne et activité médicale'.[1] 'In Christian doctrine,' he writes, 'death . . . does not figure as the end of a normal process, but as the result of a state of things disordered from the beginning.' The order established by the Creator was indispensable to life; man's violation of it, therefore, necessarily leads to his death. But in His mercy God delays this outcome. He comes to man's aid. He heals his wounds. He protects him, in spite of

[1] In *Theologische Zeitschrift*, October, 1945, Verl. Friedrich Rheinhardt, Bâle

himself, against the dangers into which he has run. In short, He grants him a respite, and in this respite our life is situated. The doctor, even the non-Christian one, is in this sense God's fellow worker: he helps to retard death, to prolong this 'respite of debt', during which a man may find Jesus Christ, and receive through faith the promise of forgiveness, of victory over death, and of resurrection.

All this we shall be examining in detail in the course of the succeeding chapters. The first point is that the world created by God was perfect. At the end of the account of the Creation, we read: 'And God saw everything that he had made, and, behold, it was very good' (Gen. 1.31). In Psalm 19, already quoted, in which the poet sings of the wonders of Nature, he adds: 'The law of the Lord is perfect' (Ps. 19.7). I think that that does not mean only the moral law, but also the order instituted in Nature by God in the beginning. The central idea of the Bible is that this original order has been upset by man's disobedience, so that the world in which we live, and our own nature, are 'out of order'; consequently, we cannot last, we are doomed to die. The re-establishment of order is only possible if God intervenes once more, and this He does in history in accordance with His purpose: God's intervention begins with His covenant with the people of Israel, is continued in the ministry, death, and Resurrection of Jesus Christ, in the history of the Church, and it will be consummated in Christ's return.

This notion of disturbance in the order of Nature is what is lacking in the Naturists. And that makes them somewhat naïve and servile in their attitude to Nature, in a way that is impossible in the person who takes the Biblical point of view.

The world in which we are living is very different from the perfect world willed and created by God. It is a fallen, tainted, troubled world; this is stated in the well-known account in Genesis, which we are going to study; but the view taken there persists throughout the Bible. 'And the Lord God took the man, and put him into the garden of Eden to dress it and to keep it. And the Lord God commanded the man, saying, Of every tree of the garden thou mayest freely eat' (Gen. 2.15-16). So in this primitive order God gives man his work and his food, both of them beneficent, normal and necessary to his life.

The story adds: 'but of the tree of the knowledge of good and evil, thou shalt not eat of it: for in the day that thou eatest thereof thou shalt surely die' (Gen. 2.17). We know how the serpent came and said to the woman: 'Ye shall not surely die: for God doth know that in the day that ye eat thereof, then your eyes shall be opened and ye shall be as God, knowing good and evil' (Gen. 3.4-5). According to the Bible, then, evil and death do not come from God. God actually sought to preserve man from them by requiring of him strict submission to the perfect order of life. Man's disobedience is his claim to be his own god, to judge good and evil for himself, to conduct his own life. Thus he cuts himself off from God, disturbs the order of perfection, and the inevitable consequence is death.

Professor Ellul, who is a lawyer as well as a theologian, has pointed out[1] that we have here not a punishment meted out by God, but a 'sanction', by which he means an unavoidable consequence of man's behaviour. The sentence, 'In the day that thou eatest thereof thou shalt surely die', at once appears less as a threat than as a warning. It is like a notice giving warning that it is dangerous to touch high-tension cables: the sanction is death. Verses 17 to 19 of this chapter of Genesis show that the sanction is also physical and social suffering, symbolized by the pains of childbirth and the difficulty man will have in winning his bread.

The suffering of man is also the suffering of God. That is always my reply to those who tell me that they can't believe in God in the face of all the suffering that goes on in the world. God is the greatest sufferer; the state of the world causes Him so much suffering that we are told that 'it repented the Lord that he had made man on the earth, and it grieved him at his heart' (Gen. 6.6). Throughout the Bible evil and death are the enemies of God; 'the devil', we read, 'that had the power of death' (Heb. 2.14), a power hostile to God, which He will annihilate in the end: 'death and Hades were cast into the lake of fire. This is the second death, even the lake of fire' (Rev. 20.14)—that is to say, the death of death.

This warning from God that we have read, 'In the day that thou eatest thereof thou shalt surely die', may seem to contradict the idea of a respite put forward above. But the reader will

[1] *Op. cit.*

remember the double aspect of death of which I spoke at the beginning of this chapter: spiritual death and physiological death. The moment man disobeys, he cuts himself off from God; this is the spiritual death, sin, which enters into him. Here we have the best definition of sin, the definition which throws most light on our moral and spiritual life: 'sin is everything that separates from God and from our fellow men'.

But, we said, the two aspects of death are inseparable: spiritual death, entering into man, will be manifested sooner or later in his physiological death; from that moment he is condemned to death. Professor Courvoisier's 'respite' is situated between these two events.

In this respect, the experiments in the artificial culture of living tissues carried out by Carrel and his pupils have revolutionized our ideas. Previously, it had been thought that, from the scientific point of view, we should die because we were made of organic tissues that were destined to die, that it was the death of the parts that brought about the death of the organism as a whole. Such is by no means the case, since these parts, suitably cultivated, can continue to live indefinitely beyond the time that they would have died if left in the organism. It is therefore the destiny of the organism as a whole that governs the death of the parts.

The mystery of that destiny remains, nevertheless, the mystery of death; the mystery of sin. Why did man, having been created perfect, cut himself off from God, compromising thus his own life? I shall return later to the problem of the connection between sin and disease. And then, in the end of the day, the Biblical perspective shows that we must simply accept that we cannot understand the whole of God's mysteries. I hope, however, that I have helped some doctors to understand better many of the Bible passages insistently quoted by theologians, passages which frequently repel them: 'the wages of sin is death' (Rom. 6.23); 'servants . . . of sin unto death' (Rom. 6.16); 'the sin, when it is full-grown, bringeth forth death' (Jas. 1.15); 'Therefore, as through one man sin entered into the world, and death through sin; and so death passed unto all men, for that all sinned' (Rom. 5.12).

21

THE MEANING OF
DISEASE

CONTINUING our story, we find that the first consequence of this separation from God is fear (Gen. 3.9-13). Adam hides amongst the trees. Note in passing that it is worth while for us to ask ourselves what are the trees behind which we hide in order to escape our insecurity or our moral responsibility: they range from our university degrees and our reputation to the State or our poor health. God calls us as we hide, as He called Adam: 'Where art thou?' Adam replies: 'I was afraid, because I was naked.'

This reference to Adam and Eve becoming aware of their nakedness has an obvious sexual significance. But, as I showed earlier, those whose psychological complexes incline them to exaggerate the importance of sexual sin see this interpretation only; they identify the Biblical idea of original sin with the sex instinct. The truth is that this story clearly shows that it is because of his spiritual separation from God that man has got into difficulties, in sexual matters as in every other sphere.

To me the word 'naked' here seems to mean equally 'unprotected'. In wishing to be his own god, man discovers his weakness and insecurity; in wishing to judge for himself how to use the power God had given him, he becomes aware of the disasters he risks. Look how 'naked' men feel in regard to the atomic bomb! Dr. Stocker[1] sees yet another meaning in this nakedness. For him, it is the nakedness of the soul which has lost salvation. That is why, he adds, when we find salvation again, we may speak of being 'clothed' with it.

The insecurity of a man's life will be underlined especially by

[1] A. Stocker, *Etudes sur la psychologie de la personne*, Œuvre de Saint-Augustin, St. Moritz, 1942

disease. 'Disease is a sign of the death which is to come', writes Professor Courvoisier. 'Every disease has in it the germ of death.' Doctors, at any rate, will not contradict him! Although in health men repress as far as they can their terror of death, it reappears with the slightest disease. When, in our consulting-rooms, they ask us in as detached a tone of voice as they can manage: 'Well, Doctor, is it serious?' we know well enough what they mean. They mean: 'Is there any risk of my dying from it?'

They ask it, furthermore, more willingly and more often when the disease is obviously slight. When it is more serious the dialogue is less explicit. But there always is a dialogue, more silent or less so, between the doctor and the patient on this subject; for the meaning of disease for every man is that it reminds him of the threat of death that hangs over him; it is the *memento mori* of the ancients.

If his wife shows us to the door and chats for a moment about her recent trip to Italy, the patient at once wonders if we are exchanging pessimistic remarks about him which we do not want him to hear.

Again, I have learned to be a little distrustful of people who say: 'Doctor, you must tell me the truth. I am strong. I prefer to face it.' They are not always as strong as they claim to be. The strongest usually do not hide their fears; they allow us to become aware of them indirectly, and they like us to speak to them indirectly, too, with the utmost tact.

Mlle. S. Fouché of Paris, who has devoted her life to the rehabilitation of the crippled and the sick, made an investigation among two hundred patients of what they expected from the doctor. When I heard their replies read out I was deeply moved. The men were more realistic than the women: what they expected first and foremost from the doctor was to be cured. But in all the replies three themes reappeared with striking urgency and regularity. They wanted the doctor to pay real attention to their suffering and distress, to treat them as human beings and not as guinea-pigs, and to tell them the truth about their disease, about its probable duration, and what his prognosis was. The desire to be told the truth was put first by the majority of those consulted. But many of them added that they did not want the truth to be told them brutally, so that they were cowed and shocked by it, but gently and tactfully, so that they might be helped to accept it.

The problem of telling the truth about the prognosis is indeed a difficult one. Dr. Schlemmer has made an interesting study of it, which I recommend.[1] Dr. Rist[2] has taken a categorical stand, saying: 'To enter into a conspiracy with the relatives to keep from the patient the very thing he has come to the doctor for, the truth, is in my opinion an unpardonable breach of duty.' But he adds frankly: 'And yet how often we succumb to it!' I must also confess that I have not always been able to tell a patient seriously ill what I thought about his condition. And I have always had in such cases, like Dr. Rist, a feeling of failure and guilt.

But in fact I have always felt that my fault lay farther back, that it was less in this silence, which was after all imposed by charity, than in not having been able earlier, when the patient was not so near death, to establish close contact with him and to create that climate of spiritual fellowship without which the truth cannot be told. It is in speaking of the meaning of things that we enter into this fellowship, giving the patient an opportunity of talking to us about the things that are weighing on his mind, long before he has reached the last extremity. Since every sickness is a reminder of our mortal state, it is easy to recall this Biblical meaning of disease before it has become serious. We speak then of death as the great unknown, for which we must all be ready, doctor as well as patient; for, after all, who can be certain that I shall not die before my patient does?

But let us admit it: there is a streak of cowardice in all of us, doctors and patients alike; each one of us, and more strongly than we care to confess, puts up a stubborn resistance against tackling the essential, tragic and insoluble problems of suffering, disease and death. This honest man-to-man discussion which Mlle. Fouché's patients demanded, and in which they expect the doctor to take the first step, requires courage to start and to continue without hedging. It inevitably brings up problems in which the doctor himself is often in the dark. There are many doctors

[1] André Schlemmer, 'Doit-on dire la vérité à un mourant?' in *Le Christianisme au XX* siècle, 10 and 17 November, 1944
[2] E. Rist, *La morale professionnelle du médecin*, Masson, Paris, 1941

who hold high professional ideals, who long with all their hearts to profess a humane medicine. But can they, without a religious faith? For if they are not fully convinced that their own life has a meaning, how can they approach the questions their patients put to them about human destiny? It is then that they are so easily tempted to change the subject of conversation. All they need to do is to admire the bunch of carnations on the table, or to talk of some X-ray photograph from which they are expecting to get valuable information. The awkward discussion, which the patient desires, and which the doctor fears, is avoided.

There is another obstacle, which has to do with our vanity. The patient has appealed to me to heal him. Obligingly to reveal to him the resources at my disposal, to stress the beneficial effects of the medicines I have prescribed for him, to pass on to him the definite information about his disease which I derive from my laboratory tests, will indeed keep up his morale; but it is also more flattering to myself than communicating to him my anxieties and uncertainties. To talk to him about the possibility of death is in some way to confess to him that there is a risk of the confidence he has placed in me being mistaken. At this point one cannot but have a feeling of serious guilt. We feel the same whenever we measure the limits of our technical resources.

So, when the disease is not serious, it is easy to avoid the problem of death, and to keep up morale by assuring the patient of his recovery. And if the condition of the patient worsens, it will be perhaps too late, too difficult, too disillusioning, too painful, abruptly to forsake an optimism which has been too complacently indulged in. For many doctors, the morale of a patient is nothing other than his confidence in his recovery. As long as this is probable, all is well. But when it becomes improbable, there is nothing to do but bolster it up fallaciously. It is too late then to call on quite different moral resources, grounded in faith, which give the patient courage to look reality in the face.

On the other hand, many sick people feel rebellious because they consider their illness to be an unexpected accident which they do not deserve. In the Biblical perspective, they may come to see the truth that death and disease are a necessary destiny.

The Meaning of Disease

Let us put it quite frankly: they are even normal. Here again the Bible is completely realistic:

> For affliction cometh not forth of the dust,
> Neither doth trouble spring out of the ground;
> But man is born unto trouble,
> As the sparks fly upward (Job 5.6-7).

When my wife broke her leg two years ago, she said to me: 'The hospitals are always full; it is only right that for once it should be my turn to go there.' It is, then, life and health which turn out to be the unmerited gifts, and the prolongation of life and the re-establishment of health, for which medicine labours with all its strength, are seen to be a blessing from the merciful God, a respite, a stay of execution. We may ask why God grants us this respite. It can only be that He wants us to use it to come nearer to Him, laying hold through faith on His promises of eternal life.

I have received today a letter from a brother doctor whom a major surgical operation has snatched from otherwise certain death. 'To you', he writes, 'I can say that I really feel that Providence intervened, wishing to make me understand that I am being allowed to go on living for a very special purpose. That will lay many obligations upon me, and so I shall be very much in need of the continued prayers of friends like you.'

So, if we are the kind of doctors we ought to be, not absorbed entirely by the technical problems of the case, but having a care for the patient as a person, if we penetrate with affection into the secret places of his heart, where he is troubled by the problems of the meaning of sickness and of death, a quiet understanding is established, which deepens as the disease worsens. We feel then that we have not departed from the truth; the patient becomes increasingly aware of the increasing danger without our ever having to break it to him brutally.

For, after all, medicine is not so certain that we can ever formulate a fatal prognosis. Death is always only a more or less probable eventuality, which stands in our path as well as in that of our patient. This sense of our common destiny establishes a real fellowship between us. These questions about the meaning of illness and death concern us as much as they concern our

173

patient; we are taking part together both in the tragedy of our human condition and in the miracle of salvation.

There is, indeed, nothing more impressive for the doctor than thus to accompany a patient who has become a dear friend and who is walking in full knowledge of his condition to meet death; a patient who remains human, who does not repress or hide his moments of rebellion or distress, but who at the same time is deepening his blessing of faith.

I am reminded of a young woman who worked with me for several years, a woman who had been severely tested, but whose trials had greatly strengthened our spiritual fellowship, and who, after a few days of most painful illness, was taken, in the flower of her youth. Many sick people shut their eyes to their condition because they lack the faith which will enable them to face its seriousness. But she had that faith and, thanks to it, that realism. It was wonderful how she used the last few days of life that God granted her. One by one she called to her bedside all the people to whom she had something to say before leaving this earth; and her great concern was the peace of the world: 'People ought to pray much more for peace,' she would say. This thought was reverently taken up by her father, and became the source of a great movement of prayer for peace.

True courage—the courage which has its roots in faith—is that which listens to what God is saying to us through disease and the threat of death. If this is our attitude, sickness and death will take on meaning for us, they will have something to teach us, something to bring to us, and they will also help to make us revise our scale of values.

Every sickness is a crisis of life. Every sick person who calls for our help is one who has suddenly become aware of his fragility. 'What is your life?' says St. James. 'For ye are a vapour, that appeareth for a little time, and then vanisheth away' (Jas. 4.14). He is at the same time discovering the fragility of everything that once filled his life: work, money, affections, instincts, and pleasures. If he has regarded them as duties and blessings sent by God, the sudden stoppage caused by the sickness will be easier to bear: he still has God, and will wait upon new blessings from Him in the spiritual retreat that sickness can become. But if, on the other hand, he has made them his gods, if he has thrown himself frantically into them in order to distract and dope himself, then suddenly and tragically he is faced with the true problems of life, and of his own life. Sickness sets him face to face with God. For, as Hippocrates said, 'all diseases are divine and all diseases are human'.

He hates being alone. He thought he was strong, but finds he is weak. It is God's opportunity, referred to by Jesus: 'They that are whole have no need of a physician, but they that are sick' (Matt. 9.12). The sick person calls the doctor; he talks to him of his troubles and asks him to relieve and heal him. But behind this appeal there always lies hidden another, deeper, less precise, more secret, often unconscious: the need for understanding, love, consolation and support; the fear of being left alone in a time of trial with all the problems it reveals or raises. As Professor Ckinzyc has said, every sick person is a man seeking a man. He needs the doctor and his technical aid; but he needs to find in him also a man and a friend, to enter into fellowship with him.

Psychoanalysts, who at first stressed the fact of healing as an emotional relief, have been attaching ever-increasing importance to the personal contact and the emotional transfer between patient and doctor. Dr. Maeder has made a notable contribution to the study of this problem.[1]

Too often it happens that we doctors cover up our sensitiveness. This love for suffering humanity, of which the whole Bible speaks, is what has made us become doctors. It should be for our patients the kindly reflection of the love of God. Most doctors are very sensitive people! I have been the confidant of too many of them not to say that here. In the public mind they are often thought to be callous. I consider it a fallacy, even in the case of surgeons; but I think also that it is to some extent the fault of doctors themselves that this legend dies hard: they have taken refuge in an impersonal scientific attitude just because they want to protect their sensitiveness.

They are afraid of encouraging the patient to become emotional about himself, or of building up in him an over-sentimental attachment to his physician. These are real dangers. But I

[1] Alphonse Maeder, 'Sur la psychologie du contact affectif et ses différentes formes', in *Revue suisse de psychologie et de psychologie appliquée*, 1949, Vol. VIII, No. 2, Hans Huber, Berne

do not think we avoid them any better by closing our hearts to our patients. Even in those neuroses in which flight into disease plays, consciously or unconsciously, an essential part, an artificial hard-heartedness increases the patient's emotional demands instead of helping him to adopt a more courageous attitude.

I am not here advocating sentimentality or mawkishness. By nature, by upbringing, and by the Calvinist environment in which I grew up, I am a person of extreme reserve. At times I even suffer for it; but we must be unaffectedly ourselves, neither more nor less. An Italian colleague, when I send him a patient, may, with the exuberant impetuosity of his race, take him by the arm and 'old fellow' him. It would not ring true if I did it.

But whatever the apparent diversity of our natures, I am here speaking of the heart, which is not to be either flaunted or concealed. And if we are sincere we shall recognize that it is not always the fear of our patient's reactions that prevents us from laying ourselves open in this way, but concern about our own reactions, a sort of modesty about our sensitiveness.

I shall never forget one of my first impressions in medicine. I was a student at the time, attached to a children's clinic. I was under a houseman who soon became my firm friend. He seemed to me then to be well on in his career: he had taken his doctorate. On the day I started with him, he had just witnessed a death from tubercular meningitis. I found him in the library, a prey to an overwhelming emotion. 'I can't stand it!' he told me. 'It's an awful death. Hour after hour of groaning, of frightful pain that nothing will relieve. That child's eyes staring at nothing, and all I could do was to stand there helpless, watching death coming relentlessly nearer, and so slowly. And the father and mother waiting there, and one has nothing to say to them. . . .'

His words made a deep impression on me: so one could be a doctor without ceasing to be a man! Many people since have said to me: 'I could never be a doctor; I can't bear seeing people suffer.' I think the best doctors are those who cannot bear to see suffering, and who try to bring relief and healing in spite of the limitations of our means, and who pursue their vocation in spite of the suffering it imposes on them.

There are indeed some awful deaths. Professor P. L. Mounier-Kuhn was talking to us recently about them, for they are frequent in his speciality, diseases of the ear, nose and throat. Watching such a death, the doctor experiences within himself an acute conflict. He longs to put an end to the intolerable, useless suffering, and yet he is under an absolute obligation, imposed by the Bible (Ex. 20.13) and by human conscience—an obligation 'which governs our profession', as Dr. Rist writes,[1] 'and which is the reason for its existence: the obligation to protect and to safeguard life to the utmost of our power'.

And then there are all those times when the doctor is suddenly called to the bedside of a patient in the throes of an acute crisis—as in thrombosis, for example. Of course, he can act, he can make an emergency injection. And how good it is, when in the grip of emotion, to be able to act! Nevertheless, he always feels at such a moment that there is more at stake than he can cope with, that he is watching a gigantic struggle being fought out between the forces of life and the forces of death, in which his own puny intervention can have but little effect. Then perhaps in his heart he will turn to prayer; and at that point prayer is of more avail than action.

[1] *Op. cit.*

22

THE MISSION OF
THE DOCTOR

D ISEASE does not always end in cure or in death: it
may be prolonged and become chronic, or it may leave
behind it a permanent infirmity. We all know the long
chain of problems attached to these two terms—chronic illness
and infirmity. It was Professor Mounier-Kuhn again who underlined the importance of a medicine of the person in oto-rhino-
laryngology, for instance. If a man loses the power of hearing
or speech, it probably means that his career is finished, and in
any case his social and family relationships will be profoundly
affected. And what is one to say of the blind, the paralysed, the
limbless and many more who are for ever condemned to live
a diminished life of inaction and dependence on others?

Clearly, when the doctor can do no more to heal, his task is
not over. It is much more difficult and thankless, but just as
necessary. He has to help the cripple to accept the inevitable and
to engage in the struggle to adapt himself as far as may be, so
that he is not allowed to lose his share in the life of the community. It is often thought that these two things are incompatible
—that the cripple who accepts his infirmity must cease the
struggle for reintegration, and that to fight must mean to revolt
against the infirmity. Experience proves otherwise. If the cripple
revolts and complains, he cripples his spirit also, and shuts himself off from outside contacts, becoming hard and inadaptable.
But in so far as he succeeds, helped by his faith, in accepting his
infirmity, he relaxes, and finds in himself new energy to live in
spite of everything, and often an extraordinary capacity to overcome his difficulties.

I say 'helped by his faith' because I am becoming more and
more convinced that on the human level acceptance is all but
impossible. Stoicism, of course, teaches acceptance. But Stoical

acceptance has always about it a hard inhumanity which is quiet different from Christian acceptance. In his study of pagan and Christian attitudes to death,[1] Charles Favez has clearly demonstrated this contrast between Stoicism and Christianity, and how in the ancient world the Christians showed themselves to be more human: 'Sure of being able to offer true consolation, they do not hesitate to give free rein to their sensitiveness: they understand and excuse tears.' But, of course, it is not by preaching acceptance that we shall help our patients, but rather by understanding how difficult acceptance is for them, and by confessing that in their place we should feel the same rebelliousness. This brings us back to the mission of the doctor.

In cases of cronic disease, the patient expects of us that we shall really share in his sufferings, travelling with him in it faithfully to the end. He wants us to help him to live notwithstanding, and to help him to die. That seems to me to sum up the whole of medicine—helping men to live and to die.

A few days ago the medical superintendent of a large sanatorium said to me frankly: 'Just think how hard it is to come day after day for weeks and months to the bedside of some of those in the ward without ever being able to bring them good news or to suggest for them the operation whose success they can see in others around them.' If the patient asks about his condition, or whether he has still a long time to wait, the doctor feels these questions as if they were reproaches, as if the delay were his fault. How great, then, is the temptation to space out one's visits in order to avoid these painful interviews, or else to do what I call playing tricks: to affect humour or artificial high spirits, to make small talk so as to crowd out more serious topics. The chronic invalid is very sensitive. Such tricks do not deceive him. He feels that his doctor is no longer his travelling companion, but is holding himself aloof. The doctor holds himself aloof in order to protect himself from being hurt. The invalids who are always complaining are almost easier to deal with, for they provoke an active reaction; but the gentle ones, whose eyes only ask their unspoken questions—how hard it is to face for long the infinite confidence of their gaze.

[1] Charles Favez, 'L'attitude païenne et l'attitude chrétienne devant la mort', in *Les Cahiers Protestants*, 1943, No. 7, La Concorde, Lausanne

To all these things the Bible has its answer: 'Have this mind in you, which was also in Christ Jesus' (Phil. 2.5). The Bible also brings the Master's answer: 'Whosoever doth not bear his own cross, and come after me, cannot be my disciple' (Luke 14.27). Bearing our cross means especially bearing without fainting the pain of seeing the suffering of our patients. I received recently a letter from a woman doctor who told me of an experience she had just had. Called to the bedside of a man with a lung disease, who was able to breathe only with difficulty, and who could hardly speak, she realized that he did not want a flood of words from her, nor exhortation, nor even sympathy; he wanted real, deep, burning companionship. She spent with him a whole hour of complete silence, and that hour is for her now one of the most beautiful of her life.

Everything that I have said regarding chronic invalids and the infirm is true also of neurotics, whose treatment is so often long-drawn-out. It is easy to sympathize on our first contact, to penetrate whole-heartedly the neurotic's life problems, to share his feelings in the shocks he has suffered and which have made him the invalid he is. But when relief is slow in coming, when one finds oneself constantly up against the same false reactions, the same stubborn obsessions, the same anxieties, when he gives vent to his weariness and his discouragement, it becomes a heavy burden to bear. But it is not the patient who is burdensome; it is the disease. But he is quick to think that it is he who is weighing on us and not his ills!

The other day I was overjoyed to see a woman whom I treated for ten years for most distressing neurotic obsessions. She was always afraid that I should weary of her; she even blamed herself for not being able to bring me success to crown my efforts on her behalf. Sometimes, after one of our sessions together, the veil would be lifted, the agonizing distress would disappear, only to return a day or two later, often worse than ever, and we would have to start all over again. Then suddenly one Good Friday the thing happened: she felt that she had been sent peace, and the anxiety disappeared. That is some time ago now, and the new-found freedom has been maintained: she is living a new life. She came to thank me for persevering with her all through the long tunnel of those ten years of agony. An interesting medical detail in this case is that the psychological trouble was accompanied by physical disturbance, in particular a stubborn condition of anaemia. Throughout all those years preparations of iron or of liver-extract had never succeeded in raising the level of haemoglobin above 55 per cent. Now it is a fact that three weeks after the final disappearance of the psychological symptoms, and without her having undergone any further anti-anaemic treatment, the haemoglobin level was found to be 78 per cent.

But technical treatment and human sympathy are not enough. The mission of the doctor is wider still. Helping a person to live does not mean only helping him to bear his life, but helping him to grow, and to solve his problems. Every disease compels the patient to turn in upon himself, and to examine his life, and for this also he needs his doctor. If sickness in general is a sign of our frailty, of the disorder that has broken into the world, and of our mortal nature, each particular case of sickness has its own peculiar meaning, closely linked to this general meaning. The patient may discover this meaning by himself, for it is only found by listening oneself to God; but the doctor helps by giving him an opportunity of talking, by surrounding him with his care and understanding, and sometimes by bringing him the witness of his own experience.

Job saw his sickness as a test through which God sought to strengthen his faith (Jas. 5.11). St. Paul saw his as a thorn in the flesh which God would not remove from him, in order to keep him from pride, so that in his weakness he would rely only on God's strength (II Cor. 12.7). David, taught by the prophet Nathan, saw in the sickness and death of his son a divine punishment (II Sam. 12.1-14). David had used his royal power to take Uriah's wife from him, after he had seen her bathing and become enamoured of her. When he knew she was pregnant, he had had Uriah brought back from the battle-front and had granted him leave, hoping that he would go to his wife, and thus make her pregnancy appear lawful. But Uriah did not go to her. 'My comrades,' he says, 'are encamped in the open field; shall I then go into mine house, to eat and to drink, and to lie with my wife?' (II Sam. 11.11). Even after prolonging his leave and making him drunk, David had had no more success. Then he had sent Uriah to his general, Joab, with a letter saying: 'Set ye Uriah in the forefront of the hottest battle, and retire ye from him, that he may be smitten, and die' (II Sam. 11.15). And Uriah had been killed.

As soon as we begin to listen to the confidences of our patients, we find that they discover something about the meaning of their illness. This is especially so in the case of neuroses. One of my patients once said to me: 'I see now that I shall never be cured of my neurosis until I have learned what God is seeking to teach me through it.' As we know, many illnesses have a symbolic meaning: muscular spasms in the throat or attacks of asthma may symbolize a feeling of being suffocated in one's family or social life. Repeated attacks of phlebitis in the legs may symbolize a fear of moving forward in life. I know of a doctor who has long suffered from an unexplained pain in the heel; but he tells me that he knows its symbolic meaning: he allows his life to weigh on him too heavily. A certain woman has displayed the alternating organic and nervous disturbances described by many writers; she has discovered that all her successive troubles have a common meaning connected with her fear of life and her negative attitude towards it.

I treated a man suffering from total arrhythmia, which had resisted every form of treatment. Who could guess at the respective parts played in such a case by organic and by functional factors? But he found out its meaning. The arrhythmia began when he came back to his native town, where he was surrounded by the memories of a childhood crushed under maternal domination. Having realized the fact, he brought all this heavy load of bitterness and laid it at the foot of the Cross. I took his pulse: it was regular.

One further case, a man suffering from furunculosis. He was soon able to confess to me that the boils were, as it were, a physical expression of all the bitterness he was nursing in his soul as a result of repeated quarrels with his wife.

Disease also has its purposive aspect. By this I mean that it frequently seems to be aimed at a definite end, even though the sufferer may be unaware of it. I do not need to insist on the 'flight into disease', often described since Freud, in which the patient is trying to win affection which he does not receive when well. There are more subtle cases. Take, for instance, that of a man who in childhood suffered from his father's failure in business and the social discredit which this brought upon the family. From then on a fierce will to succeed in life took hold upon him, and spurred him on to climb all the rungs of promotion in the firm he had joined. At last the long-awaited day came when he was appointed its director. That very day he fell seriously ill. But that illness has borne unexpected fruit: he sees now that he was the unconscious victim of this personal will to success, which possessed and enslaved him and whose power has at last been broken by his illness. Through it he has become aware that ever since his childhood God has been calling him to give up to Him this will of his. And now instead of fighting God's call, he is able to respond to it.

Or take another case, a man who was the victim of a serious motor-cycling accident. He has not yet recovered, even after months in hospital and several operations. He was brought up in a Christian home. The day came when he rebelled against the narrowness and formalism of his upbringing. He threw every thing over, God included. But one day as he lay in bed in hospital he suddenly saw his accident as a sort of Damascus Road. It was God who had stopped him in the mad career that his life had become, the same God whom he had learned to know in his childhood, in spite of the errors of his Church, and to whom he unconsciously longed to return. Now he has found Him again, and is preparing to undergo yet another operation in quite a different state of mind from before.

It does not have to be an exceptional occurrence. The most ordinary case has its echoes in the depths of the heart. A few days ago a workman engaged on the construction of a garage for the house next door rang my door-bell: he had cut his hand with a saw. Disinfection, a couple of stitches and a dressing —what could be simpler? It was an almost automatic routine. But we chatted while I was busy: 'Have you seen those planks that the boss is making us saw up?' the injured man asked. 'They've come straight off the trees; they're so wet it's practically impossible to do anything with them.' So in that unfortunate saw-cut there was something other than a mere accident. There was the man's irritation against his employer. When we are irritated by our work, our efforts become unco-ordinated and jerky

—and thus the accident had happened. Talking with him further, I learned that this workman was not a carpenter by trade, but a precision mechanic, and he had been given the sack unjustly. His irritation against his present employer was in part due to the fact that he was carrying over on to him the rancour which he had previously harboured and repressed.

It is clear that every illness and every accident reveal problems, sometimes of vital importance, in which physical, psychological and spiritual factors are closely interwoven. Of course, the doctor is not to take the place of the minister of religion, though he can often usefully work in with him. But neither can he refuse to try to understand the tortured minds and hearts his patients bring him.

There will be forged between doctor and patient a real human bond, and this is important medically in physical as well as nervous diseases. It is only as he discovers this whole background of problems in the life of the patient that the doctor really begins to understand him, his disease, and all those psychological and spiritual factors which impinge upon it and so are vitally important in the formulation of a prognosis. And then the doctor disposes of physiological and psychological knowledge which the cleric usually lacks. He is thus able to help—even in religious matters—certain patients with whom the minister of religion would be at a loss what to do. We must remember that man is an indivisible unity, and so the vocation of the doctor and that of the pastor cannot be kept in watertight compartments. The same is true as regards the respective spheres of the doctor and the teacher.

Sometimes the doctor may exercise a profound influence on his patient by a straightforward declaration of his faith, for such a declaration will have more effect than if it came from a clergyman. Let us be frank about this: problems of the sort we have been discussing in connection with cripples, chronic invalids, neurotics and others who are suffering from life's harshest blows can find a solution only in Christian faith. Thus a verse from the Bible may afford real relief—and the only true relief—like, for example, that in which the prophet Isaiah anticipates Christ's succour: 'Surely he hath borne our griefs, and carried our sorrows' (Isa. 53.4). Dr. Maeder said to me one day that the doctor must learn to handle his Bible as he handles the pharmacopoeia.

But we do not have to be continually talking about God. A doctor once asked me at a medical conference whether I prayed with each one of my patients. I was astonished at his question! I am reminded of a patient who turned to me on the doorstep and said: 'Doctor, I'm grateful to you for having put God into my life.'

'But I can't remember ever having discussed the subject with you,' I replied.

'That's true,' he said. 'Probably it has more to do with my having read Lecomte du Nouy's books recently.[1] But I still feel that it is the result of our talks together, and that it is because of them that I have read those books in quite a new frame of mind.'

A married couple came to consult me about their marital difficulties. I saw either one or the other or both together a large number of times. I became passionately interested in the psychological problems which underlay their difficulties. One day the wife, while staying abroad with some friends, happened to pick up one of my books, and learned that I was a Christian, a matter on which I had had no occasion to speak to her. She began to read the Bible and underwent a real conversion. When she came back it was to bring me a confession of her faults, and almost to blame me for not having spoken to her before of the Christian life she was now discovering.

We doctors are not called upon by God to preach. Our task is rather to listen and to understand. If we give our patients an opportunity of speaking of what is in their hearts, they will get to know themselves better; they will discover what are the real problems they have to face, and perhaps see the meaning of their sickness.

But what are we to do, faced with this flood of problems to which science has no answer and which exhortation does not suffice to resolve? I think that the best thing to do is to speak to our patients about our own experiences, our own difficulties, faults and failures, and about the blessings we have received. We should not, of course, overdo all this, but follow that just measure to which God prompts us. A personal bond, a realization of our brotherhood as men, will be created between us and

[1] See his *Human Destiny*, Longmans, Green & Co., London, 1949

them. They will see that they are not alone. If we have not had to face precisely the same difficulties, we have faced very similar ones; to some we have been given a solution; some are still with us, and we are still seeking through faith a solution to them; and there are some that we shall always have to bear as our cross. We are brothers in wretchedness and in blessing. One can only help others by giving them a bit of oneself.

In this way, speaking from the heart, we set up that reciprocity which the Bible teaches. The Bible contains much teaching and exhortation; but it contains even more of personal experiences.

We should know nothing of that searching hour spent by Moses (Ex. 3, 4) at the beginning of his ministry, when God spoke to him out of the burning bush, if he himself had not spoken of it. He told how he tried to resist God, and all the objections he put forward before giving in to His call. We should know nothing of the prophet Isaiah's radical experience when he received his commission from God if he had not told us himself how he became aware of his own sin, and knew that God was purifying him. We should know nothing of the internal struggles of Jeremiah (Jer. 20.9) and of many another of the men of the Bible if they themselves had not revealed them. And the account of the Temptation of Christ (Luke 4.1-13), which we have discussed at length, would be unknown to us had He not Himself given it to His disciples. So even Jesus Christ told of His experiences and His struggles. He told His disciples of His anguish before the Cross: 'My soul is exceeding sorrowful, even unto death' (Matt. 26.38). And the theologian St. Paul, whom no one can suspect of subjectivism, refers constantly to his personal experience (Gal. 1.11-24).

If, following the example of these men of the Bible, we speak from our hearts, we help our patients to understand their illness. But it is still they themselves that make the discovery. It is a subjective, personal matter. It is not possible to compile a systematic classification of the meanings of various diseases. Professor Ellul,[1] quoting our Lord when He said of His friend Lazarus' sickness: 'This sickness is not unto death, but for the glory of God' (John 11.4), concludes that there are two classes of disease, those that are unto death, and those that are for the glory of God.

[1] *Op. cit.*

My readers will by now be able to see that I could not subscribe to such a theory. Diseases can be classified scientifically, but not spiritually. Every case is particular and personal. Besides, Lazarus did really die.

Similarly, we are told that King Hezekiah was 'sick unto death' (II Kings 20.1-11). The prophet Isaiah came to confirm the fact: 'Thou shalt die.' But God heard the King's prayer and sent Isaiah back to him to tell him: 'I will heal thee.' So the 'meaning' of a sickness is not an abstract scientific idea that can be classified. It is concerned with the word which God speaks to us, and which may change from one moment to the next, for God is a living God.

To seek the meaning of things is to bind ourselves to the living God, to live with Him, to listen to what He tells us through life, through sickness, and through the threat of death. It is to look the problems of life and death squarely in the face.

Thus we see Jacob (Gen. 48, 49), at the age of 147, call to him his well-beloved son Joseph; he reminds him of the great experience of his life: how God blessed him at Luz, and promised him that this blessing would also be on his posterity. Then Jacob transmits the blessing to his sons and grandsons, and says to them, 'Behold, I die' (Gen. 48.21). To each he gives advice and instructions, he arranges his burial, and he dies.

And thus we see the prophet Elisha, already 'fallen sick of his sickness whereof he died' (II Kings 13.14), dissuading King Joash from weeping over his imminent death. He concerns himself rather with the people's welfare, and announces to the King the victories which God promises soon to grant him.

23

SIN AND DISEASE

L ET US LOOK at another impressive account of a death
—that of Moses. God Himself gives him warning of it:
'Behold, thy days approach that thou must die' (Deut.
31.14). Nevertheless, 'his eye was not dim, nor his natural force
abated' (Deut. 34.7). God speaks to him at the same time of His
people, that rebellious people whom Moses has mastered at the
cost of countless struggles, leading them to submit to their God.
And God says that the people will forsake Him, and break the
covenant He has made with them (Deut. 31.16).

Nevertheless, this people is to go, in accordance with God's
promise, into the land of Canaan, towards which Moses has
been leading them for the last forty years. God sends him to the
top of Mount Nebo, to look from afar at the promised land.
And God says to him: 'Die in the mount . . . as Aaron thy brother
died . . . because ye trespassed against me in the midst of the
children of Israel' (Deut. 32.50–1).

What then? Is not Moses the great servant of God? We are
told of him that the Lord knew him face to face (Deut. 34.10).
How well the phrase shows the personalism of the Bible! Did he
not show himself untiring in God's cause, unbending in 'his
struggles against the people? Those forty years in the desert are
filled with the incessant revolts of the people and the fierce
energy of Moses, as each time he constrains them to repent and
to continue their journey under God's leadership. If the journey
has been so slow and so long that death is going to overtake
Moses before his goal is reached, it is surely more the people's
fault than his. And now God is announcing to Moses his pre-
mature death, indicating that it is the price he must pay for sins
committed 'in the midst of the children of Israel'. Will not Moses
revolt against the injustice of it? Far from it: he sings a glorious
song of praise: 'Ascribe ye greatness unto our God. The Rock,

his work is perfect; for all his ways are judgement' (Deut. 32.3-4).

This story brings us back to the grave problem of the relationship of disease, death and sin. We have already spoken of it in Chapter 20, but we must now go more deeply into it, for it is a problem that troubles everyone. We have said that the Bible affirms that there is a link connecting disease, death and sin. But it is speaking of a general connection—intelligible only in the perspective of human interdependence—and not of a strict connection between a particular sin and a particular illness or death, at least not in every case.

Looking across from Mount Nebo at the land of Canaan, which his people but not he will enter, Moses might well feel himself the innocent victim of that people. In spite of all his courageous striving, the people had repeatedly aroused God's wrath by their rebellions. And now it was he, Moses, who was to be the victim of it.

But the Bible is personal without being individualistic. It is the individualist who protests: 'It is not just, because it is not my fault!' He does not recognize human interdependence, the consciousness of which makes us into persons. As we saw in Chapter 16, the condition of the integration of the person is the recognition of the link which binds man to Nature and to society.

The greatness of Moses lies in the fact that he had made himself so much one with his people that he could not say: 'It is not just, because it is not my fault.' The faults of his people, although he never ceased to combat them, he felt to be his responsibility. Ought not he to have fought better, followed God better, fulfilled better the vocation of leader to which he had been called by God? Vocation implies responsibility. He was indeed a victim, but he felt himself responsible as well.

Perhaps I may be permitted to illustrate all this with a personal experience of my own. I had had a serious motor-car accident. My wife and one of our children had been injured. My uncle, who had brought me up after the death of my father, had been killed. That night my brain turned over and over the feverish thoughts that assailed me. Legally, I was not responsible: I was the victim of Fate. There had been a heavy shower, perhaps a patch of oil on the road, and my car had skidded. But I had paid no attention, a little while before, to a notice warning drivers of the slippery road surface. I was not travelling very fast; but half an hour earlier I had been delighting in my skill in driving at speed.

Above all, I felt that all this interior discussion would in no wise bring me peace. Even if I could without reticence have gathered together all the arguments exonerating me from responsibility, they would not have exonerated me. I was indeed a victim, but I was to blame as well. If I had been in closer contact with God, more open to His inspiration, He would doubtless so have led me that this thing would not have happened. That very morning, in haste to get away, I had cut short my prayers; and the prayers I had said had been only an imitation of prayers.

That is sin, to be out of contact with God, to be separated from Him and from His guidance. And there again we feel ourselves to be victims, because it is the inevitable lot of humanity, and yet we feel ourselves at the same time to be responsible—that we are to blame. That night I realized that it is absolutely impossible by intellectual processes to separate that of which we are the victims from that for which we are to blame. It is not a matter for analysis; it is beyond all analysis. And then, in the pleasure I take in driving, I am one with the modern world with its swarms of cars and its patches of oil, increasing the risk of death; I am a part of it; I belong to it and I help to create it, to make it what it is; like all other men, I am responsible for it as well.

Finally, though we can make amends for some of the wrongs we have done, there are others which are irreparable, particularly when a death has occurred. That night I felt and understood the meaning of the Cross of Christ: that the Cross is the reparation for the irreparable; that we all bear a burden in which are mingled inextricably that of which we are the victims and that for which we are to blame, but that we can lay down this entire burden just as it is at the foot of the Cross; for the Cross is at one and the same time forgiveness where we are guilty, and true relief where we are the victims.

A simple image may help to make this clear. The world is like a great ship on which we are all embarked without having wished to be so, and which, from time immemorial, has been disabled. In the beginning, through disobeying the captain's orders, the crew handled the ship badly, and it was holed. Since then, urged on by the instinct of self-preservation, or sometimes by a noble ideal, the crew has been feverishly trying to repair the damage. But the very fever, fear and confusion that reign create tumult, and the ship is handled worse than ever, so that even constructive efforts result in further damage. The sailors argue about the best method of effecting the repairs, and these arguments add to the disorder and confusion; the noise of them makes it impossible to hear clearly the captain's orders.

In this ship, each one is a victim, a victim of the fateful diabolical chain of events, a victim of the wrongs of others; but each is at fault also, and contributes, even with good intentions, his share to the general tumult, to the bad handling of the ship, and to the panic. And the disaster which threatens each one is bound up with all the disorder. Each feels his responsibility since each must strive to avert it, and yet none can be judged to be more responsible than another.

This was what I realized that night after my accident. It brought me to my knees before the Cross. Was not the meaning of this accident for me just what God had made me realize through it? Since that night I see more clearly than ever I did before the tragedy of human life. I have understood how inexorable it is, and how there is no other help than the grace of God: *ave Crux, spes unica.* One of my patients once said that sin can lead only either to despair or to God.

Since that time it has been given to me to serve my fellow men with an ever-deepening understanding of their needs. Men and women of all ages and conditions have come to me bearing a burden made up of that inextricable mixture of guilt and suffering. There are indeed in their lives some things of which they can truthfully say they are the victims, and some for which they really feel themselves to blame. But when we look closely at these things we find that the frontier between them is far from being clearly demarcated.

Take, for example, this man, the victim of a jealous termagant of a wife. He can detail to me for hours all he has suffered; and it is the truth. It is true that he is the victim. But that does not afford him relief; it is no solution for him. But through all his complaints I can at last perceive also in him a feeling of responsibility. He had a high idea of what marriage should be. That his home has become what it has is his own failure as much as that of his wife. We all know ourselves to be responsible for the way our wives behave; none of us can escape the question: 'Could I by acting differently have helped her to become something other than she is?'

Or take the case of the weak-willed man who takes refuge in falsehoods. He comes to confess them in my consulting-room. He feels himself to be guilty, and yet he feels himself to be the victim of all manner of circumstances—his heredity, his education, the events of his life.

It is evident that on this view the great debate between the Freudians and the theologians loses all its force. The former accuse the latter of treating the victims as if they were guilty, and *vice versa*. I believe that we shall understand men only when we admit that both are right—that all men are at once both guilty and victims.

I am reminded of a woman who came to me after having been treated for a long period by a Freudian psychiatrist. His absolute denial of the fact of sin had been very good for her, for as often happens with people who are a prey to deep-rooted obsessions, she was inclined to see in her sufferings a sign of God's condemnation of her. But this had not freed her from the real feelings of guilt which were intimately associated with her obsessions. Without consciousness of sin there is no room for grace, and she still longed for forgiveness. I spoke to her one day about these two aspects of the soul: about the pathological mechanisms of which we are the victims, and the sins of which we are guilty. I spoke also of doctors who see only the mechanisms, and theologians who see only the sins. She at once replied: 'We must see both.'

There are psychoanalysts who do succeed completely in making a synthesis between these two aspects of the person. I shall never forget the first words I heard from the mouth of Dr. Maeder of Zurich the first time I met him. He had just been converted to Christianity. He was witnessing to his experience, and began with these words: 'For more than twenty years I had been caring for men's souls without seeing the most important fact about the life of the soul—namely, sin.'

Now, if evil has two aspects, grace has also two aspects. The

Bible, in affirming that there is a link between human ills and
human guilt, gives the same answer to both. The account of the
healing of the paralytic by Christ is well known (Luke 5.17-26).
Before healing him, our Lord said to him: 'Man, thy sins are
forgiven thee.' At this the hostile bystanders began to murmur
against Him. Then He healed him: 'I say unto thee, Arise, and
take up thy couch, and go unto thy house. And immediately
he rose up before them.' This incident is often quoted in connection with the relationship between sin and disease as evidence
that the forgiveness of sins is the condition of healing, or, what
is still more serious, as evidence that the sins of the paralytic
were the cause of his paralysis. But Jesus did not say that at all.
As He healed the sick man, He told His adversaries expressly
that He was doing it in order to show them that He had 'power
on earth to forgive sins', having asked them, 'Whether is easier
to say, Thy sins are forgiven thee; or to say, Arise and walk?'

It is quite clear from this account that Jesus is proclaiming His
double power of forgiveness and healing, and that these two are
bound up together. We shall return later to the subject. Throughout the Bible the healing of disease is presented as the symbol of
God's grace which at the same time purifies the soul of its sin.
Thus, while avoiding completely any suggestion of a causal link
between the sins and the paralysis of the sick man, Jesus dealt at
once with both.

Unhappily, we do find isolated Christians, or the adherents
of certain Christian sects, who claim that there is a causal link
between a man's sin and his sickness. I was once told that a sister
in a religious order brought a sick person one of my books and
said to him: 'Here. Read this book, and you will realize that
you must be a sinner, because you are ill.' That anyone should
think me capable of writing such a thing! Quite recently I have
heard about a most distinguished Christian man who devotes
much of his energies to the subject of healing through prayer,
but who maintains that all physical disorder is a sign of a corre-
sponding moral disorder, and that if healing does not follow
prayer, the cause of failure lies in this moral disorder. Professor
R. Siebeck of Heidelberg lays down[1] the general connection
that exists between disease and sin, since the doctor is faced with

[1] *Op. cit.*

'the fact that man's wretchedness is apparent not only in disease, but also in sin.' But he adds: 'How often do we find sins without disease, and diseases without sin! . . . Endless harm is done by this idea of a relationship of cause and effect between the two. Countless despairing people have had to undergo indescribable suffering and torture of mind simply because their ills have been thought to be the result of their actual sins. Consider what great strides forward have been made in medical science since first it struggled free from the clutch of prejudices of this sort.'

It is true that we cannot over-emphasize the harm done by such theories, completely unsupported as they are by the Bible. Indeed, the opposite is the case, for once, when our Lord's disciples asked Him concerning a man born blind, 'Rabbi, who did sin, this man, or his parents?' Jesus replied: 'Neither did this man sin, nor his parents' (John 9.2-3). We could hardly have a more explicit declaration.

There is another passage that enables us to see the mind of Christ on this subject. He was speaking to His disciples about some Galileans who had been massacred by Pilate, the Roman Governor. He said: 'Think ye that these Galileans were sinners above all the Galileans because they have suffered these things? I tell you, Nay: but, except ye repent, ye shall all in like manner perish. Or those eighteen, upon whom the tower in Siloam fell, and killed them, think ye that they were offenders above all the men that dwell in Jerusalem? I tell you, Nay: but, except ye repent, ye shall all likewise perish' (Luke 13.2-5).

In thus denying categorically that the victims of such calamities are greater sinners than other men, Jesus denied the existence of a direct causal link. But in adding 'Except ye repent, ye shall all likewise perish', He affirmed the existence of the general connection of which we have spoken, namely, the fact that misfortunes, political massacres or accidents are signs of the disorder that has broken into the world, and also calls to repentance.

The striking thing about this text is the way in which our Lord turns us from the sin of others to our own sin. His disciples are wondering if the Galileans or the victims of Siloam were greater sinners. Jesus turns their minds from these thoughts of self-righteous judgement, and brings them back to the consideration of their own sin and their own need to repent.

That is the whole spirit of the Gospel. All the misunderstandings that bedevil this problem of the relation between sin and disease are rooted in this Pharisaical spirit that judges others (Matt. 7.1), so relentlessly combated by Jesus Christ. They arise when we try to treat the problem as an objective one, speaking of direct causality, discussing the sins of the sick—the sins of other people. The Bible, as we said at the beginning of this book, compels us to cast aside our modern mentality, with its scientific notions of causality. For when it speaks to us of sin, it means our own sin. It urges us to repent of our own sins.

The reader may perhaps raise as an objection Christ's words to a man whom He had cured beside the Pool of Bethesda. Meeting him later, He said to him: 'Behold, thou art made whole: sin no more, lest a worse thing befall thee.' In my opinion, we are not necessarily to see in this injunction the assertion of a direct link between this man's sin and his infirmity. Jesus is simply using the occasion of the tangible blessing received by the man in his healing to urge him to mend his ways. And it is worth noting that it is only after having healed him that Jesus thus exhorts him.

Think of all those sick people who flocked to Jesus. He never repulsed them; He never told them they must first repent. His calls to repentance were directed to everybody, and especially to the healthy and the self-satisfied. But with the sick His first care was to afford consolation, relief and healing.

There is here a clear lead for the doctor. The patient who comes to him does not want a sermon or an exhortation to repentance, but help in his suffering. The doctor must never be like Job's friend, who said to him: 'Who ever perished, being innocent?' (Job 4.7). We can well understand Job's vehemence to his friends: 'Ye are all physicians of no value' (Job 13.4).

It would be wrong for us ever to speak to our patients of their sin, or even to suggest to ourselves that there might be a connection between this sin and their illness. 'Charity', says St. Paul, 'thinketh no evil' (I Cor. 13.5, A.V.). If they themselves broach the subject, it is another matter. We shall be coming back later to the therapeutic value of confession. On the other hand, when the patient is healed we can often show him that his recovery is a blessing granted by God, and turn his thoughts to the new responsibilities that this involves.

Life, Death, Disease and Healing

We see once more that double aspect of grace, manifesting itself at the same time in healing and in forgiveness, in a passage already quoted from St. James's Epistle: 'Is any among you sick? let him call for the elders of the church; and let them pray over him, anointing him with oil in the name of the Lord: and the prayer of faith shall save him that is sick, and the Lord shall raise him up; and if he have committed sins, it shall be forgiven him' (Jas. 5.14-15). Once again we have an assertion of the link between the two aspects of grace, without the remotest suggestion of a causal link between sins and disease.

I cannot quote that text without being reminded of a poor, neurotic woman, a prey to terrible nervous anxieties, who on the basis of this text appealed to the elders of the sect to which she adhered. They refused to administer the unction of oil which she asked for, on the ground that her nervous anxieties were the result of sin and not of disease, and that they called for repentance rather than intercession.

24

THE MEANING OF
AFFLICTION

THE BIBLE, while affirming the existence of a general connection between sin and affliction, never sees health and prosperity as a measure of holiness or faith. In the Biblical perspective all men are sinners: 'There is none righteous, no, not one' (Rom. 3.10). He who thinks himself less sinful than his neighbour is further than he from the Kingdom of God, as Jesus shows by His parable of the Pharisee and the Publican (Luke 18.9-14). 'The last shall be first, and the first last', He says (Matt. 20.16). Troubles come indifferently to the good and the wicked; God's gifts also are for all. 'All things come alike to all', says the Preacher, 'there is one event to the righteous and to the wicked' (Eccl. 9.2). And Jesus echoes him: 'Your Father . . . maketh his sun to rise on the evil and the good, and sendeth rain on the just and the unjust' (Matt. 5.45).

The spectacle of the 'prosperity of the wicked' (Ps. 73.3) exercises many of the Biblical writers. 'Righteous art thou, O Lord, when I plead with thee', cries Jeremiah, 'yet would I reason the cause with thee: wherefore doth the way of the wicked prosper? wherefore are all they at ease that deal very treacherously?' (Jer. 12.1). To Jeremiah both the Bible and modern analytical psychology reply that there is wickedness and treachery in the hearts of all men, and that none of them lives at ease.

But if we study the Bible honestly we shall come across numerous passages also where a specific affliction—an accident, an illness, a bereavement, a death—is represented as being the direct consequence of a fault, or even as a punishment for it. In Chapter 20 I quoted Professor Ellul's remark in reference to the 'thou shalt surely die' of Genesis. In his view this is not a threat of punishment, but a solemn warning given by God to man on the risks he would run if he tried to free himself from the wise laws of his Creator. That is, of course, true, generally speaking; but the theory cannot account for numerous other texts. Especially in the Old Testament God is often pictured as a 'jealous God' (Ex. 20.5), a God of wrath, who is provoked to anger by the sinner: '[Let no one] bless himself in his heart, saying, I shall have peace, though I walk in the stubbornness of mine heart, to destroy the moist with the dry: the Lord will not pardon him, but then the anger of the Lord and his jealousy shall smoke against that man, and all the curse that is written in this book shall lie upon him, and the Lord shall blot out his name from under heaven' (Deut. 29.19-20).

I could multiply such quotations: 'And God saw the earth, and, behold, it was corrupt. . . . And God said unto Noah, The end of all flesh is come before me; for the earth is filled with violence through them; and, behold, I will destroy them with the earth' (Gen. 6.12-13). Nevertheless, from the first pages of the Bible onwards, this terrible God allows Himself to be moved, as witness the magnificent account of Abraham's intercession on behalf of Sodom (Gen. 18). But there are other texts: 'But if ye will not hearken unto me, and will not do all these commandments . . . I will appoint terror over you, even consumption and fever' (Lev. 26.14 and 16). 'They have moved me to jealousy . . . for a fire is kindled in mine anger . . . I will heap mischiefs upon them' (Deut. 32.21-23). 'The Lord hath spoken: I have nourished and brought up children, and they have rebelled against me. . . . Why will ye be still stricken, that ye revolt more and more? The whole head is sick, and the whole heart faint. From the sole of the foot even unto the head there is no soundness in it; but wounds, and bruises, and festering sores: they have not been closed, neither bound up, neither mollified with oil' (Isa. 1.2, 5-6).

This wrathful and jealous God is indeed the God of many of our patients. It is incredible the predilection that neurotics and melancholics can have for these parts of the Bible. They seem to be incapable of finding in the Bible anything else at all. The doctor who has a real affection for such sufferers can scarcely refuse to discuss these disturbing problems on the grounds that they are the province of the theologian rather than the doctor.

Here, in addition, are some particular cases. There is the sister of Moses and Aaron, Miriam, smitten with leprosy for having been jealous of her sister-in-law (Num. 12.10). There is Gehazi, Elisha's servant, also smitten with leprosy as a punishment for his lies and his greed (II Kings 5.27). There is King Jehoram, smitten 'in his bowels with an incurable disease' (II Chron. 21.18) for having introduced the worship of false gods, and King Uzziah, smitten with leprosy for having allowed himself to be carried away by his pride and having profaned the temple (II Chron. 26.19). There is Eli the priest, to whom the young Samuel announces (I Sam. 3.18) his imminent death as a punishment for the theft of the offerings committed by his sons, 'and he restrained them not' (I Sam. 3.13). And there is King Ahaziah, to whom the prophet Elijah announces that he will die as a result of his accident, for having wished to consult Baal-zebub, the god of Ekron, in the matter (II Kings 1.4). I have already referred to the sickness and death of David's adulterine son.

In the New Testament, mention must be made of the suicide of Judas Iscariot (Matt. 27.5), the death of Ananias and Sapphira (Acts 5.1-11), and in particular a passage in St. Paul. He is stigmatizing the disorders that have crept into the Church in Corinth, where the celebration of the Lord's Supper has been turned into an orgy. He adds: 'For this cause many among you are weak and sickly, and not a few sleep' (I Cor. 11.30).

As I said in Chapter 2, we must see in all these texts the personal witness of men who have become aware of the greatness of God and of the enormity of sin. They are all illustrations of St. Paul's saying: 'Be not deceived; God is not mocked' (Gal. 6.7). It is in this sense that they speak to us, even if some of them do leave us somewhat uneasy.

But what the Bible does boldly assert is that God suffers in all these ills that His children bring down upon themselves by their disobedience: 'For he doth not afflict willingly, nor grieve the children of men' (Lam. 3.33). Twice the prophet Ezekiel repeats what God has charged him to say: 'As I live, saith the Lord God, I have no pleasure in the death of the wicked; but that the wicked turn from his way and live: turn ye, turn ye from your evil ways; for why will ye die, O house of Israel?' (Ezek. 18.32 and 33.11). And the whole Bible speaks of God's special love for the afflicted, a love which is particularly expressed by the Beatitudes of Christ (Matt. 5.1-12).

God does not will sickness and death. Evil does not come from Him, but from His enemy, Satan, from the devils. Throughout the Bible, healing and raising from the dead are represented as victories of God over His enemies. 'The last enemy that shall be abolished is death' (I Cor. 15.26). And since until then death is inevitable, God opens for us, by the Resurrection of Jesus Christ, the way to our own resurrection: 'As in Adam all die' (that is to say, like Adam, as a result of sin) 'so also in Christ shall all be made alive' (I Cor. 15.22).

According to the Bible, evil comes from Satan, who is sometimes called the devil (Matt. 4.1) (that is to say, he who divides), sometimes the serpent (Gen. 3.1), the tempter (Matt. 4.3), the evil one (Matt. 13.19), the murderer (John 8.44), he who has the power of death (Heb. 2.14), the power of darkness (Col. 1.13), the prince of the devils (Matt. 12.24), the enemy (Matt. 13.28), the father of lies (John 8.44). I may perhaps be permitted in this connection to digress on an interesting detail. The Bible condemns one of the most widespread of modern sins—the sin of statistics (I Chron. 21.1). It attributes to Satanic inspiration David's idea of numbering Israel, in order to feed his pride. The thing 'displeased God' (I Chron. 21.7). Of course, when we compile our statistics of deaths we shall not readily be accused of having a similar motive!

But if Satan is the great enemy of God, in the Bible he is also His servant. The opening of the Book of Job shows us him in the midst of the heavenly spirits assembled around God, and conversing with Him (Job 1.6-7). He has power only in the measure to which God grants it to him (Job 1.12, 2.6). So St. Paul sees in the 'messenger of Satan' who buffets him an instrument of God (II Cor. 12.7). Similarly, God calls Nebuchadnezzar, the great enemy of His people, 'my servant' (Jer. 43.10). It is in this sense that we may understand the strange passage in Isaiah to which Jesus Himself alludes, where God says to the prophet: 'Go . . . make the heart of this people fat, and make their ears heavy, and shut their eyes, lest they . . . understand with their heart, and turn again, and be healed' (Isa. 6.9-10).

What does it mean, if not that the trials of affliction are part of God's loving purpose for the redemption of the world? Such is without doubt the Biblical view. The purpose of God, for humanity in general as for the life of each of us, has none of the quality of an inexorable fate. Man enjoys real liberty. And yet, in the light of faith, we realize that even the ills that befall us, though not willed by God, even our own faults (which are disobedience of Him), contribute to the accomplishment of His purpose for us. Affliction, then, has other meanings besides that of punishment for sin. Christ's Passion is proof of this, 'who did no sin' (I Pet. 2.22). Jesus Himself explained to His disciples that His Passion was in accordance with God's purpose, 'that the Son of man must suffer many things, and be rejected of the elders, and the chief priests, and the scribes, and be killed, and after three days rise again' (Mark 8.31).

The plagues of Egypt were likewise in accordance with God's purpose (Ex. 7). An Egyptian, abandoned by an Amalekite because he was sick, serves as a guide to David, according to God's purpose (I Sam. 30.11-20). Again, the Apostle Paul, arrested and brought in chains to Rome, sees in these events God's purpose, that he may preach the Gospel there (Phil. 1.12-13). I could quote many other declarations by St. Paul, who always sees his afflictions as the road by which God Himself is leading him. 'Through many tribulations,' he says, 'we must enter into the kingdom of God' (Acts 14.22).

Here doctors have plenty of testimony to add. They see sick people alight with joy, and hear them speak of the wonderful fruits their afflictions have borne. 'I had forgotten God, when things were all right with me,' one of my patients said to me. The words were simple, but they came from the heart. She was echoing Pascal, in his prayer for the good use of disease: 'Thou didst give me health that I might serve Thee, and I put it all to worldly use. Now Thou sendest me sickness to correct me; let me not use it to avoid Thee through my impatience.'

The Apostle James writes: 'Count it all joy, my brethren, when ye fall into manifold temptations; knowing that the proof of your faith worketh patience' (Jas. 1.2-3). Have you never found yourself saying of a hard-hearted man, 'You can see that he has never suffered'? There is a certain inner evolution of the being that only affliction seems capable of producing.

Affliction is revealing, too. We are told of King Hezekiah that he 'prospered in all his works. Howbeit in the business of the ambassadors of the princes of Babylon, who sent unto him to inquire of the wonder that was done in the land, God left him, to try him, that He might know all that was in his heart' (II Chron. 32.30-1).

In this connection I am always reminded of those most realistic words of Christ: 'He that hath, to him shall be given: and he that hath not, from him shall be taken away even that which he hath' (Mark 4.25). We see believers whose faith is wonderfully increased in affliction, so that they can say with Job: 'The Lord gave, and the Lord hath taken away; blessed be the name of the Lord' (Job 1.21). And we see also embittered people whose bitterness only increases in affliction, whom it provokes to rebellion.

This seems to be the meaning of suffering, in the Bible, that it is a school of faith. This is the whole message of the Book of Job. 'Happy is the man whom God correcteth' (Job 5.17). And the Epistle to the Hebrews quotes Proverbs, 'Whom the Lord loveth he chasteneth' (Heb. 12.6; Prov. 3.12), and the Revelation takes up the saying: 'As many as I love, I reprove and chasten' (Rev. 3.19). We find it in St. Peter: 'You . . . are kept through faith. . . . Wherein ye greatly rejoice, though now for a little while, if need be, ye have been put to grief in manifold trials, that the proof of your faith, being more precious than gold that perisheth though it is proved by fire, might be found unto praise and glory and honour' (I Pet. 1.5-7). And again in St. Paul: 'We are pressed on every side, yet not straitened; perplexed, yet not unto despair; pursued, yet not forsaken; smitten down, yet not destroyed . . . for our light affliction, which is for the moment, worketh for us more and more exceedingly an eternal weight of glory; while we look not at the things which are seen, but at the things which are not seen' (II Cor. 4.8-9, 17-18).

There are many sick people who can exclaim with Hezekiah: 'Behold, it was for my peace that I had great bitterness' (Isa. 38.17).

Finally, our study of the meaning of affliction must bring us to the subject of death. Beyond and in spite of all we have said, death is clearly thought of in the Bible as a blessing from God.

Cast your mind back to the account of the Garden of Eden which we studied earlier. Side by side with the tree of the knowledge of good and evil there also grew, in the middle of the garden, 'the tree of life' (Gen. 2.9). We are told that God drove Adam from the Garden, after the Fall, in order to prevent him from touching also the tree of life: 'Lest he put forth his hand, and take also of the tree of life, and eat, and live for ever' (Gen. 3.22).

What is the meaning of this? We may take up again Professor Courvoisier's expression: as a result of his disobedience, man finds himself in a disordered world. By preventing him from living eternally, God preserves him from the worst fate of all, that of living for ever in this world of suffering and strife.

On board our ship, in the midst of the confusion and despair, what is there to do except to go on eternally repairing the breaches in her side? Of course it must be done. Of course suffering must be relieved, the sick healed, and life prolonged as far as possible. But it is only a temporary expedient: it merely prolongs the suffering; nothing would be worse than to live on board the ship for ever.

This is why we feel ourselves to be 'sojourners and pilgrims' on the earth (I Pet. 2.11); as Christians, we know that 'our citizenship is in heaven' (Phil. 3.20). These, let us note, are not the words of defeatists; they come from the pens of the Apostles Peter and Paul, the great fighters, the most energetic builders of the Church.

We are indeed promised eternal life, but in a restored world, freed from suffering. It is the central theme of our Lord's own teaching, and He returns to it constantly. It begins in this life, in so far as He lays hold upon us. But it will be fulfilled only beyond death.

Thus the image of the 'tree of life' reappears twice in the Bible in prophetic visions of the restored world; firstly in that of the prophet Ezekiel: 'And by the river upon the bank thereof, on this side and on that side, shall grow every tree for meat, whose leaf shall not wither, neither shall the fruit thereof fail: it shall bring forth new fruit every month . . . and the fruit thereof shall be for meat, and the leaf thereof for healing' (Ezek. 47.12). Secondly, in the Revelation: 'In the midst of the street thereof, and on this side of the river and on that was a tree of life, bearing twelve crops of fruit, yielding its fruit every month, and the leaves of the tree were for the healing of the nations' (Rev. 22.2, R.V. marg.).

So death has its use. It is a blessing from God. Through it we inherit eternal life in a world where 'neither shall there be mourning, nor crying, nor pain any more' (Rev. 21.4). Has not every doctor at some time seen death as a merciful blessing, after awful agony? Pilate, we are told, marvelled that Jesus was dead already (Mark 15.44).

25

THE MEANING OF HEALING

WE HAVE SEEN that disease and death are symbols of the disorder that has broken in upon the world as a result of sin. And, as I pointed out in Chapter 11, the word symbol is to be taken not simply as meaning a poetic image, but as a tangible sign bound up with the thing symbolized.

In the Bible, healing—every case of healing—is the symbol of redemptive grace and a manifestation of it. 'The healing of disease', writes Professor Courvoisier,[1] 'is always represented as God's victory, and more particularly as God's victory won in Jesus Christ over sin and death.' Professor Ellul says:[2] 'Healing is always both bodily and spiritual.' Healing and salvation are constantly associated: 'Heal me, O Lord, and I shall be healed; save me, and I shall be saved,' cries Jeremiah (Jer. 17.14). And the Psalmist sings: 'Bless the Lord, O my soul; and all that is within me, bless his holy name. Bless the Lord, O my soul, and forget not all his benefits: who forgiveth all thine iniquities; who healeth all thy diseases' (Ps. 103.1-3).

When Solomon, having completed the building of the Temple, is addressing to God his magnificent prayer of consecration, he asks God to succour them with His blessing in all their troubles —calamity, disease, and sin: 'If there be in the land famine, if there be pestilence, if there be blasting or mildew, locust, or caterpiller; if their enemy besiege them . . . whatsoever plague, whatsoever sickness there be; what prayer and supplication soever be made by any man, or by all thy people Israel, which shall know every man the plague of his own heart, and spread forth his hands toward this house: then hear thou in heaven thy dwelling place, and forgive' (I Kings 8.37-9).

Isaiah prophesies the end of both disease and wickedness: 'Then the eyes of the blind shall be opened, and the ears of the

[1] Op. cit.   [2] Op. cit.

deaf shall be unstopped. Then shall the lame man leap as an hart, and the tongue of the dumb shall sing. . . . No lion shall be there, nor shall any ravenous beast go up thereon, they shall not be found there; but the redeemed shall walk there' (Isa. 35.5, 6, 9).

When the disciples of John the Baptist are sent to ask Jesus if He is indeed the Christ, He replies, in evident allusion to these prophecies: 'Go your way and tell John the things which ye do hear and see: the blind receive their sight, and the lame walk, the lepers are cleansed, and the deaf hear, and the dead are raised up, and the poor have good tidings preached to them' (Matt. 11.4-5). Jesus performs His miracles of healing in order to relieve the suffering of those who appeal to Him, but He always performs them in order to show forth God's power as well: 'If I by the Spirit of God cast out devils, then is the kingdom of God come upon you.' 'The healing of the sick and the proclamation of the Gospel go . . . together':[1] Jesus sends His disciples 'to preach the kingdom of God, and to heal the sick' (Luke 9.2).

Similarly, during the early days of the Church, when the Apostles Peter and John have healed a man lame from birth, Peter takes the opportunity of preaching Christ to the crowd: 'By faith in his name hath his name made this man strong, whom ye behold and know: yea, the faith which is through him hath given him this perfect soundness in the presence of you all' (Acts 3.16).

The gift of healing played a large part in the primitive Church (I Cor. 12.9). Professor Weizsäcker[2] of Heidelberg has pointed out that it was regarded as being as valid a proof of apostolic authenticity as the 'sound doctrine' (Tit. 1.9). He holds that the Church has been guilty of intellectualist distortion in retaining the 'sound doctrine' while almost entirely neglecting the gift of healing. The Roman Church has nevertheless remained more faithful to it in attaching as it does considerable importance to the cures connected with Lourdes and with the lives of the saints. In recent years there have been several movements started within the Protestant Churches aimed at reinstating the gift of

---

[1] Jaques Courvoisier, *op. cit.*

[2] Viktor von Weizsäcker, 'Zur Frage der "christlichen" Medizin', in *Tutzinger Aerztebrief*, No. II, Tutzing am Starnberger See

healing in its rightful place. The well-known English pastor and psychoanalyst Leslie Weatherhead has written an interesting report[1] on his prayer-meetings for the healing of the sick, in which he records some remarkable results, even in cases where the sick people were unaware that they were being prayed for.

The questions raised for doctors by supernatural phenomena are dealt with in an interesting book[2] by Professor H. Urban of Innsbruck. He deals especially with the case of Thérèse Neumann.

But as we shall presently see, the Bible does not set supernatural over against natural healing. It does not even distinguish between them. It accepts all healing as God's gift. Paul says of the sickness of Epaphroditus, his 'brother and fellow-worker and fellow-soldier': 'For indeed he was sick nigh unto death: but God had mercy on him; and not on him only, but on me also, that I might not have sorrow upon sorrow' (Phil. 2.27). And Paul's (possibly natural) immunity from the effects of a viper's bite, recorded by his doctor friend, Luke, is taken as confirming his spiritual authority (Acts 28.5). In the familiar passage that speaks of the 'great cloud of witnesses' (Heb. 12.1) who were victorious through faith, the author of the Epistle to the Hebrews writes that they 'stopped the mouths of lions, quenched the power of fire, escaped the edge of the sword, from weakness were made strong' (Heb. 11.33-4). And then there are the words of our Lord Himself: 'Thy faith hath made thee whole'—that is to say, 'Thy healing is a manifestation of the faith that binds thee to God.'

Let us go back for a moment to the general meaning of healing which, following Professor Courvoisier, I described in Chapter 20. Healing is a sign of God's patience. He has compassion on man, intervening in the disordered state of Nature, in order to postpone the inevitable outcome. He wishes to protect man against disease (Ex. 23.25), to heal his wounds (Jer. 30.17), and to prolong his days (Prov. 3.2), to grant him a stay

[1] L. D. Weatherhead, *Healing through Prayer*, Spiritual Healing Booklets, No. 1, Epworth Press, London, 1946

[2] Hubert J. Urban, *'Übernatur' und Medizin*, Tyrolia-Verlag, Innsbrück-Vienna, 1946

of execution, a respite of debt, in which period our earthly life is situated.

The Bible abounds in accounts of healing. There is the healing of Abimelech (Gen. 20.17), that of the Israelites bitten by the serpents (Num. 21.6-9), that of Naaman, by Elisha (II Kings 5.1-19), and that of King Hezekiah, whose gratitude was but short-lived (II Chron. 32.24-5).

Then there are Christ's acts of healing. Many of them are reported collectively (Matt. 8.16; 12.15; 14.14; 14.36; 15.30-1). He healed lepers (Matt. 8.1-4; Luke 17.12-19); a woman suffering from a haemorrhage (Mark 5.25-34); a man with dropsy (Luke 14.1-6); an epileptic (Luke 9.37-43); two paralytics (Matt. 9.1-8; John 5.2-47); a crippled woman (Luke 13.11-13); a man with a withered hand (Matt. 12.10-13); the Apostle Peter's mother-in-law, when she had a fever (Luke 4.38-9); the daughter of the Canaanitish woman (Matt. 15.22-8); the centurion's servant (Luke 7.2-10); the nobleman's son (John 4.46-53); several blind people (Matt. 9.27, 20.30-4; Mark 10.46; John 9); a man who was both blind and dumb (Matt. 12.22); two men with mental disease (Mark 5.1-17; Luke 4.33-7); and, in the Garden of Gethsemane, He healed the High Priest's servant (Luke 22.50-1).

Finally, acts of healing by the Apostles. Here again many of them are reported collectively, as, for instance, the sick people who were brought out into the streets through which Peter was to pass (Acts 5.15). I have already mentioned the lame man cured by Peter and John (Acts 3.6-8). Aeneas the paralytic was healed by Peter at Lydda (Acts 9.32-5). A cripple from birth was healed by Paul at Lystra (Acts 14.8-10), and the father of Publius was cured of dysentery, also by Paul (Acts 28.8). These spring at once to the mind, but they do not exhaust the list.

We may add the chief cases of raising of the dead reported in the Bible, apart from our Lord's own Resurrection: that of the widow's son at Zarephath, by Elijah (I Kings 17.17-24); that of the Shunammite's son, by Elisha (II Kings 4.33-7); and that of the man who was cast into Elisha's sepulchre (II Kings 13.21). Jesus raised Lazarus (John 11.1-46), the daughter of Jairus (Matt. 9.18-26), and the only son of the widow of Nain (Luke 7.11-15). Lastly, there is the raising of Tabitha by St. Peter at Joppa (Acts 9.36-43).

It is of special interest to us doctors that this conjunction of spiritual, psychological, and physical effects in the divine action is not only doctrinal and theoretical, but has every appearance of being organic. We see in it the beneficent effects of the action of the Spirit upon the body, grace flooding into the whole person: 'The word of God is living, and active, and sharper than any two-edged sword, and piercing even to the dividing of soul and spirit, of both joints and marrow' (Heb. 4.12).

The fact is, as I showed in *Médecine de la personne*, that God's laws of life lay down those conditions that are most favourable to health. I shall not return to the subject here (Dr. Mentha has written an excellent little book on it[1]), except to quote three passages from Proverbs: 'My son, attend to my words, incline thine ear unto my sayings . . . for they are life unto those that find them, and health to all their flesh' (4.20, 22). 'Fear the Lord, and depart from evil: it shall be health to thy navel, and marrow to thy bones' (3.7-8). 'A merry heart is a good medicine: but a broken spirit drieth up the bones' (17.22).

At this point we must consider the physical and psychological effects of confession and absolution. I have at times been accused of over-emphasizing the importance of confession, as if the whole cure of souls were contained in it. I speak from my own experience as a doctor. Without neglecting the good effects of sympathy, exhortation, advice, and doctrinal teaching, I am convinced that, from the medical point of view, none of these can be compared in importance with confession.

Many functional disturbances, and, in the long run, many organic lesions as well, are the direct consequence of unresolved remorse. That this is so is shown by the fact of their abrupt disappearance or reduction after confession. One has seen, for instance, cases where long-standing insomnia, palpitations, headaches, disorder of the digestive organs or of the liver have disappeared overnight after the confession of a lie or of an illicit love-affair.

I could give very many examples, especially of patients who have come to visit me only once—often from a great distance—with the sole purpose of finding someone to whom they could

[1] Henri Mentha and a team of doctors, *Lois de la vie*, Librairie de l'Université, Geneva, 1951

confess a sin that has been weighing upon them for years. They are often bewildering cases, in which I have done nothing, practically said nothing; for which I have done no more than silently pray. Or perhaps I have by a few kindly questions helped them to make their confession more concrete. There remained nothing for me to do but to remind them in one way or another that 'if we confess our sins, he is faithful and righteous to forgive us our sins, and to cleanse us from all unrighteousness' (I John 1.9). In many cases I have had neither time nor opportunity to make a medical examination or to prescribe a medicine, and yet, a little while later, I have received a letter telling me that some morbid symptom that no medical treatment had been able to cure has disappeared, either at once or gradually.

There is no worse suffering than a guilty conscience, and certainly none more harmful. It has not only psychological effects —it acts as a clog upon vitality, and has far-reaching repercussions on general health. The tremendous joy brought by forgiveness plays a correspondingly important part in causing the medical effects that I refer to. In the healing by Jesus of the paralytic, which we studied in Chapter 23, we may think that the assurance that the sins were forgiven possibly created conditions favourable to the cure that followed it. But I do not think that this psychological explanation accounts for all the facts. It seems that there is a current of physical life which is re-established on contact with God.

The psychological effects are considerable, one of the most important of them being the removal of the feeling of inferiority which often accompanies unresolved remorse.

A woman came to consult me. Physically, she had suffered from various maladies, one after another, and psychologically she was the victim of a serious inferiority complex, resulting in hesitation, lack of mental concentration and memory, and unsociability. An orthodox course of psychological treatment would be a lengthy affair. We had discussed the possibility only for a moment or two when she burst out with the confession that she had come especially to unburden her conscience of a matter that had weighed on it for more than twenty years. Originally she had been more sinned against than sinning, but she had not had the courage either to confess or to make amends, and the memory of it still obsessed her. A year later I received a wonderful letter from her, describing the radical transformation that had taken place in her life, her health, her state of mind, and her social behaviour.

There must in our modern world be large numbers of men and women who are seeking a confessor, especially in Protestant countries, where concrete confession is neglected. Doctors are willingly trusted, even by those who are prejudiced against the Church. They may thus, from being mere confidants, become in a true sense confessors. The only condition, in my experience, is that they themselves should be in the habit of confessing, for no one becomes a confessor otherwise. This is a matter about which men's hearts have a sure intuition.

But for Roman Catholics as well the doctor can be an instrument whereby God brings them back to the Confessional.

I recently met, after a long interval, a medical student who once came to consult me. He was the victim of obsessions of a hypochondriac nature, and had already seen several other doctors. I might mention, in passing, that a succession of such cases recently has brought forcibly to my notice that there are numerous students in our medical faculties who are in need of psychiatric treatment. But they are able to pass through the whole of their course, coming into close contact with the most eminent specialists—even specialists in psychiatry—without the fact being noticed, so little interest is taken in them as persons. They are made to sit examinations to test the medical knowledge they have acquired; but psychological health is as important to the practice of medicine as medical knowledge.

This student found no difficulty in telling me about his life and about various sentimental affairs experienced in the last year or two. He had cultured literary tastes; words came easily to him. He was a Roman Catholic, and was in the habit of engaging in long arguments with his fellow students in defence of his faith. I listened with a keen interest to all he had to say. But later that evening I was worried. I was to see the young man for a further hour on the morrow. It seemed likely that we should have another animated and interesting discussion, but that no real progress would have been made by the time he left Geneva.

It happened that that same evening we received a visit from a couple of old acquaintances. Before they left they suggested to my wife and me that we should all say some prayers together. Naturally, in our silence before God, my thoughts turned to my medical student. It was borne in upon me that for our discussion to be fruitful I ought frankly to suggest to him as well that we should spend some time in silence waiting upon God. As soon as he arrived next day I told him what I had felt about our previous day's conversation, and he confessed that he had had the same feelings. After half an hour, during which we talked on all sorts of interesting subjects, yet without seeming to get anywhere, I made my suggestion.

We remained silent together. After a long time he broke the silence: 'The thing that worries me most is that I pretend to be the champion of the Catholic faith, while the fact is that since my first Communion I have never once gone back either to confession or Communion.' A moment later he added: 'I know one person who is going to be glad about this—my best friend. He told me he prayed every day that I would go back to confession. But as the years passed I became more and more afraid of taking the crucial step.'

We had twenty minutes left. And what a wonderful twenty minutes they were. We had left the abstractions, the dialectic, and the literary peaks behind us. He spent the time making his plans. His greatest preoccupation was to find an understanding confessor. I reminded him that St. François de Sales recommended that a confessor should be chosen from 'among a thousand and even ten thousand'. But I added that if we really want to find one, we always do. And when I saw him the other day, he told me of the wonderful welcome given him by the confessor he had chosen, who had taken him into his arms and kissed him like the father of the Prodigal Son.

That reminds me of a young woman, a devout Roman Catholic, who had felt she had a missionary duty to bring a young atheist to belief in God. But the opposite had happened: he had caused her to lose her faith, and had turned her away from her religious duties. She repeated to me all his intellectual objections, which she had made her own. But I have learned that it is not on that ground that souls are brought to God. I asked her if it would not be better for her to go back to her Church. She was thoughtful for a while, and then she said: 'But where can I find in this town a confessor who would understand?' 'God will be able to send one to meet you on your road,' I replied.

She went back to the town where she lived, and began to wander about the streets. A man came up to her. 'You seem to be looking for something. Can I help you?' 'I am,' she replied. 'I'm looking for a confessor.' 'I am he! I am the University Chaplain.' You can imagine her astonishment.

I could give many more examples. Dr. Josef Miller[1] has made an interesting study of the relation between Catholic confession and psychotherapy. Everything confirms what the Bible tells us, that confession and repentance are essential steps towards the health of the soul. 'Confess therefore your sins one to another, and pray one for another, that ye may be healed' (Jas. 5.16). The Bible gives us examples as well: 'I have sinned against heaven and in thy sight,' says the Prodigal Son in the parable (Luke 15.21). 'Lo, I have sinned, and I have done perversely,' cries King David (II Sam. 24.17). 'I was speaking, and praying, and confessing my sin and the sin of my people,' says the prophet Daniel (Dan. 9.20). 'Many also of them that had believed came, confessing, and declaring their deeds', we are told of the Church in Ephesus (Acts 19.18).

But the Bible supplies the answer also. It brings us the assurance of forgiveness, of which that great confessor, the Curé d'Ars, so strongly urged us never to be in doubt, from the story of the scapegoat (Lev. 16.21), in which Dr. Baruk[2] sees a fundamental psychological law, through the message of the prophets: 'I have blotted out, as a thick cloud, thy transgressions, and, as a cloud, thy sins' (Isa. 44.22); 'Though your sins be as scarlet, they shall be as white as snow' (Isa. 1.18); and the song of the Psalmist: 'Thou hast forgiven the iniquity of thy people, thou hast covered all their sin' (Ps. 85.2); and Jesus Christ Himself: 'But while he was yet afar off, his father saw him, and was moved with compassion, and ran, and fell on his neck, and kissed him' (Luke 15.20); to the cry of the Apostle: 'There is now therefore no condemnation to them that are in Christ' (Rom. 8.1).

[1] Josef Miller, S.J., *Katholische Beichte und Psychotherapie*, Tyrolia-Verlag, Innsbruck-Vienna, 1947
[2] *Op. cit.*

The doctor who has had this experience is called upon to witness to it when one of his patients makes a confession to him. Of course, he will not omit, in the case of a Roman Catholic, to send him back to his confessor, for the Roman Church does not recognize the validity of absolution except when pronounced by a priest clothed with the authority conferred by the Apostolic Succession. In this matter the Roman Catholic Church bases its belief on Christ's words to the Apostle Peter: 'I also say unto thee, that thou art Peter [Petros], and upon this rock [petra] I will build my church; and the gates of Hades shall not prevail against it. I will give unto thee the keys of the kingdom of heaven: and whatsoever thou shalt bind on earth shall be bound in heaven: and whatsoever thou shalt loose on earth shall be loosed in heaven' (Matt. 16.18-19).

26

THE MEANING OF
MEDICINE

WE HAVE SEEN that healing is an effect and a sign
of God's mercy, extending the term of our life. And
so, as Professor Courvoisier writes, the vocation of
medicine is 'a service to which those are called who through their
studies and the natural gifts with which the Creator has endowed
them . . . are specially fitted to tend the sick and to heal them.
Whether or not they are aware of it, whether or not they are
believers, this is from the Christian point of view fundamental,
that doctors are, by their profession, fellow workers with God. . . .
because their activity is itself a sign of God's patience. It is not His
will that men should be lost, but that they should all come to the
knowledge of His Son and of His salvation.'

This is the meaning of medicine for us. From this it derives its
greatness and its beauty. And it is also this that lays upon us such
a heavy load of responsibility. 'Sickness and healing are acts of
grace', writes Dr. Pouyanne.[1] 'The doctor is an instrument of
God's patience', writes Pastor Alain Perrot.[2] 'Medicine is a
dispensation of the grace of God, who in His goodness takes pity
on men and provides remedies for the evil consequences of their
sin', writes Dr. Schlemmer.[3] Calvin described medicine as a gift
from God.[4]

Thus every doctor, Christian or not, is a collaborator with God,

[1] *Op. cit.*
[2] *Notes sur la signification que la Révélation biblique donne à la mort*, unpublished
[3] André Schlemmer 'Médecine', in *La foi chrétienne et l'Université*, 'Foi et
Vie' Books, 139 Bd. Montparnasse, Paris
[4] Jean Calvin, *Contre la secte phantastique et furieuse des libertins qui se nomment
spirituels*, Op. VIII, p. 246, 1545

as Ambroise Paré said, in these well-known words: 'I tended
him. God healed him.' Some of my colleagues may be thinking
that, in repeating the affirmations of these theologians and doctors,
I am breaking down doors that are already open. I do not think
so. It is important to have a solid conviction as the basis of action,
and to be sure that it is in accordance with God's purpose. As I
showed earlier in this book, there are Christians who condemn
medicine in the name of their faith; and others who hesitate to
have recourse to it, as if one had to choose between God's help
and that of the doctor. I should like to give another charming
quotation from Ambroise Paré, in which he well expresses this
marriage of intellect and faith, technology and prayer: 'The
Marquis d'Auret had a bullet wound in the joint of his knee and
seemed at death's door. . . . Howbeit, to give him courage and a
good hope, I told him that I should soon set him on his feet. . . .
When I had seen him I went for a walk in a garden, where I
prayed God that He would grant me this grace, that the Marquis
be healed, and that He would bless our hands, and the physics
that were needed to fight so many complicated maladies. . . . I
discoursed in my mind on the means I must adopt to do this.'

To know ourselves to be called by God is to believe in our
vocation with as much conviction as St. Paul when he declares
himself to be 'separated unto the gospel of God' (Rom. 1.1).
And it is St. Paul who speaks of the 'diversities of ministrations'
(I Cor. 12.5). Our profession is a priestly ministry. I should like
to see the Church consecrating doctors just as it ordains its
ministers. This would be in conformity with the gospel. It is
this conviction which makes us give ourselves with our hearts
and minds and souls to our vocation—with our 'spiritual hearts',
as Dr. Stocker says,[1] quoting Pascal.

Even when the doctor believes he is obeying only his own
feelings, his compassion for human suffering, he is at that
moment the instrument of the divine compassion: Jesus 'saw a
great multitude, and he had compassion on them, and healed
their sick' (Matt. 14.14). Even the prophets who speak of God's
wrath tell us that He repents of His anger: 'For I will not contend
for ever, neither will I be always wroth. . . . For the iniquity of
his covetousness was I wroth and smote him, I hid my face and

[1] A. Stocker, *Amour et sensualité*, Œuvre de Saint-Augustin, St. Moritz, 1951

was wroth: and he went on frowardly in the way of his heart.
I have seen his ways, and will heal him: I will lead him also,
and restore comforts unto him and to his mourners. . . . I will
heal him' (Isa. 57.16-19).

And so the command rings out in our ears also: 'Heal the
sick' (Matt. 10.8). We all know the parable of the Last Judgement
(Matt. 25.31-46), in which Jesus takes as His criterion not this or
that sin, but the charity or the hardness of the heart. And he
adds: 'Inasmuch as ye did it unto one of these my brethren, even
these least, ye did it unto me' (Matt. 25.40). Similarly, the prophet
Ezekiel castigates the shepherds of Israel: 'Ye feed not the sheep.
The diseased have ye not strengthened, neither have ye healed
that which was sick, neither have ye bound up that which was
broken, neither have ye brought again that which was driven
away, neither have ye sought that which was lost' (Ezek. 34.3-4).

We have here the whole task of medicine, which is not only to
heal, but also to protect the weak: 'Ye shall not respect persons
in judgement; ye shall hear the small and the great alike; ye shall
not be afraid of the face of man' (Deut. 1.17). Again, medicine
is to bring back to obedience those who are neglecting the laws of
life: 'Thou, O son of man, I have set thee a watchman . . . therefore thou shalt hear the word at my mouth, and warn them from
me. . . . If thou dost not speak to warn the wicked man from his
way, that wicked man shall die in his iniquity; but his blood will
I require at thine hand' (Ezek. 33.7-8, A.V.).

The Bible makes no distinction between spiritual and temporal
action, between supernatural and natural healing. The Bible, of
course, preceded scientific medicine and so could make no
allusion to it; but it is not silent on the art of healing. I have
already quoted the passage in Ecclesiasticus (38.1), which speaks
of the physician as created by the Lord. Isaiah uses a cake of figs
to cure King Hezekiah (II Kings 20.7); our Lord applies clay to
the eyes of a blind man (John 9.6); music was used to calm King
Saul when he was suffering from mental disease (I Sam. 16.16).
Mention is made in the Bible of plants that are used for healing
(Ezek. 47.12), of the oil that is poured on sores (Isa. 1.6), of the
balm that is applied to wounds (Jer. 8.22), of wine used as a dis-
infectant (Luke 10.34), of appliances for containing fractures
(Ezek. 30.21), of therapeutic baths (John 5.2), and of the calling

in of physicians (Jer. 8.22). St. Paul concerned himself with Timothy's diet (I Tim. 5.23), and invited his companions to recruit their strength by taking some food on board their ship buffeted by the storm, adding: 'This is for your safety' (Acts 27.34). There are also many instructions regarding rest (Ex. 20.8), fasting (Acts 27.9), and on feeding (Deut. 14), many of which have a medical basis, as, for example, abstention from alcohol during pregnancy (Judg. 13.4).

Thus the doctor collaborates with God through his remedies, his techniques, and the skill of his hands, as well as through his intercession for his patients (Jas. 5.14), by his personal asceticism (Matt. 17.21, R.V. marg.), by the laying on of hands (Luke 4.40), and the unction of oil (Mark 6.13). 'And I find occasion here', writes Ambroise Paré, 'to praise God for that it hath pleased Him to call me to the work of medicine, which is commonly called surgery, the which may not be bought with gold or silver, but rather only by virtue and by long experience. Nevertheless it is stable in all countries, for the cause that the sacred laws of medicine are not subject to those of Kings and Princes, nor to the changing ordinance of time, as having their origin from God, 'whom I beseech that it please Him to bless this mine undertaking, that it be to His eternal glory.'

I should like further to call attention to the words of St. Paul —words which the doctor may make his own—on dedication, even to death, to the service of others: 'So then death worketh in us, but life in you' (II Cor. 4.12). But however great his knowledge and his dedication, the doctor does not always succeed in snatching his patient from death. I have already spoken several times of the 'death complex' in doctors. Those who have no other conscious source of vocation than their zeal for the relief of suffering find the death of their patients very hard to bear. They feel it to be a personal failure.

It is appropriate here to recall what I have said about death also being considered, in the Bible, as a blessing and as one of the elements in God's purpose. The doctor who in tending the sick is conscious of being God's instrument will be fired with an equal zeal, but will also accept more easily the death of a patient. Professor Courvoisier speaks of this at the close of his study. He writes: 'It is the same God who is there . . . whether the patient lives or dies. That is why success and failure are . . . elements of one and the same truth.'

We are shown David fasting and spending the night lying on the ground when his son is sick, then rising and eating when the child is dead (II Sam. 12.15-23). It is in this sense also, I think, that we are to understand the words of our Lord: 'Leave the dead to bury their own dead' (Matt. 8.22). The dead no longer belong to us. They are in God's peace. Let us turn towards the living. I should like to stress the psychological importance of the Biblical view on this point. We often see families in which a member who has passed on still holds a place that ought to be taken by the living. There are parents, for example, who have lost a child, and who make him the centre of all their thoughts. It can become a sort of religious cult, having serious consequences for the remaining children.

But it is clear that to accept death we must believe in resurrection. I am very sorry for those of my colleagues who do not. Their vocation must be a singularly disappointing one, always striving to prolong lives which will inevitably finish in an endless night of death.

There is no need to emphasize that on this subject the Bible is categorical. It assures us of God's final victory over death: 'He hath swallowed up death for ever' (Isa. 25.8); 'Death shall be no more' (Rev. 21.4); 'I will redeem them from death: O death, where are thy plagues? O grave, where is thy destruction?' (Hos. 13.14). The Bible promises us the resurrection of our whole person: 'He that raised up Christ Jesus from the dead shall quicken also your mortal bodies' (Rom. 8.11).

But the Bible does more than promise. It shows us the bodily Resurrection of Jesus Christ as the proof of its affirmations: 'Reach hither thy finger, and see my hands; and reach hither thy hand, and put it into my side: and be not faithless, but believing. Thomas answered and said unto him, My Lord and my God' (John 20.27-8).

St. Paul in his discussion with the Corinthians lays great stress on this proof of our resurrection by that of Christ: 'If there is no resurrection of the dead, neither hath Christ been raised. . . . If in this life only we have hoped in Christ, we are of all men most pitiable. But now hath Christ been raised from the dead, the

firstfruits of them that are asleep' (I Cor. 15.13, 19-20). To
Timothy he writes: 'Christ Jesus . . . abolished death, and brought
life and incorruption to light' (II Tim. 1.10).

There are many more texts that I could quote, but I will desist,
not wishing to desert the sphere of medicine for that of theology.
It is, however, impossible to over-emphasize the concrete practical
importance of this certainty to the doctor at the bedside of a
dying man. When science has done all it can do, when the doctor
is, as we said before, accompanying his patient to the gates of
death, this inner conviction of the certainty of resurrection is the
only true consolation that remains. Whether, at God's instance,
he voices it, or whether he communicates it only by his own silent
confidence, he is the messenger of hope: 'Neither death, nor life,
nor angels, nor principalities, nor things present, nor things to
come, nor powers, nor height, nor depth, nor any other creature,
shall be able to separate us from the love of God, which is in
Christ Jesus our Lord' (Rom. 8.38-9).

Reassurance and consolation. It has been said of medicine
that its duty is sometimes to heal, often to afford relief, and
always to bring consolation. This is exactly what the Bible tells
us that God does for suffering humanity. Sometimes God heals,
but not always. But He gives relief, He protects and sustains us
in times of affliction; and His consolation is unending. Here too
we may say that the doctor in his vocation works hand in hand
with God.

We spoke of healing in the preceding chapter. As for God's
protection when we are in affliction and even when we are in
rebellion, there is an interesting Biblical reference. When Cain
had murdered Abel (Gen. 4.3-15), God said to him: 'What hast
thou done? the voice of thy brother's blood crieth unto me from
the ground. And now cursed art thou . . . ; a fugitive and a
wanderer shalt thou be in the earth.' And yet when the terrified
Cain says to Him: 'Whosoever findeth me shall slay me,' the
Lord replies: 'Whosoever slayeth Cain, vengeance shall be taken
on him sevenfold. And the Lord appointed a sign for Cain, lest
any finding him should smite him.'

Thus, in the Biblical perspective, although affliction and disease
are bound up with sin, and although they are occasionally
represented as the expression of the wrath of God, man still

remains under His protection; even when man is cursed, he is never completely abandoned. A particular illustration of this truth is furnished by the forty years spent by the Israelites wandering in the desert. Rebellious as they were, and always earning God's maledictions, they nevertheless also enjoyed His succour in their afflictions: 'The Lord thy God . . . humbled thee, and suffered thee to hunger, and fed thee with manna' (Deut. 8.2-3). God tried them, but they remained His people and lived under His protection.

This is the experience of every believer. This is the meaning of God's answer to St. Paul when the Apostle asked for healing and was not granted it: 'My grace is sufficient for thee' (II Cor. 12.9). We find it in the mouth of the Psalmist: 'Yea, though I walk through the valley of the shadow of death, I will fear no evil; for thou art with me' (Ps. 23.4). This certainty of divine protection whatever happens fills the whole Bible: 'Fear not, for I have redeemed thee; I have called thee by thy name, thou art mine. When thou passest through the waters, I will be with thee; and through the rivers, they shall not overflow thee: when thou walkest through the fire, thou shalt not be burned; neither shall the flame kindle upon thee' (Isa. 43.1-2).

Nowhere does the Bible promise us exemption from sickness, suffering, or temptation. *Gratia non tollit naturam, sed perficit*, wrote St. Thomas Aquinas. The Bible is realistic, showing us human life as it is: 'Man is born unto trouble' (Job 5.7). In the Bible, man is neither taken out of the world nor removed from contact with evil, but at that very point he is assured of God's care. Jesus, making His great prayer to the Father for the disciples whom He was about to leave, said: 'I pray not that thou shouldest take them from the world, but that thou shouldest keep them from the evil one' (John 17.15). And He said to the Apostle Peter: 'Simon, Simon, behold, Satan asked to have you, that he might sift you as wheat: but I made supplication for thee, that thy faith fail not' (Luke 22.31-2). And so in St. John's memorable words we read of how Jesus re-established this same Peter, dejected after his great denial (John 21.15-19).

God comforts and consoles. St. Paul calls Him the 'God of all comfort; who comforteth us in all our affliction' (II Cor. 1.3-4); and in a magnificent phrase God speaks through Isaiah: 'As one whom his mother comforteth, so will I comfort you' (Isa. 66.13). There is another fine passage, in Ezekiel, which sets forth God's mercies: 'I myself will feed my sheep, and I will cause them to lie down, saith the Lord God. I will seek that which was lost, and bring again that which was driven away, and will bind up that which was broken, and will strengthen that which was sick' (34.15-16).

Our Lord said: 'Come unto me, all ye that labour and are heavy laden, and I will give you rest' (Matt. 11.28). God does not shelter us from pain. He bears it with us. He enters into it and takes it upon Himself. That is what the Cross of Christ means 'By whose stripes ye were healed' (I Pet. 2.24), of whom Isaiah spoke:

> *Surely he hath borne our griefs,*
> *And carried our sorrows:*
> *Yet we did esteem him stricken,*
> *Smitten of God and afflicted.*
> *But he was wounded for our transgressions,*
> *He was bruised for our iniquities:*
> *The chastisement of our peace was upon him;*
> *And with his stripes we are healed* (Isa. 53.4-5).

In that magnificent Chapter 40 of Isaiah the prophet speaks of the consolation of God (Isa. 40.1, 6, 7, 10, 17): 'Comfort ye, comfort ye, my people . . .'; and he speaks of the frailty of man: 'All flesh is as grass, and all the goodness thereof is as the flower of the field: the grass withereth, the flower fadeth'; and, finally, of the matchless majesty of God: 'Behold, your God! Behold, the Lord God will come as a mighty one. . . . All the nations are as nothing before him; they are counted to him less than nothing, and vanity.'

I have not tried to hide from the reader that, in spite of all the light thrown upon it by the Bible, the problem of pain, sickness, and death remains for us an impenetrable and overwhelming mystery; and that in fact here and there we can find in the Bible contradictory witness, answering to the varying experiences of believers before a problem that they do not understand. But the Bible itself does not claim to solve the problem. It lives it with us, and proclaims throughout the littleness of man and the greatness of God. It asserts that man cannot penetrate God's secrets, or contend with his Creator (Job 40.2).

It is at this point that the Bible reveals most profoundly the 'meaning' of suffering, disease, and death. They are to bring us to our knees before the absolute sovereignty of God. Such was Job's experience. The Bible may tell us in one place that God sends disease, and in another that He sends healing, here that death is His enemy, and there that death is His mercy; in so doing it is concerned to proclaim His almighty sovereignty: 'He hath torn, and he will heal us' (Hos. 6.1). 'I form the light, and create darkness; I make peace, and create evil' (Isa. 45.7). 'See now that I, even I, am he. . . . I kill, and I make alive; I have wounded, and I heal' (Deut. 32.39). 'Out of the mouth of the Most High cometh there not evil and good?' (Lam. 3.38).

The Bible proclaims the sovereign liberty of a God who keeps His secrets, and has no account to render to men, a God of glory. None understood this better than St. Paul: 'he hath mercy on whom he will, and whom he will he hardeneth' (Rom. 9.18). But a little further on St. Paul adds: 'God hath shut up all unto disobedience, that he might have mercy upon all. O the depth of the riches both of the wisdom and the knowledge of God! how unsearchable are his judgements, and his ways past tracing out! . . . For of him, and through him, and unto him, are all things. To him be the glory for ever' (Rom. 11.32-3, 36).

That other great believer, Moses, had already long before had the same experience (Ex. 33.12-23). Daunted by the difficulties of the task to which he had been called, he cried out to God to show him His glory. God answered him: 'I will be gracious to whom I will be gracious, and will show mercy on whom I will show mercy.' And He said: 'Thou canst not see my face: for man shall not see me and live. . . . Thou shalt stand upon the rock: and it shall come to pass, while my glory passeth by, that I will put thee in a cleft of the rock, and will cover thee with my hand until I have passed by: and I will take away my hand, and thou shalt see my back: but my face shall not be seen.'

We too can see God only from behind. We shall see Him face to face only in Heaven (I Cor. 13.12). Only in Heaven shall we understand. But we can see the traces of His glory. The impenetrable mysteries with which in medicine we are daily surrounded, the marvels that we discover in each body and each soul, the immensity of the insoluble problems set for us by every one of our patients—all these things give us some idea of how great must be the glory of God. We are faint and tremble at it, like Daniel at his vision (Dan. 8.27); but it is only the glory of God, and the reflections of it that we see, that give meaning to our life.

PART FOUR

THE CHOICE

27

LIFE OR DEATH

THE TIME has come for us to gather together the threads that we have picked up from many places in the Bible. We have said that life, health, and good are declared to be the fruit and the symbol of contact with God; death, disease, and sin the result of separation from Him. The Bible is full of the antagonism between the two. Many striking texts illustrate this: 'See, I have set before thee this day life and good, and death and evil . . . therefore choose life, that thou mayest live, thou and thy seed' (Deut. 30.15, 19).

The Bible sets a choice before man. Man lives in a world in which is being waged a gigantic battle between God and Satan, between life and death. Moment by moment, every thought, every feeling, every action implies a choice between the two contestants. In dedicating himself to the preservation of life, the doctor is putting himself at God's service. Here again, in his choice of methods, the doctor must always try to act in accordance with God's purpose. To conform to the will of God is to contribute to the healing of the world; to depart from it is to add to the train of evil which weighs upon us all.

Man is given a free choice. That is what makes him a person, responsible before God. It is often thought that the Bible is full of 'thou shalt'—authoritarian obligations laid upon him, making him less than adult. This is not at all the case. The Bible calls for man's own freely willed adherence. The 'thou shalt' of the Bible is preceded by an 'if' understood: 'If thou choosest life, then thou shalt . . .'

I do not mean by this remark to water down the demands made by the Bible; they are absolute: 'Be ye therefore perfect, even as your Father which is in heaven is perfect' (Matt. 5.48, A.V.). But their very character of absoluteness proceeds from the idea of choice; for to choose is to say 'Yes' or 'No'. There is no middle way. The least compromise in our lives separates us from God. We deal then, in the Bible as in medicine, with a matter of life and death.

This inescapable choice is found everywhere in the Bible: 'Whoso findeth me findeth life. . . . All they that hate me love death' (Prov. 8.35, 36). 'Thus saith the Lord', says Jeremiah, 'Behold, I set before you the way of life and the way of death' (Jer. 21.8). Jesus Christ takes up the theme: 'Wide is the gate, and broad is the way, that leadeth to destruction, and many be they that enter in thereby. For narrow is the gate, and straitened the way, that leadeth unto life, and few be they that find it' (Matt. 7.13-14). St. Peter, preaching the Church's first sermon, quotes Ps. 16: 'Thou wilt not leave my soul in Hades. . . . Thou madest known unto me the ways of life' (Acts 2.27, 28). I could quote many passages from St. Paul: 'For the mind of the flesh' (that is, of fallen man, separated from God) 'is death; but the mind of the spirit' (of man reconciled to God) 'is life and peace' (Rom. 8.6). Too numerous to list are all the passages identifying life and love, death and hate: 'Blessed is he that considereth the poor: . . . The Lord will preserve him and keep him alive' (Ps. 41.1, 2). 'We know that we have passed out of death into life, because we love the brethren. He that loveth not abideth in death' (I John 3.14).

We see how the whole Bible echoes the text from Deuteronomy which I quoted at the beginning of this chapter. Many other passages from the same book state the choice in unequivocal terms: 'Behold, I set before you this day a blessing and a curse; the blessing, if ye shall hearken unto the commandments of the Lord your God, which I command you this day: and the curse, if ye shall not hearken . . .' (Deut. 11.26-8). 'And it shall come to pass, because ye hearken to these judgements, and keep, and do them, that the Lord thy God shall keep with thee the covenant and the mercy which he sware unto thy fathers: and he will love thee, and bless thee, and multiply thee: he will also bless the fruit of thy body and the fruit of thy ground, thy corn and thy wine and thine oil, the increase of thy kine and the young of thy flock . . . there shall not be male or female barren among you. . . . And the Lord will take away from thee all sickness' (Deut. 7.12-15). Do you see how we have not left medicine, and still remain in the perspective of incarnation? The divine blessing bound up with obedience, and the divine curse, bound up with disobedience (see also the well-known text, Ex. 20.6), are not abstract states of mind. It is a question of fertility and protection against disease: 'If thou wilt diligently hearken to the voice of the Lord thy God, and wilt do that which is right in his eyes, and wilt give ear to his commandments, and keep all his statutes, I will put none of the diseases upon thee, which I have put upon the Egyptians; for I am the Lord that healeth thee' (Ex. 15.26). One more quotation, from Leviticus: 'Ye shall therefore keep my statutes and my judgements: which if a man do, he shall live in them' (18.5).

The man who will choose life must let himself be permeated through and through with the Word of God: 'These words, which I command thee this day, shall be upon thine heart: and thou shalt teach them diligently unto thy children, and shalt talk of them when thou sittest in thine house, and when thou walkest by the way, and when thou liest down, and when thou risest up. And thou shalt bind them for a sign upon thine hand, and they shall be for frontlets between thine eyes. And thou shalt write them upon the door posts of thy house, and upon thy gates' (Deut. 6.6-9).

What do my brother doctors think of this? I imagine that there are some among them who make plenty of mental reservations when they read these texts. Is it really true that this austere piety creates life? They, like me, will doubtless have seen individuals and families who put it strictly into practice, and remind us rather of death than life; mummified, crystallized families, lacking any spark of spontaneity or joy; Protestant families, in which the Bible is read morning and evening, grace is said both before and after meals, and church never missed on Sundays; Roman Catholic families which attend Mass daily, follow all the offices, observe all the fasts and recite all the prayers; sectarian families whose members, thinking to obey God, deprive themselves of dancing, non-religious reading, see no plays or films, and wear no pretty clothes. But they are families in which all this great effort, sincere and praiseworthy though it be, bears no living fruit; in which piety has become a crushing suffocating burden; families in which this great discipline has become so much a part of them that they cannot escape from it, and all liberty is dead; in which the discipline is imposed with particular rigour upon the children, who have chosen nothing, or for whom the choice has not been a free one, but rather suggested to them by their surroundings, and who are beset by a dull and gnawing anguish; families, in short, whose members believe that these rigid observances ensure their salvation, while remaining unaware of the presence of subtler and more elusive sins: jealousy, bitterness, tyranny, and pitiless judgement of those who do not practise the same austerity.

Some of my colleagues will doubtless have treated, like me, many of the neurotics that abound in such families as a result of constraint and repression being substituted for free will and self-control. For example, I remember a tragic case of maternal domination, a girl of twenty-five, on whom her mother used Biblical quotations as a slave-driver uses a whip, stifling every breath of real life in her with texts, such as: 'Children, obey your parents in the Lord: for this is right' (Eph. 6.1). I could give many more examples. The fact is that this whole problem of the meaning of life and death, which perhaps seems rather too theological to some of my readers, is actually a medical one: the question is whether religion quickens and exalts life or whether it stifles it.

The gospel is full of the struggle of Jesus with the Pharisees, who were scrupulous in their observance of God's commandments. He calls them 'whited sepulchres' (Matt. 23.27). They sincerely believed that they had chosen life, and imposed upon themselves the most detailed observance of the law. But they became the slaves of the letter of the law, fettered by formal piety. They symbolize death, with which Christ, the symbol of life, is in uncompromising conflict: 'It is the spirit that quickeneth,' He said to His disciples (John 6.63). And St. Paul, himself a Pharisee (Phil. 3.5), liberated by Jesus Christ, echoed Him: 'The letter killeth, but the spirit giveth life' (II Cor. 3.6).

One can well understand how Paul could confess: 'The commandment, which was unto life, this I found to be unto death' (Rom. 7.10). In this poignant paradox we see that St. Paul, too, had noticed that strange reversal of things of which we were speaking just now: that the law of God, instead of creating life, can in the end strangle it. Moreover, the Apostle speaks from his own experience; he had known the reversal and suffered its stifling effects. But in this text he is not only condemning the religious formalism that we have just been denouncing. The importance of his experience is much more far-reaching, as we shall see. That experience was the fundamental fact of his life. He makes it the theme of his Epistle to the Romans, an Epistle that has an important bearing on the understanding of the Biblical perspective.

It is worth noting that not once throughout His ministry did Jesus win over a Pharisee, not even Nicodemus, who was secretly sympathetic towards Him (John 3.1-21). After His death their hatred continued unabated, and they persecuted the infant Church. One of the leaders in these persecutions was Saul of Tarsus, the future St. Paul. He was a sincere man who had really tried to 'choose life', and had therefore chosen the sect that was most ardent and loyal in its observance of the law. But he was not a satisfied Pharisee. He was tortured by doubts: there went on within him a terrible conflict of a sort that might well arouse the interest of a doctor or a psychologist.

I am not watering down the miraculous nature of the event that took place on the Damascus Road. St. Paul lays great stress on it (Gal. 1.11-17): it ran counter to all his conscious thoughts and expectations that Jesus Christ's call should break in on him: 'Saul, Saul, why persecutest thou me?' (Acts 9.4). But it is to the troubled soul that God speaks, and the trouble of such souls is as it were an intuitive prologue to the drama that will be enacted when God intervenes. This is the witness of all those who have experienced conversion. They realize afterwards that for a long time before they had been troubled by the problem that was suddenly to become the point on which their conversion was to hang.

St. Paul too was to become aware, after his conversion, of the struggle that had been going on within him, and which goes on within every pious man who desires to choose life and to attain it through obedience to God, but who has not found Jesus Christ. He was able to describe it so clearly and so poignantly in the Epistle to the Romans because he had himself lived through it. He had wished to choose life, and to that end to observe the law; he felt, as we said just now, that a real choice excludes compromise. But who can serve God perfectly? 'To will is present with me', he wrote, 'but to do that which is good is not. For the good which I would I do not: but the evil which I would not, that I practise. . . . It is no more I that do it, but sin which dwelleth in me' (Rom. 7.18-20).

Saul of Tarsus faced despair: if, to obtain life, the law is to be observed without any compromise, then life must always escape our grasp. For no man since Adam has been free of those impulses towards disobedience which we feel to be woven into our nature. We can understand the Apostle's cry: 'Through one man sin entered into the world, and death through sin; and so death passed unto all men, for that all sinned' (Rom. 5.12).

One further point: 'Where there is no law, neither is there transgression' (Rom. 4.15). This echoes the words of Christ: 'If I had not come and spoken unto them they had not had sin' (John 15.22). I often think of those words of St. Paul in connection with patients who are the victims of unconscious impulses: where there is no consciousness, neither is there sin. But what the Apostle meant was that the law, which had been instituted in order to give life, aroused sin, and through sin, death.

St. Paul became aware of the conflict that had gone on within him when he was a pious Pharisee because he had found the solution to it: the grace and pardon of Jesus Christ. 'Where sin abounded, grace did abound more exceedingly' (Rom. 5.20). But the part to be played by the law is none the less necessary. Powerless to produce life, because incapable of being kept perfectly, the law brings men indirectly to life through the very conflict it arouses. By convincing men of their incapacity to obtain life however great and sincere their efforts, it drives them on to their knees. Grace, as Jesus often said, is for the humble and not for the self-satisfied (Luke 18.9-14). 'So that the law hath been our tutor to bring us unto Christ, that we might be justified by faith' (Gal. 3.24).

That is the crux of the matter. Either we expect to win life through our own efforts or else we recognize our incapacity and look only to grace. I have tried in this book to show the unity of the Bible. But on this point, which belongs to Christianity alone, and distinguishes it from Judaism, the New Testament has advanced decisively beyond the Old. The Old Testament is neither unimportant, nor has it been abolished by the New (Matt. 5.17); it is the tutor of which the Apostle speaks. But it leaves man in the torment of the dilemma of that choice which is at once necessary and impossible.

This decisive step between the Old and New Testaments broadened at the same time the promise of life and blessing. It freed it from the Jewish nationalism to which it had hitherto been linked. The original promise made to Abraham had not been so restricted: 'In thee shall all the families of the earth be blessed' (Gen. 12.3). But to fulfil that purpose, God had made a particular covenant with the people of Israel (Ex. 34.27), and they had come to believe that they had a permanent monopoly of His blessings.

In a vision (Acts 10), God showed Peter, thoroughly Jewish as he was, that the promise of life and blessing, henceforth linked with faith in Jesus Christ, was addressed also to the Gentiles. We know the difficulty Peter had in persuading his brethren in Jerusalem to accept the idea (Acts 11.2-3); yet they ended by saying: 'Then to the Gentiles hath God granted repentance unto life' (Acts 11.18). But when St. Paul was led by God to his great missionary work among non-Jewish peoples, demanding from them only that they should have faith in Jesus Christ, St. Peter fell back into his old nationalist prejudice. He complains against St. Paul, who resisted him openly (Gal. 2.11). There was a continual emancipation—first from the burden of the law, and then from social prejudices.

The importance of all this for psychotherapy is incalculable. All neurotics are weighed down by the burden of the very efforts they make to live, and by the feeling they have of the absolute demands that are made on them, plunging them into the despair that St. Paul describes. That is the tragedy of neurosis, that the efforts that ought to bring life only thrust it farther away. The very intensity with which the neurotic longs for life, for justice, for affection, for perfection, deprives him of those things, and of the courage to fight against his neurotic propensities. Preaching to him a morality that is after all only relative will bring but momentary relief; it is no true answer.

I am not, of course, saying here that there is no difference between the conflicts of neurosis and the moral conflict described by St. Paul. That would again be to identify sin with disease. The former are pathological, and occur only in certain persons as a result of circumstances of which they are the victims, while the latter is a part of human nature and is common to all men. The first are due to the unconscious misdirection of automatic impulses, whereas the second is the result of the conscious struggle against our natural desires. But in their ambivalence the two situations are analogous. There is an analogy too in the fact that the solution to each lies in liberation. The conscience of every sensitive person tells him that there is an absolute moral law. At the same time we must accept the reality of our own infidelity to it. This is the dilemma from which a way out must be found.

The way out is to be found in the personal encounter with Jesus Christ. The old dilemma remains; life is contact with God, and death is separation from Him. But for the cold, impersonal system of the law, seeking in vain to safeguard this contact through a vigilant but impossible obedience, the New Testament substitutes a living Person: Jesus Christ. In Him God comes to us instead of waiting for us to go to Him, as soon as we dare to acknowledge that we are incapable of doing so. God Himself is in Christ, restoring the contact.

The thing that daunts us in the view of the law given by the passages from Deuteronomy quoted above, is the anxiety behind it all. It is here that it is allied with neurosis. If life is conditional upon strict obedience to all God's commandments, it is bound to be poisoned and obsessed by the anxiety of seeing all this effort crumble at the least disobedience. The joy of liberty is killed, and man becomes a slave and not a person. But if life comes from above, and not from our fruitless efforts, if it flows from the contact re-established with God through Jesus Christ, freely given by God, forgiving and supplying our insufficiency, then that life will be sure, stable, peaceful, and free from anxiety.

This is the only answer to the problem of life and death. The whole of our inquiry into the meaning of medicine leads us to this: we are collaborators with God. He uses us to postpone death, prolonging life in order to procure that merciful respite of which we have spoken. The sole purpose of our labour is to give our patients a supreme opportunity of encountering

Jesus Christ, and of binding themselves ever more closely to Him through faith.

For in the last analysis all our activity is but a temporary expedient. We are but repairing breaches which are continually made again. Our cures, symbols of God's grace, do not remove, but only postpone the threat of death. Our victories over this sin or that do not deliver us from sin, which always reappears, nor do they preserve us from ultimate judgement. Until death we are obliged to live in this imperfect world, where tares are mixed with the wheat (Matt. 13.24-30), where victory alternates with defeat, where the forces of life and the forces of death contend together.

Our cures and our victories are, as St. Paul says (II Cor. 1.22), an earnest of grace and of Heaven. Only in Heaven shall we know the fullness of physical, psychological, and spiritual health. But already here on earth we are given by Christ the earnest of the Spirit, so that we may fix our hearts immovably on Him, finding in Him the source of eternal life: 'I am the resurrection, and the life: he that believeth on me, though he die, yet shall he live' (John 11.25).

28

THE HIGHEST GOOD

THIS PERSONAL LINK with Christ is what we call faith. Given such faith, the choice is always life. But we do not put our faith in a system that will procure life, but in a Person who incarnates it, Jesus Christ.

Jesus Christ is the incarnation of life; He is life. There are many texts to show that He Himself declared that He personifies it and gives it to all who believe in Him: 'I am the way, the truth, and the life: no one cometh unto the Father, but by me' (John 14.6; see also John 3.16; 6.35, 40, 47; 17.1-2, etc.). The disciples bear the same witness: 'Lord, to whom shall we go?' cries St. Peter. 'Thou hast the words of eternal life' (John 6.68; see also John 1.4; I John 5.12; Rom. 5.17; Phil. 1.21).

I want to stress the personal character of the bond between Jesus Christ and ourselves, as shown in the gospel. Life under the Old Covenant had its majesty and its awe, but it was distant and inaccessible. In the New Covenant, life personified in Jesus Christ comes close to us, concrete, accessible, and personal: 'The life was manifested, and we have seen, and bear witness. . . . That which we have seen and heard declare we unto you also, that ye also may have fellowship with us: yea, and our fellowship is with the Father, and with his Son, Jesus Christ: and these things we write, that our joy may be fulfilled' (I John 1.2-4).

Let me take an illustration from my own profession. Practising medicine in its technical aspect, we write prescriptions. They may be compared to the law of the Old Testament. In them we lay down what medicines the patient should take and the things he should do in order to get well. It is useful, but cold and impersonal. When we are aiming at practising a whole medicine, a medicine of the person, which will help the patient to live, and awaken the forces of life within him, the important thing is no longer the prescription, but the personal bond between him and ourselves. We ourselves are involved; we exercise a personal influence upon the patient. This bond may be compared to the personal contact of the Christian with Jesus Christ, which the New Testament gives us, and into which God enters, in Jesus Christ. This is what makes Christianity a religion of the person, and Christian theology a theology of the person.

But this is more than an illustration. In the intimate personal relationship that we have with Jesus Christ lies the secret of the relationship which is established also between our patient and ourselves. In the measure to which that relationship with Christ develops, our medicine becomes a medicine of the person. What is distinctive of Christianity is that personal attachment to Jesus Christ.

I remember well a certain occasion, when I had already become a Christian. I believed in Jesus Christ, and loved Him. I took an active part in His Church, and communicated with Him at His Holy Table. But it was God, and not Jesus Christ, who occupied the centre of my devotional life. Of course, He is the same God; but in Jesus we see God more intimately and more nearly, 'being made in the likeness of men' (Phil. 2.7). With Him there can be established a more familiar relationship than with the Father alone. There came a day when I was granted a vivid realization of this. I often used to visit, on Church business, an old pastor who never let me go without praying with me. He would address his prayers to Jesus, and I was struck one day by his extreme simplicity. It was as if he were continuing aloud an intimate conversation that he was always carrying on with Him.

When I got back home I talked it over with my wife, and together we asked God to give us also the close fellowship with Jesus that that old pastor had. Since then He has been the centre of my devotion and my travelling companion. He takes pleasure in what I do (cf. Eccl. 9.7), and concerns Himself with it. He is a friend with whom I can discuss everything that happens in my life. He shares my joy and my pain, my hopes and fears. He is there when a patient speaks to me from his heart, listening to him with me and better than I can. And when the patient has gone I can talk to Him about it.

This is no magical Utopia that I am describing. I know full well the dark places that remain, my own unfaithfulness in this

continual trysting with Jesus. That is our human nature. Jesus
Christ does not take our humanity from us; He comes down into
it, so that I can bring my difficulties and failures to Him, and that
also helps to maintain our fellowship.

That is the unshakable rock of the Christian life (Ps. 62.2).
We remain weak, uncertain, troubled, and disappointed in the
great task of service to mankind entrusted to us by Christ.
Often we set about it in the wrong way, and bungle it. Often we
think we see our way clearly, and rush wholeheartedly into the
half-seen task, only to come up against snags and disappointments.
Sometimes it is our friends, our brethren, even our Church, that
disappoints and hurts us. But Jesus Christ remains. He stands there
beside us, always ready to receive us, to forgive us, and to set us
on our feet again. As soon as we come once again into contact
with Him, life wells up in us: 'Whosoever drinketh of the water
that I shall give him shall never thirst; but the water that I
shall give him shall become in him a well of water springing
up unto eternal life' (John 4.14). This is the 'river of water of
life' of which Revelation speaks (22.1). In the great battle for
life waged by medicine, Jesus Christ appears as the living source
of life. In place of the attempt to repair the breaches and undo our
mistakes by moral effort alone, He substitutes a powerful stream,
'that what is mortal may be swallowed up of life' (II Cor. 5.4).

And it is this that gives to life its savour. Without it, whatever
happiness we find in life, and whatever we do in it, is just vanity
(Eccl. 2). This is the true source of power for life—but how often
we are in fact moved by 'bitter jealousy and faction' (Jas. 3.14).
The true life is the life that is guided by Him (Ps. 73.24), in which
every decision is discussed with Him in prayer: 'Woe to the
rebellious children, saith the Lord, that take counsel, but not of
me' (Isa. 30.1). That means taking counsel over everything which
concerns our personal, family, and professional life; over the
organization of our time, the use of our money, and over every
therapeutical operation, whether it be by the lancet or by the
spoken word.

But let us make no mistake here: Jesus Christ is an exacting
master. He gives life, but the price to be paid is the abandonment
of our own lives. 'If any man would come after me, let him deny
himself, and take up his cross daily, and follow me. For whosoever

would save his life shall lose it; but whosoever shall lose his life for my sake, the same shall save it' (Luke 9.23-4). A little farther on He is even more explicit: 'If any man cometh unto me, and hateth not his own father, and mother, and wife, and children, and brethren, and sisters, yea, and his own life also, he cannot be my disciple' (Luke 14.26). The Apostle John reports a similar utterance: 'He that loveth his life, loseth it; and he that hateth his life in this world shall keep it unto life eternal' (John 12.25).

This absolute demand made by Jesus Christ is not a tyrant's caprice. It is a profound truth, a law of life to which He also submitted in accepting the Cross. The reader will remember our study of the Temptation in the wilderness in Chapter 14. We said there that Jesus knew that His very life was at stake in the choice He made; the choice between magic, that is to say a service of God which aims at procuring glory and success, and faith, that is to say a service of God which, along the path of humility, leads 'even unto death, yea, the death of the cross' (Phil. 2.8). It is because He made that choice Himself that He can also demand it of us.

We can see now that with the choice of which we have been speaking in the preceding chapter there goes another, deeper and more costly. We are not faced only with the primitive choice between life and death, but with a choice between natural, physiological life, and supernatural, eternal life. Two further quotations will make clearer the nature of this dilemma: Jesus is speaking about a rich man whose farms had prospered, and who was making many plans as to what he would do with his wealth. 'But God said unto him, Thou foolish one, this night is thy soul required of thee; and the things which thou hast prepared, whose shall they be? So is he that layeth up treasure for himself, and is not rich toward God' (Luke 12.20-1). Another of the sayings of Jesus throws still more light on the meaning of this parable: 'For what shall a man be profited, if he shall gain the whole world, and forfeit his own soul?' (Matt. 16.26, R.V. marg.).

'The whole world' includes life and health. To win eternal life we must care about it more than this life; we must hold to Jesus Christ more than to this life; we must not cling to this life. That is a truth which is not only theological. It has considerable practical importance for medicine.

In the new perspective that Jesus Christ opens out before us, life and health are not the greatest blessing, any more than wealth, happiness, or pleasure. The substance of many of the texts I have quoted up to now has been to show that obedience to God will bring happiness, health, and prosperity. Now Jesus tells us that we must be ready to renounce all those things for His sake. But the two statements are not opposed. There is no contradiction, as Christ has shown: 'Seek ye first his kingdom and his righteousness; and all these things shall be added unto you' (Matt. 6.33).

Nevertheless, a new step forward has been taken here; a new element has been introduced, and it has its importance in medicine. For many doctors life is really the highest good. For them the struggle to preserve life is an end in itself, the sole purpose of medicine. They profess a kind of metaphysic of life, which soon becomes a religion in which life is the god they worship.

If we accept the Biblical view we strive equally hard to preserve life, since God calls us to do so. But it is no longer the final goal. We cannot consider ourselves as doctors without considering that we are also believers. I have tried to show throughout this book that we cannot ignore medicine on the pretext that salvation is more important than health. And, further, so far from being less doctors because we are no longer concerned only with health, the truth is that we are more fully doctors. This was made clear in the story I told at the beginning of this book about my sick colleague. He came to see me because he was worried about his health. But there was something else that was worrying him —the inner conflict of conscience which was hampering his life and health, as well as his spiritual destiny.

Naturally, I was glad that through setting his life in order he found his health improved; but I confess that I was even happier that he came back to Jesus Christ and to his Church, for that is the most important thing, more important than life and health themselves. I trust that the reader will not think that I am here setting medical against spiritual well-being. I have, on the contrary, sought to show in this book how closely they go together; that our medical activity has its place in God's purpose; and that personal fellowship with Jesus Christ can have an effective medical value.

But in spite of all our efforts, old age, disease, and death will have to be faced. Then the man for whom life and health are the highest good will turn in despair to the doctor, expecting from him more than as a doctor he can give. But though the doctor can no longer give him youth, healing, and life, he can help him to find a new scale of values. He will necessarily find himself called upon to witness to his faith, if he is really trying to practise a whole medicine. His first duty is, of course, to give medical attention; sometimes to heal, often to afford relief, and always to console. But since life, health, healing, relief, and consolation are not the highest good, he is called on to add his witness in one way or another, however discreetly and soberly, to his technical action. There are many doctors who would be quite ready to give their lives for their faith in times of persecution, and yet in everyday life they show the greatest timidity in telling their patients what Jesus Christ is for them. But we all know this timidity, even those of us who are most committed. We are quick to call it modesty—a flattering term. Ought it not sometimes to be called cowardice? Ought we not more often to point out to our patients that the health to which we are trying to restore them is only a means to an end, and that the highest good is fellowship with Jesus Christ?

Let me give a simple, concrete example that will show the reader the medical importance of this new perspective. The other day there came to my 'free consultation' an old lady whom I am always glad to see. Punctilious, shrewd, and sensitive, she has a strong and lively faith. She has lived a life of service. She longs with all her heart to be guided in all things by Jesus Christ, and to that end she asks for my help. But her strength is failing with advancing years. That is a thing she must accept, and she does accept it. But how far is she to go before drawing the line? She told me of a distracted young woman who had come to her for help. She had had a long and serious talk with her, but it had left her very tired. Had it been too much for her? Ought she to give up undertaking such interviews in the interest of her own health?

I told her what I have said here, that health is not the highest good. There will perhaps be some among my brother doctors who object to that, and who will accuse me of betraying medicine. But then if our only goal is the preservation of health, irrespective of the use our patients make of their lives, what meaning is there in it? 'Health', writes Professor Siebeck,[1] 'is not an end in itself: it is significant only in so far as life itself is significant.'

There is obviously no simple answer to this problem of the end and the means. A proper balance must, of course, be preserved. I should indeed be betraying the vocation to which Christ has called me if I suggested to my patients that they need not bother about their health so long as they were living useful lives. But there is also the danger that the doctor for whom health is the highest good may be doing harm to his patients. Without actually saying it in so many words, but by the exaggerated concern he shows, he suggests to them, to a greater or lesser extent, that illness is the greatest of all calamities. In such cases a great fuss is made even of the most trifling indispositions, and conserving one's strength and strict observance of a diet become real obsessions.

This brings me to another aspect of the problem, more important still. I refer to the attitude of the patient towards illness and death. If we overestimate the value of life and health, we encourage rebellion against sickness and death. In order for affliction to be borne patiently, it is clear that a certain spirit of detachment, from oneself and from worry about one's health, as well as from life itself, is necessary. Only a person who has come to know that the highest good is fellowship with Jesus Christ can aspire to such detachment. There is, of course, nothing in the Bible that authorizes the Christian to desire or to seek suffering. But when it comes, it brings him nearer to Christ, who also suffered.

This I have found to be the only effective source of calm and serene acceptance of unmerited suffering. The fact is frequently witnessed to in the Bible: 'For what glory is it', writes St. Peter, 'if, when ye sin and are buffeted for it, ye shall take it patiently? But if, when ye do well, and suffer for it, ye shall take it patiently, this is acceptable with God. For hereunto were ye called: because Christ also suffered for you, leaving you an example, that ye should follow his steps' (I Pet. 2.20-1). St. Paul writes: 'In everything commending ourselves, as ministers of God, in much patience, in afflictions, in necessities, in distresses, in stripes, in

[1] *Op. cit.*

imprisonments, in tumults, in labours, in watchings, in fastings' (II Cor. 6.4-5). And again: 'Be patient in tribulation' (Rom. 12.12).

But fellowship with Christ does not only make us able to accept; it is also a source of healing energy. Remember the question put by Jesus to the sick man by the Pool of Bethesda: 'Wouldest thou be made whole?' (John 5.6). Some of my readers no doubt will consider such a question superfluous, but my brother doctors will not agree with them, knowing as they do how many sick people come to see them lacking any real will to be made whole again. Look at the reply this man made to our Lord's question: 'Sir, I have no man . . . to put me into the pool.' He laments his misfortune; he complains of lack of help; he expects help only from others; he does not give a thought to the healing energy within himself. Jesus awakens it with His question. Similarly, by His question to the blind men, 'Believe ye that I am able to do this?' (Matt. 9.28), He awakens their faith and the energy that comes with it.

It is above all when faced with death that men find that personal fellowship with Jesus Christ is their only true succour. As I have said, in the Biblical perspective death remains a thing to be feared. A vague, impersonal religion which believes only in an aloof Creator does not bring much comfort to a dying man. Only he whose heart is stayed fast upon the Resurrected Christ can echo the words of St. Paul: 'All things are yours; whether . . . the world, or life, or death, or things present, or things to come' (I Cor. 3.22). 'With all boldness, as always, so now also Christ shall be magnified in my body, whether by life, or by death. For me to live is Christ, and to die is gain. But if to live in the flesh, if this is the fruit of my work, then what I shall choose I wot not. But I am in a strait betwixt the two, having the desire to depart and be with Christ; for it is very far better: yet to abide in the flesh is more needful for your sake' (Phil. 1.20-4). Shortly before his arrest he says to his old friends, the elders of the Church in Ephesus: 'I hold not my life of any account, as dear unto myself, so that I may accomplish my course, and the ministry which I received from the Lord Jesus' (Acts 20.24). He is echoing his Master's words: 'I am the good shepherd. . . . I lay down my life for the sheep' (John 10.14, 15).

The Choice

Of all the feelings in the hearts of men, fear of death is the most tenacious. I do not think that anything can completely eradicate it. But the martyrs have proved that a profound personal fellowship with Jesus Christ enables men to confront it victoriously. 'Be not afraid of them which kill the body,' said Jesus, 'but are not able to kill the soul' (Matt. 10.28).

Jesus Christ knew suffering, death, and Resurrection. The highest good is our fellowship with Him, even more precious in sickness than in health. Death will not break it. It will come into its fullness after our own resurrection. In the dark tragedy amidst which we live our daily lives together, both patients and doctors, the Biblical view of life is the only true light, because it comes to us from God. Speaking of the Scriptures, the Apostle Peter writes (II Pet. 1.21): 'Men spake from God, being moved by the Holy Ghost.'

INDEXES

INDEX OF SUBJECTS

ABORTION, 126, 158
Adultery, 62, 65, 67, 69
Astrology, 102
Atom bomb, 27, 169

BIBLE, REALISM OF, 19, 72, 134, 159, 173, 202, 221
Bible-study, 16, ch. 2, 29, 33
Birth-control, 155, 158-60
Body, attitude to the, 59-61, 65
Bossey, 20-2

CELIBACY, 160-1
Chance, 14, 33, 36, 57, 83, 87, 143
Chastity, 159-60
Chronic illness, 178-9
Church, 64, 116, 119, 166
Confession, medical effects of, 209-14
Conversion, 65, 231
    of St. Paul, 83, 230-2
Creation, the, 42, 58-9, 64, 139, 166
Cross of Christ, 18, 20, 59, 114, 116, 163, 182, 190-1, 201, 222, 239

DEATH, 16, 17, 61, 142, 143, 148, ch. 20, ch. 21, 178-9, 186-9, 202-4, 218-20, 223, ch. 27, 239, 241-4
Devils, possession by, 105
Diagnosis, ch. 1
Disease, meaning of, 12, 14-16, 57, 98, 104, 106, ch. 21, 181-4, 186-7, 223
Doctor-patient relationship, 27-8, 50, 170-4, 184, 185-6, 236-7
Dreams, ch. 9
    Freud's, Jung's and Maeder's interpretations of, 71-4
    in the Bible, 70, 73

EVIL, 61, 105, 167, 200, 221

FALL, THE, 27, 42, 68, 79, 166-9, 203
Forgiveness, 69, 192-3, 238
Freud, Dr. S., 14, 63, 71-4, 89, 106, 182, 192

GLUTTONY, 60

HEALING, GIFT OF, 152, 206
    meaning of, 165-6, ch. 25
History, 33, 56, ch. 10
Holy Spirit, 73, 128, 141, 235, 244
Homoeopathy, 51-3

INCARNATION, 24, 42, 58-9, 129, 140, 153, 234, 236, 238

JESUS CHRIST, FELLOWSHIP WITH, 133, 161, 237-44
Jung, Dr. C. G., 14, 63, 71-4, 89, 101, 128, 131, 152, 164

LEUCOTOMY, 49
Libido, 63, 147
Life, 78, ch. 17, ch. 18, 165, 174, 177, 224, ch. 27, 236, 238-42
    eternal, 147, 148, 161, 173, 203, 235, 239
Longevity, 154-5
Love, carnal and spiritual, 58, 63, 66-8

MAEDER, DR. A., 71, 107, 150, 175, 192
Magic, combated by Bible, 107-10
    good, 107, 131
Marriage, 24, 30-2, 41, 64-7, 69, 159-61, 191
Masturbation, 60, 67, 104-5, 156

247

Medicine, meaning of, 22, 135, ch. 26
  234, 240
  specialization in, 21
Meditation, 100, 133
Miracles of healing, 98-9, 152-3, 193,
  206, 208
Monogamy, 65
Mosaic law, 29-30, 77, 108, 148, 156,
  236
Mother complex, 32, 72, 111

NATURE, 38, ch. 5, ch. 6, 76, 79, 81
  Biblical view of, ch. 7, 70, 166
Naturism, 51-3, 166
Neurosis, 14, 65-6, 92-7, 107, 157,
  180, 196, 198, 230, 233-4

PERSON, 41, 60, 68, 71, 75, 122-7
  ch. 16, 189, 236
Person, patient as, 45, 49-51, 78, 122,
  124-7, 170-3
Personality, 49-50
Pharisees, 62, 195, 230-2
Plato, 58-9
Prayer, 16, 133, 165, 177, 185, 190,
  195, 237
Primitive mentality, ch. 11, 96-8, 104,
  122, 129-30
Psychology of the Bible, 30, 32, 71-3,
  219

RATIONALISM, 74, ch. 12, 107, 110,
  119-20
Redemption, 42, 201, 205

Renaissance, 130
Repentance, 116, 194-6
Repression of instinct, 62, 65
Resurrection, 23, 59, 79, 101, 219,
  243-4

SATAN, 19, 113, 167, 200, 221, 227
Science and faith, ch. 3
  foundation of, 26
  salvation by, ch. 12, 107, 113
Scientific remedies, 44-6, ch. 6, 57,
  121
  view of the world, 14, 34-5, 39,
  43-4, 95, 97, 130
Sex, 29, 30, ch. 8, 70, 73-4, 159, 169
Sexual intercourse, 64-7, 147, 159-60
Sin, 35, 62-3, 69, 144, 168, ch. 23, 197,
  199-201, 220, 230
Soul, 21-2, 42, 59, 64, 68-9, 71, 73,
  74-5, 169, 192
Sterility, 155-6, 160-1
Suffering, problem of, 167, ch. 24, 223

TEMPTATION, 19, 221
  magical, ch. 14, 133
  of Christ, 113-15, 133, 186, 239

VISIONS, 71
Vital force, ch. 17, ch. 18 .
Vocation, 22, 24, 74, 123, 189, 216,
  218

WRATH OF GOD, 198, 216, 220

INDEX OF CASES
QUOTED

ANAEMIA, 149–50, 181
Angina, 152
Arrhythmia, 182

CARCINOMA, 46, 99
Cardiac failure, 44–5, 163
Child-birth, 47
Colour-blindness, 34–5
Cut hand, 183

DIABETES, 121

EPILEPSY, 151

FRACTURED LEG, 57
Furunculosis, 182

HERNIA, 25
Hyperchlorhydria, 151
Hypochondria, 211

INFERIORITY COMPLEX, 146, 210
Inhibitions, 140

MENTAL DISEASE, 92–3

NERVOUS DISORDERS, 25, 74, 93–4, 152, 196
Neurosis, *see* Index of Subjects

OBSESSIONS, 80, 93, 146, 147, 157, 164–5, 180, 192
Old age, 241

PARENTAL DOMINATION, 31–2, 111, 230
Penicillin resistance, 44
Pregnancy, 126

ROAD ACCIDENT, 183, 189

SEPTICAEMIA, 12
Sexual maladjustment, 66

TUBERCULAR MENINGITIS, 176
Tuberculosis, 106, 149, 150–1

INDEX OF BIBLICAL
REFERENCES

Gen.
1.1…42
1.2…58, 139
1.3, 4…139
1.26…123
1.27…41, 64, 140
1.28…26, 155, 159
1.31…166
2.7…22, 141
2.9…27, 203
2.15-16…166
2.17…167, 197
2.18-24…64
2.19…26, 126
2.24…30, 67, 159
3.1…200
3.1-19…27
3.4-5…167
3.9-10…123
3.9-13…169
3.17-19…167
3.22…203
4.1…65
4.3-15…220
4.10…147
5.5, 12…154
6.6…167
6.12-13…198
7.4…54
8.1…56
9.6…147
9.13…56
11.26…154
12.1…81, 123
12.1-3…157
12.3…233
16.4…155
17.4…76

17.5…126
17.17…155
18…198
19.31-4…155
20.3…70, 156
20.14-15…156
20.17…208
20.17-18…156
22.1-18…37
24.14, 21…82
25.7…154
28.12…70
29.15-35…72
29.17…69
30.1-24…72
31.10, 24…70
32.28…126
35.19…73
35.28…154
37.5, 9…70
38.9, 26…156
40.5-22…70
41.1-7…70
47.7…81
47.28…154
48, 49…187
50.22…154

Ex.
1.15-17…147
3.4…22, 186
6.11…81
7…201
7.11…57
14.21…54
15.26…229
18.17-18…135
18.24…134

20.2…78
20.3-5…111
20.5…198
20.6…229
20.7…114
20.8…218
20.13…147, 158, 177
21.19…148
23.25…207
33.12-23…223
33.17…123
34.17…76
34.27…233

Lev.
11, 13, 15…29
16.21…213
18.5…229
19.26, 28, 31…108
20.6, 27…108
26.14, 16…198

Num.
12.10…57, 199
21.6-9…208

Deut.
1.17…217
4.36…56
6.6-9…229
6.16…113
6.20-5…77
7.12-15…228
8.2-3…221
11.26-7…157
11.26-8…228
13.1-3…113

Indexes

Deut.—cont.
14...218
18.9-12...108
24.6...148
25.5-6...155
28.15, 27-8...19
28.58, 66...145
29.19-20...198
30.15, 19...227
31.14, 16...188
32.3-4...189
32.21-3...198
32.39...223
32.50-1...188
34.7...188
34.10...65, 188

Josh.
3.16...55
24.29...154

Judg.
6.11-40...37
6.14...81
7.2...77
7.13...70
9.15-23...56
13.4...218
14.4...82

Ruth
1.8, 16...31
4.1-13...69

I Sam.
2.34...58
3.13, 18...199
4.2-18...115
5.6...116
6.10-16...116
7.3-11...116
16.16...217
26.8, 12...82
28.7...109
30.11-20...201

II Sam.
11.11...181
11.15...182
12.1-14...181
12.15-23...219
12.18...58
13.1-22...19
24.17...213

I Kings
3.5-9...70
4.24-5...77
8.37-9...205
17.17-24...208
18.21...33
19.4, 12...55

II Kings
1.4...199
4.33-7...208
5.1-19...208
5.27...57, 199
13.3...77
13.14...187
13.21...208
20.1-11...187
20.7...29, 217

I Chron.
21.1, 7...200
29.28...154

II Chron.
16.12-13...109
21.18...57, 199
26.19...199
32.24-5...208
32.30-1...202
33.2, 6...109

Job
1.6-7, 12...200
1.21...202
2.6...200
2.7...55
3.11-13...20
4.7...195

5.6-7...173
5.7...221
5.17...202
10.12...141
13.4...195
18.14...163
40.2...223
40.4...56
42.16...154

Ps.
19.1-4...38
19.7...166
23.4...221
27.1, 6...161
41.1, 2...228
62.2...238
73.3...197
73.16...82
73.24...82, 238
85.2...213
91.11-12...113
91.16...154
103.1-3...205
104.10-15...60
139.14...58
145.16...140

Prov.
3.2...207
3.7-8...209
3.12...202
4.10...154
4.20, 22...152, 209
8.35, 36...228
17.22...209

Eccl.
5.7...75
9.2...197
9.7...237
12.7...59

S. of Sol.
3.1...58
4.1...58
7.13...72

Isa.
1.2, 5–6...198
1.6...217
1.18...213
2.22...28
6.9...81
6.9–10...200
8.19...109
25.8...219
30.1...238
35.5, 6, 9...206
38.16, 19...161
38.17...202
40.1, 6, 7, 10, 17...222
41.10...20
43.1–2...221
44.22...213
45.3...123
45.7...223
45.15...83, 134
49.1...22
53.4...184
53.4–5...222
55.11...55
57.16–19...216
61.1...135
64.1...134
66.13...222

Jer.
8.22...217, 218
12.1...197
17.5...27
17.14...205
18.1–10...81
20.9...186
21.8...228
30.17...207
37, 38, 40, 43...81
43.10...200
43.10, 11...77

Lam.
3.33...199
3.38...223

Ezek.
16.6–43...58

18.32...199
30.21...217
33.7–8...217
33.11...199
34.3–4...217
34.15–16...222
37.1–10...70
37.9...141
47.12...203, 217

Dan.
2.21...77
2.31–5...70
4.10–17...70
8.27...224
9.20...213

Hos.
6.1...223
13.14...219

Ecclus.
38.1...217
38.1–2, 9, 12–14...28

Matt.
1.20...70
1.25...65
2.9...56
2.13...70
4.1, 3...200
4.1–11...113
5.1–12...200
5.17...233
5.21–4...147
5.28...69
5.45...197
5.48...135, 227
6.13...19
6.26...56
6.33–30, 240
7.1...195
7.13–14...228
8.1–4, 16...208
8.22...219
8.23...26
8.28–34...152

9.1–8...208
9.10...63
9.12...175
9.18–26, 27...208
9.28...243
9.33...105
10.8...217
10.28...244
10.30...56
11.4–5...115, 206
11.19...26
11.28...222
12.10–13, 15, 22...208
12.24...200
12.38–9...115
13.14–16...134
13.19...200
13.24–30...235
13.28...200
13.29...56
13.55...26
14.14...208, 216
14.36...208
15.22–8, 30–1...208
16.2–3...56, 76
16.17...68
16.17–18...126
16.18–19...214
16.26...239
17.18...105
17.21...218
18.20...134
19.6...67
19.29...161
20.16...197
20.20–1...32
20.30–4...208
23.27...230
25.31–46...217
26.38...186
26.53...114
27.5...199
27.46...20, 163

Mark
4.25...202
4.31...56

Mark—cont.
5.1-17...208
5.25-34...152, 208
6.13...218
8.31...201
10.46...208
15.44...204

Luke
2.41-51...32
4.1-13...186
4.2...134
4.33-7, 38-9...208
4.40...218
5.17-26...193
7.2-10, 11-15...208
7.36-50...62
7.47...63
8.5...56
8.55...142
9.2...206
9.23-4...239
9.28-36...71
9.33...134
9.37-43...208
10.30-7...127
10.34...217
12.20-1...239
13.2-5...194
13.6...56
13.11-13...208
13.16...19
13.21...56
14.1-6...208
14.26...239
14.27...180
15.3-7, 11-32...127
15.20, 21...213
15.32...148
16.13...112
17.12-14...153
17.12-19...208
18.9-14...197, 232
19.37...116
20.50-1...208
22.31-2...221

23.35...116
23.46...59

John
1.1...58
1.4...236
2.1-11...26
3.1-21...231
3.5...128
3.8...56, 141
3.16...148, 236
4.7-26...62
4.14...238
4.46-53...208
5.2...217
5.2-47...208
5.6...243
5.14...195
5.24...148
6.15...115
6.19...26
6.35, 40, 47...236
6.63...68, 230
6.68...236
7.17...135
8.3-11...62
8.44...200
9...208
9.2-3...194
9.6...29, 217
9.6-7...153
10.4...56
10.14, 15...243
10.38...115
11.1-46...208
11.4...82, 186
11.25...235
12.25...239
14.6...148, 236
14.12...161
15.2...56
15.22...232
16.33...61
17.1...76
17.1-2...236
17.15...221
18.10...114

19.11...76
19.26-7...18
20.22...141
20.27...59
20.27-8...219
21.9...23
21.15-19...221

Acts
1.24, 26...83
2.27, 28...228
3.6-8...208
3.16...206
5.1-11...199
5.15...208
8.26...81
9...83
9.4...231
9.32-5, 36-43...208
10...233
10.9-23...70
11.2-3, 18...233
13.1-3...134
13.6-12...110
13.9...126
14.8-10...208
14.22...201
15.6, 39...134
16.9...71
16.16-19...109
17.27...83
17.28...22, 142
19.18...213
19.13-16...114
20.24...243
26.9...134
27.9, 34...218
28.5...207
28.8...208

Rom.
1.1...216
1.13-15...134
3.10...197
4.15...232
5.12...168, 232

Rom.—cont.
5.17...236
5.20...232
6.16, 23...168
7.10...230
7.18-20...232
8.1...213
8.5-8...68
8.6...228
8.11...219
8.22...42
8.28...82
8.37...61
8.38-9...220
9.18...223
11.32-3, 36...223
12.12...243
12.21...61
13.4...68
14.23...145

I Cor.
3.22...243
6.12...54
6.16...67
6.19...58
7.4...64, 160
7.5, 7:..159
7.34...161
8.1...27
9.27...60
10.21...110
10.31...144
11.30...199
12.1-11...118
12.5...216
12.7...181
12.9...206
12.12-30...58
13.5...195
13.12...223
15.13, 19-20...219
15.22...200
15.25-6...61
15.26...19, 163, 200
15.42...59
16.12-20...126

II Cor.
1.3-4...221
1.22...235
3.6...230
4.8-9, 17-18...202
4.12...218
4.16...155
5.4...238
6.4-5...243
11.28-9...161
12.7...200
12.9...221

Gal.
1.11-17...231
1.11-24...186
1.18...134
2.11...233
2.20...61, 110
3.24...232
4.4...76
5.16-20, 24-5...68
5.19...109
5.19-21...68
6.7...199

Eph.
5.25...58
6.1...230

Phil.
1.12-13...201
1.12-14...82
1.20-4...243
1.21...163, 236
2.5...180
2.6-7...58
2.7...237
2.8...239
2.27...207
3.5...230
3.20...203
3.21...59

Col.
1.13...200
1.19...140

2.13...162
4.10-18...126
4.14...63

I Thess.
2.18...134
5.21...54
5.23...123

I Tim.
3.2, 12...65
4.8...68
5.23...29, 218

II Tim.
1.2...161
1.10...220

Tit.
1.9...206

Heb.
2.14...167, 200
4.12...209
11.33-4...207
12.1...207
12.2...61
12.6...202
12.24...76

Ias.
1.2-3...201
1.13...19
1.15...168
3.7-8...26
3.14...238
4.14...174
5.11...181
5.14...218
5.14-15...196
5.16...213

I Pet.
1.5-7...202
2.11...203
2.20-1...242
2.22...201
2.24...222

Indexes

II Pet.
1.21...244

I John
1.2-4...236
1.9...210

3.14...228
4.19...78
5.12...236

Rev.
3.1...162

3.19...202
18.2...105
20.14...167
21.1...42
21.4...204, 219
22.1...238
22.2...204